All His Enemies

All His Enemies

Nelson J. Zoch

Inquiries to
Call of Duty Publications
Call of Duty Publications@hotmail.com

ISBN-13: 9781983574139
ISBN-10: 1983574139

With the exception of the principals, many of the names in this lengthy publication have been changed for obvious reasons. This is a true crime story which extended over a period of 17 years, and the after-effects of these terrible events will extend far beyond in the lives of the victims' loved ones.

DEDICATED TO:

The memories of Sherry Ann Dean Easley and Patricia Sharon Hammond Easley.

Jonathan Edward Easley who has persevered against all odds to become a credit to society and a respected husband and father.

Houston Police Detective Dan Alton McAnulty who is, in my humble opinion, as well as of many of your peers, the ULTIMATE investigator. My best to you, my friend, and also to your family.

The Murder of Sherry Dean Easley (1)

O N MONDAY AFTERNOON, June 16, 1969, Houston Police Officers Tom Mashue and Ronnie Webb, riding Patrol Unit #651, received a radio dispatch at 5:56pm to a mobile home park in the 3400 block of Campbell Road. This location was what is commonly described as a trailer park, often-times degraded to include everyone who lives there as "white trailer trash". However, this address was not at all like many people would imagine it to be and the residents were not all as some would have imagined them to be.

It was named the L&L Trailer Park and was a mixture of attractive, well-maintained mobile homes, surrounded by chain-link fences and neatly kept yards, which provided a minimum amount of privacy as well as an area for young children to play outside in the safe confines of their yard. The trailer homes were also "skirted", meaning that the area from the bottom of the trailer to the ground were tastefully covered with metal sheets, thereby hiding the storage areas underneath the trailer as well as concealing the plumbing.

When this call was given by police radio to these young Officers at 5:56pm, it was described as a "See the Complainant" in regards to a "Woman Down". It was later discovered that the call-taker in the Dispatcher's Office did not take into account the bloody scene discovered by the reporting citizen and then observed by the first responding Officers. This was a high priority response and while it was not run with red lights and sirens, the Officers proceeded as quickly and as safely possible.

This area of far western suburbia, patrolled by Officers from the just recently opened Northwest Police Substation, was in an upper middle class neighborhood commonly known as Spring Branch. The crime rate in this area was very low in comparison to other parts of the sprawling City of Houston. In fact, the Officers from HPD who requested transfers to the new Northwest Station commonly referred to it as the "Ponderosa", signifying that the crime calls they responded to would be much fewer than those in the inner city. Spring Branch, unlike the melting pot that it has become today, was in 1969 a most desirable section of Houston in which to reside.

Officers Mashue and Webb, both with just barely a year or so on the Department, responded to this call and were met by the reporting citizen, David Dean, the brother of a lady named Sherry Ann Dean Easley. He reported to Officers that he lived nearby and had gone to the trailer to check on his sister as she had not shown up earlier in the day to transport and accompany his wife Barbara to work on Monday morning.

It had been common practice for Sherry to pick up Barbara at their home nearby and drive to work together as they worked in offices next door to each other. It was also their practice that at the end of the work day, Sherry would pick Barbara up and return her to her home in the late afternoon. When David checked with Sherry's place of employment, he learned that she had not reported for work that day nor had she called in. Knowing his sister's work ethic as well as her schedule, this greatly concerned David. He could not help but think that something was wrong with this situation. Little did he know that it would become worse. It would become much worse.

After work on this Monday, David was still concerned about Sherry, and after picking Barbara up from her job, they both went to Sherry's trailer home to see if they could provide some assistance for Sherry. Sherry's car was there parked in the usual spot. David went to the front door and knocked. Upon receiving no answer, David tried the door knob and found it to be unlocked. He opened the door and looked inside towards the bedroom and saw what appeared to him to be a large amount of blood on the bed and pillow, as well as seeing part of a white leg exposed on the floor of the bedroom. He correctly assumed that this leg was that of his sister. Realizing that something had gone terribly wrong and without entering the trailer, he immediately called the police.

In Houston Police Homicide terminology, this was reported to be a Murder, one commonly referred to as a WHO-DUN-IT. In other words, unlike many bar room scenes or domestic violence cases, the suspect was not at the scene nor was the suspect immediately known. This was the real thing, a victim found dead in her own residence. The response to this type of Homicide in Houston, Texas, was and still is an all-out, no-holds-barred type of investigation.

The Homicide Lieutenant in charge of the Division was the Evening Shift Boss, veteran Homicide Lieutenant Frank Crittenden. He received the phone call from the first-responding patrol uniformed Officers, in this case Mashue and Webb. They had entered the trailer very cautiously, made their initial observations that this appeared to be a Murder scene, and then exited without disturbing anything. They then relayed their findings to the Homicide Commander on the Evening Shift, Lieutenant Crittenden.

The street Officer's immediate job is to protect the integrity of the crime scene at all costs. That is, to basically bar anyone else from inside the immediate crime scene and in this particular case, from inside the trailer. Not knowing if the trailer had been broken into, they protected the entire outside perimeter of the trailer, which also included the fenced yard. At this time, no one other than the two Officers and David Dean had gained any access to the crime scene prior to the Officer's arrival at the scene. At such time later that any evidence is gathered from inside the crime scene, knowing and documenting who had access to the surroundings prior to the recovery of that evidence becomes an issue of extreme importance. Should this investigation ever be presented in a courtroom, this matter of the protection of the scene and the chain of custody could possibly mean the difference in the outcome of a court trial.

The obvious purpose of this extreme caution is to not allow anything to be disturbed in order that any physical evidence, such as blood, fingerprints, footprints, weapons, and such to be there in the original form when the main Homicide Investigators and Crime Lab technicians arrive to conduct their investigation and gather any evidence deemed vital to the investigation. The importance of crime scene protection was stressed repeatedly in the sixteen-week Houston Police Academy that these young Officers had recently completed. They were well aware of the importance of their role and carried out their assignment as they were trained to do. This was the first such assignment for either of them. It also became naturally one that they likely would not forget. The overall brutality of the bloody scene was also a factor in these findings being forever embedded in their memories.

Lieutenant Crittenden had previously served for a number of years not only as a Homicide Detective, but he had also served in the United States Navy during World War II. Frank had served his country for nearly ten years and exited the military to be able to stay home and become a family man. Little did Frank know that his devotion to his career as a Homicide Investigator would not release him from his dedication to whatever duty he had chosen to pursue, whether it be military or law enforcement.

Frank had exited the military service, but many of those military traits he learned remained forever in his professional personality. To say that Frank was a stickler for detail and was a no-nonsense supervisor would definitely be an understatement. Frank knew his Homicide business, and it is unknown who he had on his roll call available for this type of case on that 4:00pm-12:00 midnight shift to choose to send on this important case assignment. He likely would not have had more than four pairs of Detectives to choose from and several of them would probably already have been assigned a recent Murder case over the weekend. Chances are, this being a Monday Evening Shift, he would have preferred to choose two investigators who had just returned from their weekend off and were just beginning a new work week. While this is what apparently occurred, whoever was available, he could not have chosen anyone in the division on this hot, muggy afternoon more capable than Ira Holmes and E.D. (Sonny) Combs. They received this assignment from "The Boss" at 6:30pm and proceeded directly to the scene. Rush hour traffic was somewhat over at this time and they arrived at 6:56pm.

In this case, Holmes' and Combs' initial assessment of the crime scene was one in which there was no forced entry to the trailer. The victim was found on the floor of a very small master bedroom in this well-kept and neatly-furnished mobile home. Whatever had taken place in this trailer home, the violence appeared to have been confined to this small bedroom area. Blood was smeared throughout the room, on the bed as well as on the floor and walls.

Their observation, which was considered to be expert in the eyes of many of their co-workers, was that the victim had been in bed when she was initially attacked and thereafter, she had put up a struggle. This struggle was obvious to them as they observed the defensive wounds which were noticeably present on each of her hands. It appeared that she had apparently thrown her arms up repeatedly in what turned out to be an unsuccessful attempt to ward off the attacks. By defensive wounds, it is meant that her hands and arms had suffered cuts and bruises. The throwing up of a victim's hands is known to be nothing more than a natural reaction to incoming pain. All of the observations of these veteran Detectives were based on the crime scene evidence in full view at the time.

It was later determined that she, Sherry Dean Easley, had suffered seven stab wounds to the chest, stomach, and side areas of her body. A number of these stab wounds were visible at the time of viewing at the scene, but not all. The investigators would not move any parts of the body or clothing at this time, with a more detailed observation to be held later at the Harris County Medical Examiner's Office after photos are taken and all other evidence properly recovered and documented.

At this point in such an investigation, Holmes and Combs, just as most every other Homicide Investigator, ceased referring to the victim as "she" or "her." Once a positive identification had been made, from now on and forever, "she" or "her" becomes "Sherry". Sherry can no longer speak for herself. It is up to the Homicide Detectives to speak up for Sherry. This is one of the most unique of all the many unusual characteristics of a Homicide Investigator. They willingly take on the massive responsibility of speaking for the victim, for Sherry, or whoever the victim in any investigation may be. Today, it was about Sherry, who had been quieted in a very brutal manner.

There have been many very competent Investigators working cases such as this one. However, over a period of time, the responsibility of being the deceased person's primary representative lends itself to some to be too heavy a load. These Investigators then turn to investigating other crimes, such as fraud, theft, and robbery where they have a live witness to assist them. They become very successful in those endeavors also. Holmes and Combs, both in their 40s, had not yet reached that crossroad in their life but were in actuality, nearing that point. Some would call this point in an Investigator's career as having reached the "burned out" factor. Others would refer to it as the point where they wished to continue to investigate, but possibly less serious crimes. Holmes and Combs were still ready to take on challenging assignments such as this one.

Further examination of the entire crime scene revealed that not only had there not been any kind of forced entry into the premises, but from the victim's brother, David Dean, it was learned that after he was allowed to conduct a cursory examination of the trailer, to him nothing appeared to be missing or even out of place. David's wife Barbara was also allowed to take a quick look inside. Not of the body, of course, but to just see if she noticed anything missing or out of place as well as she could recall. However, it was obvious that there were a number of items in clear view that would have been taken by a nighttime burglar whose goal would have been to obtain items to sell. The Investigators were actually silently hopeful that some items would later be found to have been removed from the scene by the perpetrator. Clues of any type were welcome. If valuables were taken from the scene by the perpetrator, the odds of determining the identity of the perpetrator are greatly increased.

Now, at this early stage of a WHO-DUN-IT investigation, Ira and Sonny conferred with each other after their immediate findings. Based upon their vast years of experience and the circumstances as they existed at this time, they had their very strong suspicions that this was a crime of passion and not one where property or goods were the motive. Homicide Investigators, by nature, on some occasions have the inclination to develop an opinion regarding the motive and/or possible suspects in a case, albeit on some occasions, prematurely. Young Investigators are routinely cautioned to not delve into an investigation with their blinders on, meaning such as a horse with blinders who is only able to see straight ahead, not sideways. Outstanding Investigators will delay this complete determination to such time when all of the facts and circumstances are known.

However, in this situation, Ira and Sonny were in agreement on their initial assessment of the evidence and circumstances known at this point. They would have bet anything that the perpetrator was someone who knew Sherry very well and, also by someone who held a great amount of animosity towards Sherry. It was apparent to them that one of their next absolutely necessary steps in the investigation would be to learn everything possible about Sherry. They needed to know all about her life and especially about her current life experiences.

The Investigation Continues (2)

I N A HOMICIDE investigation such as this, it is vital to learn intimate details about Sherry Easley. Her life, now so suddenly ended, needs to become an open book to the Investigators. Ideally, nothing should be kept from the Investigators as any small detail of her life may become extremely important. And, in this case, a family member was available to provide some of that basic information. While much, much more background information on Sherry needed to be pursued, they had somewhat of a beginning point in their investigation.

In speaking at length with the victim's brother and sister-in-law, David and Barbara Dean, it was learned that the victim, Sherry Easley, had recently gone through a very contentious and nasty divorce from her husband of six years, Jerry Eugene Easley. This conversation immediately raised concern regarding the whereabouts of Sherry's three-year old son, Jon, as Sherry had been granted by the Court full custody of her small son.

When the Detectives learned of the existence of Jon, they immediately returned to the inside of the trailer. While they and the original responding Officers had routinely searched for a suspect in the trailer, they had not been aware at that time of little Jon being a part of this equation. Being aware of previous situations where a small child had crawled off and hidden in a tiny space to be secluded during the commission of a crime, they thoroughly searched every nook and cranny inside the trailer. There was no indication that Jon was inside.

The Deans knew that Jerry Easley had visitation rights every other weekend and were thinking that possibly this past weekend was one of those scheduled times. Several frantic phone calls resulted in determining that Jon had not been returned from the weekend visitation with his Dad. On this terrible Monday afternoon in June, 1969, this news provided some initial relief that his safety and well-being was not at this moment part of this mysterious tragedy.

Support personnel were summoned to this location to process the scene for additional evidence. Crime scene Officers Vernon West and Paul Michna received this assignment and took numerous photographs of the victim at the scene and also of the entire scene, including the exterior of the mobile home and the fenced yard. They dusted for fingerprints and were able to obtain four "lifters", one fingerprint and three palm prints. They also recovered numerous blood samples from throughout the scene as well as several hair samples from the floor of the murder room. And, very interestingly, they found two fingertips of rubber surgical gloves in a pool of blood on the bedroom floor.

Also discovered when the body was removed was a broken wooden leg from the bed which Sherry had been on when she was attacked. There were originally six of these wooden supports underneath the mattress and box spring. When Sherry was struggling on the floor to get away from her assailant, the struggle became so intense that one of these legs had been forced loose. Other items recovered and tagged for further examination at the Crime Lab were two knives found in the kitchen sink, the blood-soaked bed sheets, and the gown and undergarments of the victim.

After an extensive investigation of the crime scene, the premises were then turned over to the victim's brother with the instructions for him to secure the trailer but not to re-enter until further notification from the detectives. While it was not the normal protocol for an investigation such as this in 1969, in later years, leaving the scene in custody of anyone other than law enforcement personnel would have required a Search Warrant to re-enter a crime scene in any effort to recover additional evidence that might have been in any manner admissible. Today, a crime scene such as this one would have required around-the-clock protection by law enforcement authorities until such time Investigators deemed that they were finished with the scene investigation. If the scene needed to be "sat on" for several days, so be it. This would not have been a choice or exciting tour of duty for a street cop or rookie Investigator, but it would have been absolutely necessary. The crime scene would need the same protection that Officers Mashue and Webb had provided prior to Holmes and Combs arrival. Caution would be of the utmost priority as to not potentially lose any evidence from the scene.

The victim was viewed at the scene and a cursory exam of her wounds revealed numerous stab wounds throughout the upper torso of her body. Protocol and Texas State law dictate that a victim of such a crime be transported as soon as practical to the Harris County Medical Examiner's facility, also commonly known in Harris County, Houston, Texas, as "the Morgue". This gruesome facility, which anyone who had ever visited there would certainly attest to, had an odor all of its own, and was located in the basement of the county hospital, known to cops as Ben Taub Hospital. Investigative procedures also dictate that the body should also be in the same attire as found, if any, and the exact condition as it was discovered.

Once at the Morgue, the body is preserved until such time as one of the licensed Medical Examiner Pathologists and their staff can perform a complete and thorough autopsy. This is also commonly referred to as a post mortem examination, or in Homicide cop terminology, as the "post".

While at the scene, the phone rang in Sherry's trailer. Detective Holmes answered the phone and learned it was the ex-husband's attorney, Mr. Babcox, asking to speak to Sherry. Detective Holmes, after determining who the caller was, advised him of Sherry's death. This lawyer had represented Jerry Easley in the protracted and very nasty divorce proceedings. Mr. Babcox was inquiring on behalf of his client, indicating that Jerry had not been able to make contact with Sherry regarding returning the son Jon to his Mom after the weekend visitation. It was later ascertained that Jerry had been calling Sherry's family as late as Sunday night for the very same reason. Mr. Babcox then advised that the child was still with his father at that time. This was a tremendous relief for the Dean family as this verified the information they had received earlier. Mr. Babcox volunteered to make Jerry Easley readily available to the Investigators at such time they requested. It was unknown at the time as to why Jerry Easley had not just driven the child over to Sherry's trailer. This would have seemed like the manner in which the usual exchange had been taking place.

Also, while at the scene, phone calls came in from several men who had recently dated Sherry. One of these men, Bill, was later determined to have been the last known person to have seen Sherry alive, except, of course, for the murderer. Bill told Detectives that Sherry had gone to Chappell Hill, Texas, on Saturday afternoon with him to return his young son to his mother. They had been together until 5:00pm, at which time he dropped her off at her trailer. He returned to pick Sherry up for a movie date and they were once again together up until around midnight. Sherry was exhausted from the day's activities and Bill left and went home.

Detectives also received a phone call from a man named Paul, who had worked with Sherry and who had also dated Sherry. He was calling to determine if she was all right, as they had a date planned for Sunday afternoon. He stated that he arrived as scheduled at 1:20pm that afternoon and after knocking on her door and receiving no answer, left. Paul recalled that the front fence gate was open at that time and a newspaper was still laying in her yard. Both of these men were interviewed in person following these brief phone calls. Both were very cooperative with Investigators and volunteered to take polygraph tests at a later date regarding the information they had provided.

While the Detectives working this case were attempting to maintain an open mind, at this point they were well aware that there were other possible "persons of interest" in this case. They also were very much aware that all of these individuals needed to be interviewed at length and investigated thoroughly as to any possible involvement in this heinous crime.

Knowing of Bill and Paul, they received information that there were several other potential suitors who had sought the company of this young attractive divorcee. A "To Be Contacted" list was comprised by Holmes-Combs and hopefully for other Detectives who might be assigned to assist in this Murder investigation. However, while they were attempting to maintain an open mind regarding the perpetrator, the person at the top of any such list had to be Jerry Eugene Easley.

The two seasoned Detectives left the scene late that night, knowing full well that they had quite a chore in front of them. Throughout the lengthy scene investigation, protocol was to keep Lieutenant Crittenden informed of the progress, or lack thereof. This was necessary in order that he could leave the proper notifications for the supervisors who would be commanding the Day Shift Investigators. The paperwork required to document the happenings to this point was merely one small item on the list that they were preparing in their investigative minds. They knew in their hearts that this was not going to be an easy case to bring to prosecution, even though they had persons of interest such as Jerry Easley, Bill, Paul, and possibly others also. On their drive back to the Homicide Office, Combs commented to himself and Holmes that unless Jerry Easley shows up and confesses to this crime, these other "persons of interest" needed to be interviewed and as soon as possible. This is where the Day Shift would hopefully be able to come into the investigation and assist them.

Who was Sherry Ann Dean from West Texas? (3)

S HERRY ANN DEAN was the youngest of six children born to Mr. and Mrs. J.F. Dean in the Texas Panhandle. Sherry entered the world on February 14, 1945. Her parents were tough hard-scrabble cotton farmers and had also been raised in this very economically difficult lifestyle. This area of Texas was only several hundred miles south of the infamous Oklahoma Dust Bowl of the 1930's Great Depression, which had inspired the great novel *The Grapes of Wrath*. Not long after Sherry's birth, her parents, being now in their late 30s and early 40s, came to the realization that as they aged, they would not be able to maintain this hard-life farm work. They eventually abandoned this lifestyle and made a drastic change in occupations.

Of course, a major factor in this equation was the availability of farm labor, which was usually drawn from family members, both male and female. As the family grew older and as some of the children reached adulthood, they moved on, got married, and sought stable employment away from the farm. All of these issues came to the table in the decision to change the Dean family's main occupation and provide a more stable source of income.

This lifestyle had actually become impossible at times due to the natural elements involved – drought and heat, as well as the constant high winds across the Texas plains. The drought was an important element but there was also the uncertainty of rainfall at the most critical times for crops. All of these factors, along with the uncertainty of the crop recovery season as well as the rapidly dwindling labor supply, played into the decision to make this bold and drastic change.

In this lifestyle, the ultimate goal was to be able to produce enough of a sellable cash crop for enough income and thereby be able to provide for the family and survive for another year. Many times, it became just that - survival. There was never enough money to do more than "just get by". The Deans were not owners of their land. They were what were commonly known in that era as "sharecroppers". They would live on and cultivate land that was owned by other individuals. They would reside in whatever hovel was available and then work the land. If money was available, and usually not, any improvements to their living conditions were not made as they might be forced to move on after the crop year was over. If a crop was produced, which was always an uncertainty, a portion of the crop would go to the landowner, hence the word "sharecropper". It was a tough way to earn a living.

Mr. Dean had learned of a job in the "oil patch" in Seminole, Texas, a job that provided a reasonably consistent income. Having worked on farm equipment all of his life, Mr. Dean was not afraid of hard, dirty work. He had a reasonable amount of mechanical ability, most, if not all, had been learned by trial and error, the hard way. This new employment and the somewhat consistent income were in stark comparison to the uncertainty of producing a crop each and every year.

To accept this employment, the Dean family was forced to relocate. This was very likely not a real difficult decision, as the circumstances with the farm life had become unbearable and supporting this family had become next to impossible. Moving was not so much of a problem in that the Dean family, just like their parents, were, as the old phrase went, "dirt poor". Since there was no land or house to dispose of prior to the move, the only things to transport to Seminole were some items of furniture along with personal items such as clothing. A moving van was definitely not necessary to make this move of a family of two parents and four children.

Life in the "oil patch" in Seminole, Texas, was greatly different, and to a tremendous degree, better. However, the change brought about other problems for the Dean family, which had at one time also consisted of two older daughters - Naomi and Betty. Following them were two sons, Troy and David, and after that, two more daughters, Glenna and Sherry. When this major change came about in the Dean's lives, the older daughters, Naomi and Betty, had already gotten married and left home to begin their adult lives away from their parents and siblings.

It was apparent to many in the family that marital difficulties had existed between Mr. and Mrs. Dean for some time. The financial problems and constant stress resulting from the sharecropping existence were a major segment of the difficulties. In making this move, the obvious hope was that with less stress on the financial portion of the family equation, these problems might possibly be overcome.

However, the strain of the move to Seminole only exacerbated the pre-existing conditions and raised new problems. Shortly after the move, Mr. and Mrs. Dean mutually agreed upon a separation. Mrs. Dean, being from the Panhandle area of Electra, Texas, chose to move with the children back to that area in order to be near her family of origin. While it was her hope and prayer that she and the children could survive on their own without assistance from Mr. Dean, if worse came to worse, she would have some family members to fall back on for help. Mr. Dean remained in the Seminole area due to his employment. He was still in his 40s, and with a strong work ethic, fit in very well in his new job. Mr. Dean's desire to continue supporting his family was not an issue as he was very dedicated to that responsibility. However, there were obviously very hard feelings between this couple at this time.

Electra, which is near Wichita Falls, Texas, was some 200 miles east of Seminole, which was just east of the New Mexico-Texas border. In those days, the Interstate Highway system was in the early days of construction and the trek from Seminole to Electra was a major problem for Mr. Dean to be able to visit the children. There was not a direct highway route between the two locations and the one-way trip was a five to six hour excursion. While the elder Deans likely did not care to see each other that much, Mr. Dean was attempting to continue to be a part of his younger children's lives. However, working full-time and also taking financial advantage of some very welcome overtime in the oil patch placed an even greater strain on the marriage.

Mr. and Mrs. Dean eventually divorced, a move which had been a long time in the thoughts of both. Mrs. Dean remarried shortly thereafter to a man named Harold Cones. Mr. Cones was prone to indulge in the excessive consumption of alcoholic beverages and as usual in these situations, problems arose over this matter. Mr. Cones was "a drinking man". This must have been quite an adjustment in the lifestyle of Mrs. Cones, as Mr. Dean had not been prone to any such use of alcohol. It was very likely that Mrs. Cones needed someone to help support her and the children and that was a factor in her decision to wed so quickly and especially to someone of Mr. Cone's nature. This must have been quite a cultural shock to the entire Dean family as their Dad, Mr. Dean, was vehemently opposed to such habits as Mr. Cones practiced. While this new marriage was not without a number of other difficulties, a daughter Doris was born to this union.

Shortly thereafter, Sherry's Mother, David, Glenna, Sherry, and Doris decided to move to Houston. This move was likely due to marital difficulties Mr. and Mrs. Cones were experiencing in Electra. The oldest son, Troy, had experienced his own problems after his parent's divorce and was already living in Houston, attempting to make a life of his own. Of course, Troy, being the eldest son, felt the strong need to assist his Mom and his three younger siblings as well as Doris. Mr. Cones later followed the family to Houston and Mr. Dean, in an attempt to remain in the lives of his children, found employment in Houston and moved there also.

The move to Houston, even with Mr. Cones and his accompanying problems that were also brought into the picture, turned out to be good for the three younger siblings. Their house on Railton was in the Spring Branch Independent School District, which at the time was much superior academically to the monstrous Houston School District. David began his high school days at Spring Branch High School on nearby Westview Drive. Glenna and Sherry followed David to high school. David graduated in 1958 and Glenna was three years behind David, planning to be in the graduating class of 1961. Sherry also went to Spring Branch High and was in the class scheduled for graduation in 1963.

A New Start for the Deans in Houston (4)
(Comments from Friends Mona and Susan)

T HE FIRST DAY of school in Spring Branch was traumatic for Sherry. The large number of students at Spring Branch High School just overwhelmed her. There were as many people in some classes as there had been in the entire school at Electra or Seminole. Her closest friends described their memory of Sherry as very timid and shy and along with her small physical stature, could have also been actually described as somewhat frail in appearance. Sherry had shoulder length auburn hair worn in a page-boy style. She was around five feet, three inches tall. She had a warm, caring heart, was fun-loving, and had a great sense of humor.

When her Home Economics class was over, one girl noticed Sherry to be very nearly in tears. She appeared to this girl in the class as possibly just being overwhelmed with the new situation. That was, as it was later learned, a very good observation. This girl, Mona Buffington, approached Sherry and knowing she was new in the class, welcomed her to the school. Mona also invited Sherry to go to lunch, an invitation which was not only most timely, but very, very welcome. Mona and her usual lunch bunch met each and every day to get together and engage in "girl talk" about their day and their lives. Almost immediately, Sherry and Mona really hit it off as friends. Sherry also seemed to fit in with this small close-knit group of teenage girls, which was a tremendous boost in her self-esteem from that first day at the new school. Sherry later related to Mona's grandmother, with whom Mona was living at the time that she felt that after that day in class, Mona had been sent to her as a guardian angel.

Mona and Sherry had another very important thing in common. More importantly than anything else, they were both Christians. Sherry's sister Glenna, two years older, then became friends with Mona along with a close friend of Glenna's, Shirley. These four, even though there existed a four-year spread in their ages, became a very friendly and close-knit group that seemed to always be together at church, in school, and in whatever other activities they participated in.

This new friendship with Mona assisted greatly in transforming Sherry very quickly. Following the move to Houston, and actually much prior to that, Sherry had always been known as being very timid and shy. However, her new group of friends apparently opened her up and she became much more confident of herself. Glenna was a natural at making friends very fast and their activities revolved around their church. It was there at Tallowood Baptist Church that they bonded even closer together with the addition of another neighborhood girl, Susan Finch, who was brought into the group by Mona Buffington. This group of five teenage girls had many good times in those early days at the newly organized mission congregation of Tallowood Baptist. The five of them worshipped at Tallowood on a regular basis.

Sherry, Mona, and Susan only lived several blocks apart and not having a car at the time, would walk to each other's house to visit. These were the days when, even in a large and growing city such as Houston, young females could walk their neighborhoods in relative safety during the daylight hours. This safety was possible in their Spring Branch neighborhood while it would have not been so in many other areas of Houston. Sherry was overcoming her original timidity and shyness and soon developed into a very friendly and outgoing young teen-aged girl. She was immediately accepted like another daughter to Susan's parents, Mr. and Mrs. Finch. Glenna was very well liked by the elder Finches and since none of the girls had a car, Mr. Finch would even trust the girls with Glenna driving the Finch family vehicle.

All in all, Sherry was progressing very well, not only in school, but in the social structure of her newly-found church friends. She was in her Junior year in high school in the 1961-1962 school year, an exciting time for her and her friends as well as with Glenna's friends.

Jerry Easley from Elkhart, Texas (5)

W HAT IS A narcissist? The following is a compilation from several noted sources of definitions on this subject. *A Narcissistic Personality Disorder is officially described as involving arrogant behavior, a lack of empathy for other people, and a need for admiration. This person has an excessive interest in or admiration of themselves. Narcissists think the world revolves around them. They are overly self-involved and often are vain and selfish. Individuals who are narcissistic are frequently described as cocky, self-centered, manipulative, and demanding. They may concentrate on unlikely personal outcomes, such as fame, and may be convinced that they deserve special treatment. Narcissistic individuals tend to display high self-esteem, but deep down they are very insecure.*

These definitions of "Narcissism" are derived from a variety of official sources on the subject and at this juncture of Jerry Easley's life, it is discussed as a consideration when describing his behavior throughout his life. In learning as much as possible about the early life of Jerry Easley in Elkhart, Texas, it was not thought that he exhibited any type of narcissistic behavior in those years. However, in reviewing his entire life, he definitely was leaning in that direction.

Jerry Eugene Easley was born in Elkhart, Texas, on February 11, 1941. Elkhart is a small hole-in-the-road town, so to speak, up in the Piney Woods of East Texas. It is north of Crockett, and south of Palestine, basically half-way between the two larger cities. Using the words "larger cities" is an exaggeration, even though they were in fact larger than Elkhart.

Jerry was the oldest child in a family of four children born into this Easley family. Mr. Easley was an employee of the local railroad line which ran through the area. This was a stable employment for Mr. Easley, who was able to provide a reasonably good standard of living for this family. Jerry Easley was followed by a sister, three years younger, and then by two brothers, one five years younger, and another one seven years younger. Four children, seven years apart, comprised a seemingly close family to grow up in an idyllic setting in a small city in deep East Texas.

The Easley family in Elkhart was very well-known and highly respected in the community. Mrs. Easley seemed to be a very strong parent, caring for the children while Mr. Easley worked and provided a good living for the family. According to the yearbooks at Elkhart High School in the years 1959-1966, the Easley children were very active in school and seemingly were recognized as future high-achievers, which they all four eventually developed into in their adult years.

The 1959 Elkhart High School yearbook, the Elk, listed 24 graduates. Jerry had bragged at one time that he was the Valedictorian of that class. However, no such designation of a Valedictorian or that of Salutatorian was mentioned in this book. This was very unusual for this era but small town community politics and popularity may have played a role in the decision to not honor such. Jerry's activities and accomplishments noted were FFA, Historical Club, Press Club, Basketball, Junior Class Play, Manager of the Elkhorns, and the FHA Sweetheart in his Sophomore year in 1957.

In this 1950-1960's era, FFA (Future Farmers of America) and FHA (Future Homemakers of America) were very popular organizations, especially in small rural communities such as Elkhart. Young women, many of whom never even considered attending college after high school, usually prepared to be secretaries or housewives when they met the right guy. The FHA was a means for them to learn homemaking skills that they may not have picked up at home. This was just the way life was in these small towns in the 1950s and 1960s.

Young men, some of whom grew up and lived on acreages around the community, raised an animal for either food or for showing at the County

Fair or some other livestock competition. If you lived on acreage, it was commonly referred to as "out in the country". Doing so usually qualified the young man for membership in the FFA and for the school class, which also provided a rather easy high school credit to boot. The ultimate goal in raising such an animal, whether it be a calf, pig, rabbit, chicken, or whatever, was to win a blue ribbon prize for a top quality animal. This would then provide some scholarship money donated by well-off local businessmen to be used either for another animal or for education.

It was also becoming an expectation of the young males to attend college. Even the families who were not able to finance their son's further education were encouraged to find the means to attend college. The old saying, "Where there's a will, there's a way" was repeated often by teachers who had attained their education the hard way. So it was with Jerry Easley, who while being Valedictorian was in question, was at least one of the top students in that Senior Class of 1959 of the Elkhart H.S. Elks.

After graduating from Elkhart High School in 1959, Jerry Easley continued his education by enrolling at Sam Houston State Teachers College in Huntsville, Texas, less than 70 miles south of Elkhart. It is not certain that Jerry attended the required four years at "Sam", as it is commonly referred to. He did eventually complete the degree there with a major in Chemistry.

It is known that in 1961-1962, he moved to the Spring Branch area of Houston, this being in the western suburbs. Jerry became employed at the massive Cameron Iron Works, a large world-wide conglomerate and manufacturer of oil field valves and other related steel equipment. While employed at Cameron, Jerry became acquainted with a Mr. Finch, a long-time Cameron employee who had by his hard work and knowledge risen to an important supervisory position at Cameron. Mr. Finch, a very enterprising and ambitious man, on his own initiative and considerable expense, outfitted a machine shop operation in his garage at his residence in Spring Branch. It is probable that Mr. Finch was the recipient of small farmed-out contracts from Cameron and this enabled him to do well in his shop during his off-duty hours. He had developed ideas while at work at Cameron, and with Cameron working an overtime operation, they were glad to assist this loyal employee with small contracts. This small business produced several items similar to the models from Cameron and Mr. Finch's success caused him to hire Jerry Easley on a part-time or as-needed basis.

For whatever reason, the two hit it off and became friends. It was later thought by all who know both that this was a rather odd relationship, mainly due to their totally different and far-reaching value systems. Mr. Finch, being a foreman at Cameron, likely recognized in Jerry Easley the East Texas work ethic and also saw that Jerry possessed not only the personality to work with him, but also a significant degree of mechanical skills necessary in that job.

Mr. Finch had a teen-aged daughter, Susan, who had become acquainted with a number of young high school girls her age, which at this time was 16 or 17. This close-knit group of young ladies were Christians, and after attending worship services or other church related activities, usually migrated to one of their homes afterwards. One of the usual and actually the most popular stop was the Finch residence. Mr. and Mrs. Finch welcomed these girls to their home with the likely thinking that they would be safer socializing at home.

Jerry and Mr. Finch, after working their regular hours at Cameron, would usually be at the Finch garage in the late afternoon and early evening hours working on items on Mr. Finch's machines. Jerry had a nice "ride" and, being three or four years older than these girls, began eyeing one of Susan Finch's best friends, Sherry Dean.

Sherry Dean Meets and Marries Jerry Easley (6)

J ERRY WAS FOUR years older than Sherry, who had just recently begun her junior year in high school. She was very, very attractive, with a light cameo white complexion. In addition to her constantly evolving beauty, she was fun loving with a great sense of humor. She had progressed quite a far distance from that first day at Spring Branch High in the Home Economics class where she met Mona Buffington.

Sherry was becoming an excellent student in school, and a very quick learner. Prior to Jerry coming into the picture, Sherry never expressed an interest in any of the boys they were around, either at church or school. Her core group of close friends, according to Susan Finch, were all somewhat boy crazy but none had a steady boyfriend at the time. They were considered boy crazy in the sense that their curiosity about these strange creatures was constantly growing. Shortly after meeting Jerry, Jerry recognized Sherry for the attractive young lady she was and began wooing her every chance he got. Sherry then began dating Jerry.

Sherry's close group of friends attempted to warn her, as they were well aware that she was somewhat naïve. They were attempting to look out for a friend, warning her to not move too fast with this relationship with a 21-year-old since she was only a junior at Spring Branch High School. Of course, a young 17-year-old was not too interested in listening to any warnings from even her close friends, especially since none of these well-meaning friends had ever had any serious relationships of their own upon which to base their suspicions, and certainly not equipped to tender their advice. No one, not even her closest friends or her sister Glenna, ever knew that possibly Sherry was ready to move on from the home life that she knew, one that had certainly not been happy in West Texas. Her home life had in fact improved in Spring Branch, but not actually that greatly. Her friends had even cautioned her about wanting to make a change in her life simply for the sole purpose of making a change. However, again, she was not ready to listen to the advice of her very well-meaning friends.

While Jerry was working for both Cameron and Mr. Finch, he began courting Sherry heavily. As a result of this courtship, in 1962, after Sherry's Junior year at Spring Branch, she gave in to Jerry's pursuit and they married in the summer of 1962. There was no money for a large formal wedding so Sherry and Jerry were married by a local Justice of the Peace, a not-so-uncommon practice in this era.

This very likely appeared to be a wise move to Sherry at the time. Here she was marrying a man who had graduated from high school near the top of his small class in 1959 at Elkhart High School. He was well on his way towards his degree in Chemistry with plans to continue with post-graduate studies at Sam Houston when he and Sherry married. Sherry was obviously impressed with this young man and also with the potential she saw as him being a good husband and provider for a family in the future.

Sherry chose to quit school after her Junior year to marry Jerry, which many thought to be a bad decision on her part. However, her heart, or Jerry's persistence, overruled her head and she gave in. Jerry had wooed Sherry into marriage with the promise that while he would be continuing on his degree program at Sam Houston, she too could continue her education that she had left after only the 11th grade. Being an avid reader and an excellent student at Spring Branch High, Sherry vowed to also continue her education. She did so, finishing a high school program rather rapidly and then immediately enrolling at Sam Houston also. From all accounts, other than Jerry seemingly becoming more and more controlling over every facet of Sherry's life and personality, the marriage seemed to be going well.

Jonathan Edward Easley (7)

AFTER NEARLY FOUR years of marriage, Jerry became more controlling with each passing day. Not many friends or family were close to the situation as it existed at that time. Then, a son, Jonathan Edward Easley was born to this union on April 9, 1966. To Sherry, this was a blessing in her life and provided an opportunity for her to become a loving Mother. It was unknown how Jerry felt in that regards. The marriage continued on for well over two more years.

Much more will follow regarding Jon Easley.

The Early Life of Sharon Hammond Bonham (8)

PATRICIA SHARON HAMMOND was born in San Antonio, Texas, on December 19, 1942. Her parents were Mr. and Mrs. A.E. and Freddis Hammond, a God-fearing couple who moved to Houston in the 1950s. Mr. Hammond was in the printing business, and in their early years in Houston, they lived on South Main Street. Mr. Hammond was an enterprising man and while working a full-time job in the advertising field, began a part-time printing operation in his garage.

A.E.'s ventures had been very successful in the printing business and he and Freddis had provided for their three children not only a Christian upbringing but were also able to provide for them the opportunities for further education after high school. The family consisted of three children - Patricia Sharon Hammond, born in 1942, Charles Walter Hammond, born in 1944, and the youngest child, James Richard Hammond, born in 1946. Patricia Sharon, or Sharon as she was known to family and friends, attended and graduated from the old San Jacinto High School on Holman Street. Unlike in later years prior to this school being closed, this was in a rather affluent section of Houston.

Charles and James also began high school there, but in James' freshman year, the Hammond family moved to far West Houston to a home on fashionable Memorial Drive. This placed both Charles and James in the Spring Branch Independent School District, which ironically at the time, their high schools consisted of only the top three grades, 10th, 11th, and 12th. James had begun high school in the 9th grade at San Jacinto High School, which had the traditional four grades of high school. When they moved to West Houston, James was forced to return to junior high school.

If that was not confusing enough, after James finished the 9th grade, he began his high school days once again, this time at Spring Branch High School. During his sophomore year, the Spring Branch School District was rapidly expanding and opened the new Memorial High School. Then James was redistricted to this new high school, Spring Branch Memorial, from which he later graduated.

Settling into the Memorial area, Mr. and Mrs. Hammond became active in their church which had become a way of life for all three of their children no matter where they resided. They were God-fearing parents and raised their three children in the same manner.

Meanwhile, Sharon, after graduating from San Jacinto High School, moved to San Marcos, Texas, where she attended Southwest Texas State Teachers College, a four-year University which not only trained teachers, but also provided the opportunity of an advanced education in other disciplines. Sharon was an all-around exceptional student and she was apparently a whiz at Chemistry. Before departing this University, she earned a Bachelor's Degree as well as a Master's Degree, both with Majors in Chemistry.

Having been raised in the church, Sharon frequented the Baptist Student Union at college, thereby making friends with other Christian students who were away from home and their families, many for the first time. It was there she met Gerald, a young man and student her age who was from the area around Fort Hood, Texas. Sharon and Gerald Burton Bonham, who went by the short name of Burt, hit it off very well, and in 1965, they became husband and wife. Burt had neared his degree in history at Southwest and was upwardly motivated for further studies. Sharon obtained a position at the South Texas Junior College in Houston in the Chemistry Department. Meanwhile, Burt had completed a college degree also and soon enrolled in a graduate program at Sam Houston State College in Huntsville, Texas.

At one point early in their marriage, Sharon and Burt moved in with the elder Hammonds in their spacious Memorial home. This move further elated Mr. and Mrs. Hammond, as not only were they fond of Burt, but now had their only daughter somewhat back in the family fold. This move was very likely financial but also turned out very well for all involved at the time. The young married couple regularly attended worship services in the same church in West Houston in which the elder Hammonds were actively involved.

In 1968, all appeared to be normal for the Bonham family, as both were either settled into employment in their chosen field, or in the case of Burt, well on his way to obtain the higher education he was motivated to obtain. He chose to continue his pursuit at Sam Houston University. Burt had met Jerry Easley, who was the head of the Chemistry Department at South Texas Junior College where Sharon was employed. When Burt left to continue his studies, he asked Sharon's boss, Jerry Easley, to look out for Sharon while he was away. As far as the Bonham marriage was concerned, this was later determined to be a fatal mistake. Jerry Easley took Burt's request to heart and truly did "look out for Sharon".

The Easley and Bonham Divorces (9)

THE MARRIAGE OF Sherry Ann Dean and Jerry Easley had been in disarray for some time. After the birth of Jon on April 9, 1966, Jerry became more and more controlling as he wanted to know where Sherry was at all times and did not allow, actually forbade her to have friends and spend time with them. Even stranger, he did not allow her to have any type of relationships with her Mom and siblings. And, even stranger yet, Sherry allowed herself to be controlled by her husband. Sherry's family were very hurt by this behavior, but her Mom was frightened of Jerry and apparently the Dean family nature was such that they just allowed Sherry to live her own life and did nothing to interfere nor even question this very bizarre behavior.

Jerry was very jealous regarding Sherry's friends and relatives. Included in this selfish directive of his was Susan and Mona, Sherry closest friends in high school. Jerry had correctly suspected that Susan, Mona, and probably Sherry's sister Glenna had not only advised her against marrying him, but had actively worked against this relationship. Whatever the situation was, Jerry was adamantly against his wife retaining her friendship not only with these closest of friends, but with her sister Glenna also. During their marriage, Sherry was not allowed by Jerry to dress up in any of the latest fashion styles nor could she get her hair done at a beauty shop or wear make-up. While money was not plentiful at this time in their lives, this was not at the crux of his hang-ups. It seemed that Jerry wanted Sherry the way she was at the beginning of their marriage and did all he could to hold her back. Sherry, for whatever reason, went along with this emotional abuse for several years.

This behavior continued to worsen and sometime in early 1968, life together had just become unbearable for Sherry. However, Sherry was determined to stick with the marriage for the sake of little Jon, who was about to have his second birthday. After the trouble continued and Jerry's behavior became to Sherry more and more bizarre, they separated on September 12, 1968. It seemed to many who were close to the situation that Sherry should have been the partner who filed a suit to remove herself from this marriage, but Sherry did not want to be the one to split them up. It was later believed that she was concerned about what Jon would think later as to why his Dad was not around like other kid's Dads were. She was willing to let Jerry make the decision for whatever that was worth.

If she had known what had really been occurring, she might have taken the initiative to end the marriage much sooner. While she may have suspected something was amiss, she kept it to herself and allowed Jerry to make the move. Jerry eventually became the partner that filed for divorce, which became final in December, 1968. This was actually a very short period of separation prior to it becoming final, especially for a settlement involving a young child. There apparently were not many points of contention as there normally would have been in that such a young child was in the picture. It is probable, again only speculation, that Sherry wanted out of this marriage situation as soon as possible and with as little litigation as possible to avoid running up attorney's fees.

Prior to this separation, when they left Huntsville after Jerry graduated with a Bachelor's Degree, Jerry and Sherry had moved into a trailer park on Yale Street in North Houston. At that time, they purchased the trailer home and paid for the space fee on a monthly basis, thereby accumulating a small amount of ownership equity in the home. After the divorce, Sherry was granted ownership of the trailer and had it moved to a family-type trailer park at 3403 Campbell Road. In addition to the trailer and its furnishings, she received $150.00 per month child support and an older car. This was thought to be a good move for Sherry as her Mother, a brother, and a sister all resided in the Spring Branch area. Additionally, Sherry had obtained a job in the area which was now more convenient to her residence.

However, there was a problem in that since Jerry had lived in the trailer, he had retained a key and refused to return it to Sherry, even at the urging of both their attorneys. This had to have been a bad sign and a constant worry for her. Sherry had repeatedly asked for the return of this key directly to Jerry and also by way of her attorney. Her request was denied by Jerry and her attorney's advice to Sherry was to change the locks on the doors. However, the expense involved in changing the locks eliminated that excellent idea from further consideration. This was a very troublesome situation that in hindsight could have and should have been negotiated by the attorneys involved. However, it was not. Sherry was just beginning to get her "feet on the ground" financially and must not have been able to bare the expense involved in the changing of the door locks.

After the divorce, it became obvious to Sherry that there had been more to Jerry's desire for the divorce other than their inability to get along and live together peacefully. Her suspicions were confirmed by information received from several of her friends that she had been reunited with after her separation and divorce from Jerry. Their idea of being good friends was that they had chosen to lay back and not to say anything that would sway Sherry one way or the other in her marital decisions. When they knew the marriage was over, they then came forth with what they knew or had suspected.

Through these well-meaning acquaintances, she learned that Jerry had been seeing a woman named Sharon that he had met while teaching chemistry at South Texas Junior College in downtown Houston. This relationship began in June, 1968. Sharon, who was also teaching at this institution at the time, was also married. Her husband Burt had earlier been introduced to Jerry by Sharon, who Sharon described as a co-worker. Gerald, feeling that he needed to look out for the safety of his wife, had even requested that Jerry watch out for Sharon as he was planning to move to Huntsville to continue his degree program at Sam Houston.

At the time, the parking situation at South Texas was rather dangerous due to the area of town that the college was located. The surrounding area of lower Main Street was a haven for winos and other homeless people who begged for handouts from the college students. There were also the occasional robberies and abductions that usually occurred in the night-time hours. Burt asked Jerry to make sure that Sharon was able to get to her vehicle safely each night.

Jerry did in fact look out for Sharon. Actually, he "really looked out for Sharon". In early September, 1968, Burt was commuting between Huntsville and Houston while working on his graduate degree program. During this time, Burt noticed that Sharon had become very distant to him during the limited time they were together. Burt and Sharon, now in their mid 20s, had experienced and enjoyed an active sexual relationship throughout their marriage. That was to say, up to this time. Actually, during these times in which they were apart for several days at a time, the sexual relationship was even more active when they were together for a short time. There was quite a bit of "catching up" to take care of when they had been apart for a week or so at a time.

Over a period of just several weeks, this had changed and Burt thought that something was definitely amiss. He began questioning her regarding this sudden change. Burt asked Sharon if there was another man and she became very silent. Burt then asked her if it was Jerry Easley, to which she responded that he should talk to Jerry about it. She eventually admitted to Burt that she was in love with Jerry Easley and wanted a divorce.

Jerry was neither mild-mannered nor timid when it came to his feelings toward Sharon. Burt, who was just completely taken aback by this sudden change in their marriage, set up a meeting with Jerry to discuss this matter. After meeting at a shopping mall and making small talk for a time, Jerry came right out and told Burt that he was in love with his wife and that he was "taking" her. According to Burt, those were Jerry's exact words. Jerry went on to say that he was going to file for a divorce from his wife Sherry the following day and that he was probably going to have to give up a child in doing so.

Burt, a large but an extremely even-tempered man, became very upset over these happenings but caused no problem with Jerry. He immediately called Sharon's father, Mr. A.E. Hammond, to whom he was very close.

Burt and Sharon's parents enjoyed a very close relationship, all having a strong spiritual relationship with God. Burt, somewhat embarrassed, tearfully shared with his father-in-law what Sharon had told him about wanting a divorce and also about Jerry Easley being in the picture.

Mr. Hammond, also completely taken by surprise by this sudden and upsetting chain of events, confronted his daughter regarding what Burt had shared with him. Surprisingly to him, Sharon indicated to her father that this was true and the divorce was what she desired. Mr. Hammond told her in no uncertain terms that if she was having a relationship with Easley before the divorce was final, that neither she nor Jerry would be welcome in the Hammond home or for that matter, the Hammond family.

Now, Jerry Easley, being the extremely controlling individual that he was, did not take kindly to such talk from a respectable man such as his future father-in-law was known by all to be. After being told by Sharon about what her Father had told her, Jerry demanded a meeting with Mr. Hammond and basically laid down the law to him, stating that if he did not accept him as Sharon's boyfriend, he would destroy all of the love that Sharon previously had for him and Mrs. Hammond.

These confrontations occurred in the late summer of 1968, around August. Jerry, even though not yet separated or divorced from Sherry, forbid Sharon to have any contact whatsoever with her parents and family. Jerry was calling the shots regarding both marriages and on September 12, 1968, Jerry left Sherry and Jon in the trailer on Yale Street and moved into an apartment in Spring Branch with some friends from Elkhart. Both of these high school friends, Wally Rhodes and Sidney Preacher, were experiencing issues with their significant others at the time and this worked out well for all three of them for a short time.

Sharon had already separated from Burt and was sharing an apartment with a close friend also in the Spring Branch area. It was a very convenient situation for everyone involved, that is, with the exception of Burt and Sherry. Burt was aware of what was happening but Sherry was not yet completely aware of everything that was occurring. However, she was accepting of the fact that she and Jerry could no longer stay in this marriage.

Jerry, having won the first several rounds in this battle against Burt and the Hammonds, obviously felt it necessary to flaunt his victories. He did this by attending the church with Sharon that her family and Burt also attended. Burt was an usher on one of those occasions and had the embarrassing duty to seat Sharon and Jerry for the service. Burt was also responsible at that service in the administering of Holy Communion, which required him to serve Sharon and Jerry. The sanctity of the marriage and of this Communion practice was actually being destroyed before not only their Lord, but before the entire congregation who had become aware of this situation. This was not only extremely embarrassing to Burt, but to all of the Hammond family and their many, many close church friends. This was an extremely difficult situation for all, but especially for Sharon. She was actually very close to her Father and for her to be admonished by Jerry to not have any contact with him was very conflicting to her. As honest a person as she was, she did occasionally defy Jerry and have lunch with Mr. Hammond, secretly of course.

The gauntlet had been thrown down and the line had been drawn in the sand. Of course, Burt, being somewhat of a mild-mannered man who apparently really loved Sharon deeply, decided to contest the divorce between him and Sharon. He reasoned that he would fight the divorce on the legal standing that Sharon had no actual grounds for their divorce. Even in 1968, no actual grounds for a divorce were necessary in the legal system in the State of Texas. After a brief hearing held on the matter, Burt dropped the lawsuit as he realized that this was not a winnable situation for anyone involved. The legal reasoning finally explained to Burt by his attorney was that if one of the parties wanted to dissolve the marriage, no proof or evidence of marital misconduct was necessary. Burt also was forced to face the stark realization that if a woman no longer desires to live with you, she could not be forced to. It was over, plain and simple. Their divorce was granted on March 12, 1969.

After their divorce in December, 1968, Jerry became increasingly difficult for Sherry to deal with, if in fact that had ever been possible. The past year had just been hell for Sherry as it seemed that she could do nothing to please Jerry. Jerry, in return, just became more demanding and controlling as if nothing was wrong. It was very likely, in retrospect, that Jerry's demanding personality had been such that he was attempting to drive Sherry away. Sherry had already been through her own personal hell what with Jerry's controlling personality and then on top of that, the surfacing of his infidelity.

There was court-ordered visitation with Jon and when Jerry would arrive to pick up his son, he would see Sherry who was actually becoming more liberated each day. She was having her hair done professionally, dressing in new modern-day fashions, and wearing makeup. She was growing into something that Jerry had for several years fought her from becoming. This caused Jerry to become furious, beginning an even more extreme pattern of behavior than before. Even Sherry could not have imagined the situation to become worse than during their marriage. However, it did worsen.

Sherry was constantly aware and becoming more concerned than ever regarding the situation with Jerry. It was on her mind each and every day. However, she tried to remain positive, hoping and praying that possibly most of these problems would pass with enough time. She struggled to continue with her new job and to make a new and better life for herself and her son. Also, more importantly than anything, she was determined to do what was best for Jon, the brightest spot in her life at this time. Unfortunately, each new day had Sherry wondering what new challenge Jerry would present to her.

After the Divorces (10)

FOR A MAN who was having an extra-marital relationship, it would not seem a prudent course of action to boldly attempt to intimidate the individuals you hoped would be your future mother and father-in-law. Who would attempt to begin a relationship with his future in-laws by making demands and threatening to tear their daughter's love away from them? As strange as this seemed, this was however, the approach that Jerry Easley took to endear himself to his future wife's family. Or, possibly since it worked to a great extent with Sherry's family, Jerry had no reason to believe it would not work once again in his favor.

To Mr. and Mrs. A.E. Hammond, this was not only a heartbreaking set of circumstances, it was also very frightening. To be threatened physically by a man who was not only breaking up their daughter's seemingly happy marriage, that was bad enough. However, for the Hammond family to becoming fearful of a physical confrontation was a totally new fear. They had never experienced anything close to this bizarre behavior in their lives such as this turmoil. To this mild-mannered Christian couple now in their fifties, this had to be a situation that they never would have dreamed of being involved in.

Mr. Hammond was a man of impeccable reputation, not only as a family man, but also in his church as well as in his business world of printing. While he was a patient man and even after he had been purposely provoked, this man very likely had to rely heavily on his faith to make the correct decisions through this chain of events involving his only daughter.

Jerry Easley was now living within several blocks of Sharon and it would have been very unusual if they were not cohabitating at this time as well as prior to the official dissolution of both marriages. Jerry had orchestrated the events up to this point in time and a number of his agenda items in his plan were falling into place. However, Jerry was obsessed with the next step in his grandiose plan, that being of him obtaining full custody of Jon.

Sherry was a very loving and caring Mother to Jon. Jon was her life. Of course, she was not without the dream that somehow, someway, there might possibly be that Prince Charming to surface in her life. Sure, she knew full well that this was merely just a dream at this time, that some very nice man would come along in her life and provide for her and her son the security that every Mom would be proud to have. It was a dream, and if that dream was to be, she was ready to live that dream.

Ok, all of these dreams and thoughts were OK. However, the reality was that there was this man in the past of her life that WAS NOT GOING TO LET HER GO. As Sherry emerged from this cocoon that Jerry had all but forced her to live in, this Sherry with the new look emboldened Jerry even more. To Jerry, this now ex-wife that he had despised, deserted, and cheated on was now appearing as a very attractive and desirable lady. Sherry was approached by Jerry regarding a reconciliation of their marriage. Sherry, however, knowing now full well about what had occurred prior to their marriage separation, would have no part of any such talk. Sherry's refusal to even consider any type of reconciliation was very likely the last straw for Jerry Easley. For Jerry, Sherry was and continued to be his enemy. His later utter contempt for enemies would become well known to all those who surrounded him.

Sherry had created a new life and routine for her and her son Jon. The Campbell Road trailer home was more than adequate for Sherry and Jon. Several of the closest members of Sherry's family lived nearby. She was now ready to resume those lost relationships. She felt like she had a lot of catching up to do to renew the family relationships she had so cherished in her earlier life. Sherry developed a pattern of driving her sister-in-law

Barbara to work and also home in the afternoon. They worked in adjacent office buildings so this was convenient for both. This routine included dropping little Jon off at a well-respected caregiver each and every day. For a young now 24-year-old attractive divorcee, this was the beginning of a new life that she had not been able to know while living under the domineering thumb of Jerry Easley.

Jerry had weekend visitations as ordered by the court. However, to an obsessive controlling personality such as Jerry's, this was far from sufficient. Sure, he went along with the court orders but all the while, Jerry was plotting another course of action. That course of action was to prove that Sherry was an unfit Mother. Jerry had no actual suspicion of any activity on her part that would prove such, which, by the way, would have been an impossible task in 1969. Nevertheless, Jerry was not to be denied.

Jerry began to approach any individuals that had everyday contact with Sherry. Today, in 2017, this would have been an extreme case of harassment and even stalking, both misdemeanors with serious consequences under the law. Jon's daytime caretaker, a widow lady who in her own home took care of John each day, was approached by Jerry in an attempt to prove Sherry as an unfit Mom.

Jerry soon found out, very frustratingly so, that his efforts were not becoming successful. He had even gone so far as approaching Jon's baby sitter regarding her testifying against Sherry. This became an unbearable situation for this elderly lady, who at some point in time had even told Sherry that she might need to obtain another daytime caregiver for Jon. This lady provided Jon with loving care and she actually needed the small amount of extra income this service provided to her. However, she was not able to stand up to the pressure from Jerry.

It was also learned that Jerry had even gone to Sherry's job and spoke to Sherry's boss regarding Sherry's dating activities. This was just total and outright harassment of her at her work place, but again Jerry did it on more than one occasion and got away with it, even though he was not able to learn anything negative about Sherry.

Houston Police Officer Roy Drude, a veteran of many years on the Patrol beat, answered a call for service to Sherry's trailer in April, the time frame that Jerry was on his crusade to discredit Sherry in some manner. Sherry and several family members called the police on that day in an attempt to do something about Jerry's increasingly harassing behavior. Stalking was not in the law enforcement or societal vocabulary and they were just basically advised that nothing could be done until "something was done" or a crime was committed.

Jon's pediatrician was also approached by Jerry in a bribery attempt to persuade him to testify against Sherry. Jerry even offered this health-care professional man $200 to testify that Sherry was not providing good care for Jon. The Doctor was not at all amused by this proposal and ordered Jerry out of his office with further instructions to not return. Can you imagine Jerry also approaching Sherry's supervisors and coworkers in an attempt to build a case against Sherry? This is what Sherry was dealing with in the spring and early summer of 1969. The stress must have been unbearable for Sherry, both day and night.

These bizarre actions by Jerry were obviously violations of the law should these efforts ever come to fruition. However, as Sherry had come to realize, this was all about Jerry. Should one of these proposals be agreed upon, it would likely be that person who would pay the price. Jerry would just deny any involvement and go on with his life. In Jerry's mind, this was not only the way it was but the way it should be. Little did anyone know how true Sherry's knowledge of the real Jerry Easley would later prove to be. Little did Sherry know about ALL HIS ENEMIES.

Each and every time that Jerry had contact with Sherry surrounding Jon's visitation, Jerry seethed in knowing that he no longer had control over this now attractive and well- dressed young lady. Of course, Sherry always had been attractive. She was just not allowed by this controlling husband to present herself as such.

Each new day Sherry was confronted with a new challenge, not full well knowing what action Jerry would take next to confound her life.

Sherry Easley, A Young Vibrant Divorcee (11)

I T WAS JUNE, 1969, and for Sherry Ann Dean Easley it was just one more of a seemingly never-ending succession of the typical hot and humid summer days in Houston, Texas. She was used to this type of climate, as her early childhood years were spent in the West Texas Panhandle and Plains areas.

However, this was a new era in her life, as she was just becoming adjusted to her new self, a new Sherry, that of being the young, very attractive 24-year-old divorcee. She had her modest, but comfortable well-furnished mobile home in Spring Branch. This residence was in a peaceful, serene neighborhood, a trailer park of middle-income citizens surrounded by a number of trees throughout the park. Neighbors were neither nosy nor noisy. She felt comfortable with some of them and sought to become acquainted with what she felt might have been the more family-oriented ones. She also hoped to gain new friends which might possibly give her a sense of security while living there with her young three-year-old son, Jon.

Sherry had a new job at a major, well-established oil equipment manufacturing company. At her place of employment, Sherry was the attractive newcomer to the office. She was not only very attractive, but possessed a vibrant and likeable personality. Sherry was soon reunited in friendship with several young ladies in the office that she had known back in high school in Spring Branch. And, of course, there were a number of young men her age, some older, that were immediately attracted to Sherry. She was accepted almost immediately in the office work place. Sherry's and Jon's lives in June, 1969, were a new experience for both. Sherry was ready at this time in her life to move on from her terrible marriage experience to Jerry Eugene Easley.

Beneath all of this, however, there was a deep-seated fear in her life that pervaded her every moment. This anxiety threatened her very existence on this earth. Yes, there was the joy of her life, little Jon, whom she cherished, and deep down, whom she lived for after the disappointment of a failed marriage. True, she had full custody of Jon, and had arranged for a very competent daytime caretaker while she took employment to support herself and Jon. Also true, she had a small amount of court-ordered child support to supplement the income of a divorcee who had just reentered the work force.

In many ways, life was going somewhat well for Sherry. The office work place at the Cameron Iron Works conglomerate in west Houston had exposed her to a number of young, attractive men who were seemingly lined up to ask her out on dates. In other ways, however, there was this lurking fear and ever-constant fear that Jerry was not totally out of the picture. Jerry's court-ordered visitation rights were something she would not ever even attempt to confront Jerry about. She strongly felt that this was his right as a Father and she had not planned to ever challenge that right. However, she dreaded those times when Jerry would be allowed to arrive and take custody of Jon for the weekend. She dreaded when he arrived and also dreaded those times when he would just naturally be late in returning Jon. To her, it seemed that he was tempting Sherry to raise the issue which would then cause a scene and create a larger problem. She had learned to just "grin and bear it".

Sherry was naïve in some respects, but not in all. She was well aware of the men who sought her companionship, knowing full well what most of them were all about. To the man, all that attempted to date her were recently divorced men, and most had children for which they were doing their part to support. In other words, these were men who had lived in a relationship where sexual activity was the norm of their life. Now, those same men, having lost that intimate contact with a female, were seemingly "on the prowl", hoping to regain that intimacy with an attractive young lady such as Sherry. Of course, a divorced man's desire of intimacy was not exactly what Sherry was hoping for.

Susan Finch, childhood friend of Sherry's from high school in Spring Branch, a very spiritual young single lady, lived in California and was planning to move back to Houston to be closer to her aging parents. She and Sherry had also discussed at length the possibility of her moving in with Sherry and Jon after the divorce. These were the plans but prior to this coming to fruition, Susan had employment obligations to complete and this was taking longer than she or Sherry had expected and hoped it would take.

Sandra Lee Hoover was another old acquaintance of Sherry's who worked at Cameron that she had become reunited in friendship with. She came to work there in December, 1968, and had known Sherry from high school at Spring Branch High.

Sherry was well aware of how some seemingly, well-intentioned men could be. She was "street smart" enough to know which ones were only looking for that all-important-to- them one-night stand. At the same time, there was that glimmer of hope that there might be that Prince Charming, this gentleman who might trot along at any moment on his white horse to reach down and whisk her into another existence along with Jon. After all, this would not have been the first time in history that a man out there was willing to step forth and help a very good young woman not only raise her child, but possibly even begin a new family. There was the feeling that there could just possibly be that "Mr. Right" who would be the respectful mate that she longed for, but actually had never experienced during her six years of marriage.

However, throughout all of the wishful thinking, there remained an ever pervasive fear. Of all of these thoughts, at the age of 24, she was even more preoccupied with a very troublesome aspect of her existence: This was the ever-constant presence in her life of her ex-husband, Jerry Easley.

The problems that existed in their marriage were now magnified by the possessive personality traits of Jerry. Immediately, these issues surfaced, and very rapidly, to the forefront.

It seemed that Jerry was obsessed with one primary goal in mind - to prove she was an unfit Mom. She had begun dating but always when Jon was on a court-ordered visitation. Sure, she enjoyed the companionship of some of those men she dated. No, she had not yet allowed any man to sleep over at her trailer nor her with any man at his place. She and her family as well as her close friends knew that Jerry's view of Sherry was not true. Not only was it not true, but his obsession with proving her unfit was unsettling to Sherry and Jerry's friends, and also to Jerry's own family.

Actually, many things that had occurred during their marriage were becoming more and more clear to Sherry. Everything now, just as before in his courtship of her as well as throughout their marriage, was more and more visible. And, that was this - IT WAS ALL ABOUT JERRY. It was all about Jerry's pursuit of his education, of which Sherry naturally felt was for the benefit of their financial and economic well-being and comfort. A husband with several college degrees was certainly something that Sherry felt would be of benefit to all involved. It was certainly not anything that she had known of in her own family. Honest and hard-working as they were, education had never been stressed in the Dean family. This pursuit of education by Jerry, to her, had definite positive possibilities for the long run. Sherry possessed a tremendous supply of common sense. After the failed marriage had become finalized, Sherry came to her reasoning as to what the previous six years had really been all about. The common thread that she could weave throughout their courtship and marriage was this - IT WAS ALL ABOUT JERRY.

This constant concern of Sherry's reverberated throughout her mind, not only before and during the contentious divorce proceedings, but each and every day now. As to what actions Jerry might take next took a toll on her happiness and her mental well-being. Jerry was not one bit bashful regarding his goal of proving Sherry to be an unfit Mom to Jon. He spoke to everyone he came in contact with about Sherry and what her activities were.

However, the idea in the late 1960s that a biological father could gain custody of a child for these proposed reasons was basically unheard of. There were women who had none of Sherry Easley's morals that would have been able to withstand Jerry Easley's assault on her character. Jerry Easley's East Texas upbringing could have, should have, and probably had been brought into play here; someone should have told him that he was "barking up the wrong tree." However, no one as a close friend or family member ever did so.

Sherry's Obituary (12)

The Houston Chronicle, Wednesday June 18, 1969:

EASLEY-Mrs. Sherry Ann Easley, 3403 Campbell Road, passed away Sunday morning. Employed by Cameron Iron Works. Survivors: Father, Mr. J.F. Dean, Mother, Mrs. Zelma Ellen Kimes, Son, Jonathan Edward Easley, Sisters, Mrs. Naomi Ruth Butler, Mrs. Betty Jean Leveritt, Mrs. Glenna Frances Carter, and Mrs. Doris Ellen Elkins. Brothers, Troy Wendell Dean and David Lee Dean, as well as a number of other relatives and many, many friends.

Services at 10:00am, Thursday, June 19, 1969, Waltrip Chapel, Dr. Russell Dilday officiating. Interment at Woodlawn Garden of Memories, Antoine and Katy Freeway. Waltrip Funeral Directors, 1415 Campbell Road, 465-2525.

LITTLE IS KNOWN about the attendance at Sherry's service other than it was a very large gathering of family and friends. What is known was that none of the Easley family attended. It was reported that a phone call from Elkhart was made to Sherry's sister Glenna after the Murder asking if there was anything they could do. The response to the caller was yes, "tell Jerry to turn himself in". Of course, at the time, Jerry's involvement was adamantly denied. From then on, Jon Easley, at the age of three years old, had lost all contact with his Mother's loving family.

In attempting to understand the actions of the extended Easley family in not attending Sherry's funeral, the following must also be pondered: Sherry had been a member of the Easley family for over six years prior to the divorce. There had been no known Easley family conflicts during the marriage. She was a daughter-in-law, sister-in-law, and more importantly, the Mother of the Easley family grandson and nephew, Jon.

There is an old saying that "blood is thicker than water", meaning somewhat that family is more important than anything else that might arise in relationships. This blood was obviously thicker than that which flowed from Sherry's mortally wounded body the previous Saturday night. Of course, what might have also been a factor was that the strange actions of Jerry Easley on Monday prior to her body having been discovered had not been considered. Surely, to the average person, those actions that day would have been more than suspicious to even the average person. Unless, the blood being thicker became a factor in turning a blind eye to the situation.

Jerry's Actions After Sherry's Murder was Discovered (13)

I N CONTINUING THE investigation, it was learned that at the time of Sherry's Murder, Jerry was not yet openly cohabitating with Sharon. She, along with a female friend, Peggy Brown Kelley, maintained an apartment on Johanna Street just several blocks from the apartment that Jerry lived in. He shared an apartment on nearby Woodvine Street with a couple of high school friends from Elkhart, both of whom, ironically, just as Jerry, were experiencing relationship difficulties with either wives or girlfriends.

These men, Wally Rhodes and Sidney Preacher, were interviewed shortly after Sherry's body was discovered. Interestingly enough, the following peculiarities regarding Jerry Easley's actions were noted by the interviewing Detectives:

On the tragic weekend, Wally Rhodes had been on vacation from his job for several weeks and had spent almost the entire time with his parents back in Elkhart. He returned to Houston late Sunday evening, leaving Elkhart late in order to avoid the traffic. He arrived at his apartment on Woodvine Street in Spring Branch after the two-and-a-half hour drive at approximately 11:00pm. When he arrived, Jerry, Sharon, and Jon were there. Wally wondered why Jon was still with Jerry that late on a Sunday night, but did not ask any questions. Needing to begin his new work week early the next morning, Wally went on to bed and left for work the next morning at 6:00am before Jerry, Sharon, or Jon were awake.

The next contact Wally had with Jerry was on Monday night at 9:00pm when he returned to his apartment and received a phone call from Jerry. Jerry was at Sharon's apartment on nearby Johanna Street and Jerry asked him to come over because they had something to tell him. Upon his arrival there, he said it looked like the lobby of the Rice Hotel as Jerry's Mom, his sister, and one of his brothers were all there along with Jerry, Sharon, and Jon. It was at this time that Jerry told him that Sherry was dead, which obviously very much surprised him. While Jerry did not say how she died, he did tell Wally that Sherry's family would suspect him and that since they knew where he lived, he was going to stay over at Sharon's place and it would be better if Wally did also.

Wally went along with this strange request although he wondered about why he was asked to be inconvenienced by staying away from his own apartment. However, he did so justifying it in his mind that by doing so he would avoid being questioned by the authorities. This went on for about four days, him going back and forth to get essentials. Wally wondered later at the timing of this news about Sherry, in that while she was discovered around 6:00pm, at 9:00pm, Jerry's Mom and sister were already there in Houston. Wally, while not wanting to believe that his friend had anything to do with Sherry's death, later learned that Jerry had left to go get his Mom and sister from Elkhart some six hours before Sherry's body was found, leaving Houston at around noon to pick up his Mom and sister at 2:00pm in Elkhart. Even to Wally, definitely not the sharpest knife in the Elkhart drawer, this was very strange indeed.

Wally Rhodes was also one of those individuals that Jerry attempted to enlist in his defamation of Sherry as a fit Mom. Wally turned Jerry down, telling him the only thing he could say about the care of Jon was that he was not made to mind when told to do something, not unusual for a three-year-old little boy. Wally later reluctantly agreed to take a polygraph test regarding his knowledge of the Murder. He passed the test on his being involved in the Murder, but would not answer any questions about his close friend Jerry's involvement. Actually, it was never thought that he would have been involved and that he was really only a witness to the strange events surrounding Jerry's seemingly first-hand knowledge that "something had happened to Sherry".

Another Elkhart native, Sidney Preacher, had also been residing temporarily at Wally Rhodes' shelter for estranged men. He was also questioned but had actually not been staying there at the time of Sherry's death. Both of these men admitted that they knew Jerry was romantically involved with Sharon while still married and even living with Sherry. Neither thought that was right, but felt like it was none of their business and remained quiet to Jerry regarding the affair. Both Wally and Sidney were having relationship issues, but with their East Texas-Elkhart upbringing, they knew right from wrong.

Detectives later questioned Jerry's Mom regarding the time her son contacted her on this Monday. Mrs. Easley's timeline verified that of Wally Rhodes. She indicated that Jerry was in Elkhart at about 2:00pm and they left there at 3:00pm. Jerry's words to his Mom were that he wanted her to come to Houston to take care of Jon as "something had happened to Sherry". Jerry's sister, not a resident of Elkhart at the time, just happened to be in Elkhart visiting with her Mom when Jerry called and summoned his Mom. The sister was there and basically just came along to support her Mom and brother in whatever the circumstances were. As they say in the movies, due to some of the revelations learned regarding the times involved in this notification and the hurried trip to Elkhart, the "plot was thickening". Their basic suspicions were that Jerry Easley had driven to Elkhart to bring his Mom to Houston to assist in caring for the young son because "something had happened to Sherry". The fact that this sequence of events began some six hours before Sherry's body was discovered was most puzzling to the Investigators.

TIMELINE OF JERRY'S ACTIONS ON MONDAY, JUNE 16, 1969:

12 noon: Jerry, Sharon, and Jon leave Houston for Elkhart.

2:00-3:00pm: They arrive in Elkhart to pick up Jerry's Mom to come to Houston to help take of Jon as something has happened to Sherry. Jerry's sister accompanies Jerry to Houston.

5:00pm: Approximate arrival at Sharon's apartment.

5:56pm: Call to Police from David Dean after Sherry's body was found.

The Murder Investigation
Continues (14)

HOLMES AND COMBS were both veteran Detectives and had been not only partners, but also friends and neighbors as both lived in the rural Tomball area of northwestern Harris County. Like many Houston Police Officers in this era, both had chosen to raise their families far away from the crime-ridden areas of the city they policed. Both knew the advantages and disadvantages of living 30 miles out of the city, but even with the 60 mile round trip daily commute, they believed it best for themselves and their families to be away, as much as possible, from the city they policed. At the time, they shared the use of a city-owned vehicle, which made the daily commute less expensive. The vehicle was provided to Detectives as a means for them to respond to a scene investigation in a more timely manner. It was also an important "perk" of the job itself, something that a street Patrol Officer was not able to take advantage of.

Holmes and Combs were also veterans of the military, Holmes having served his country in World War II. Combs had served in the United States Navy at the end of WWII. He was also a United States Air Force veteran of the Korean War. The plane on which he was assigned had been shot down over North Korea. The pilot was killed and Combs was injured in the crash and had thereafter been held captive for 16 months as a Prisoner of War. Combs had not surfaced from that captivity without physical problems. Being held in a four foot by six foot cage for a year-and-a-half would affect any individual. However, Sonny Combs was considered by all of his co-workers to be tougher than the average bear. He had gone through the HPD Police Academy with honors, both academically and physically. He had survived eight years on the mean streets of Houston prior to being promoted to Detective. The tradition existed at the time of both men's entry to the Homicide Division that required a vote of the existing members. While not totally binding, the consensus of the Homicide Division veterans that they would be more than willing to work with the applicant as a partner went a long way in their acceptance into this very elite fold of investigators.

Ira and Sonny, partners at this time for over four years, both knew tough times, but the scene which they were assigned to investigate this time was one which would linger in their memories for many years to come. This was unlike any of the drug-related Murder cases common to Houston. It was also much different than a barroom brawl in which someone's life was taken. This was a true victim - someone murdered in the sanctity of their own residence, someone whose peaceful rest was shattered by an unknown intruder, very likely in the dead of night. They had likely viewed more "blood and guts" through the years on Murder scenes and even at the scenes of fatal traffic accidents. However, this scene would stay with these two grizzled veterans of the Homicide Division throughout the remaining years of their careers.

When Homicide Detectives Combs and Holmes continued with their initial investigative report at the Homicide office, they worked the entire night attempting to formulate the basic outline of their Murder report. Their initial goal was to document everything they had learned up to this time and be able to answer questions thoroughly while briefing a fresh pair of Detectives as well as a Supervisory Lieutenant from the Day Shift. This would have to be a team effort to hopefully bring this case to fruition. Neither was out for the glory of clearing the case, but just as all who would be involved, there would be the common goal - bringing someone to justice for Sherry. Someone had to speak up for Sherry.

The following morning, Homicide Lieutenant Breckenridge Porter arrived for duty. The bedraggled Detectives Holmes and Combs were there anxiously awaiting his arrival and then thoroughly briefed him on what their findings and suspicions were at the time. Lieutenant Porter, also a seasoned Homicide Detective in his earlier days, summoned a Day Shift pair of Detectives to immediately become involved in this investigation. Lieutenant Porter's choice to assist Ira and Sonny on this case were Detectives Jimmy Marquis and Willie Young.

Since the entire Murder offense report had not yet been completed, Ira and Sonny attempted to thoroughly brief Lieutenant Porter and the new men, Jimmy and Willie. They went over the known and unknown segments of the investigation to this point. Numerous questions were asked of the totally exhausted scene Investigators and they were relieved at approximately 11:00am the next morning. They left to go home, catch several hours of rest, and return later the same day to continue the investigation.

Homicide Detectives are a unique breed of cops. Basically, there are several types, all being individuals who carry out their assigned duties in different manners. Homicide Detectives have the unusual task of speaking out for those who can no longer speak for themselves, those victims who meet their death at an inopportune time. Who can speak for these now silenced victims? When Ira Holmes and Sonny Combs came face to face, so to speak, with Sherry Dean Easley in those horrific circumstances that hot day in June, 1969, their main thoughts were with Sherry. Who can speak for Sherry Dean Easley? None other than these two Homicide Detectives, that's who. It was their assignment also to learn much more about Sherry, what she was like as a person and very importantly, what could have caused someone to commit this type of violence towards her?

This is an important turning point in a Homicide Detective's goal in life and the question arrives in each and every case - Can I adequately represent the victim who cannot represent themselves in this investigation?

Another type of Investigator is the dedicated professionals who can work the scene, do all follow-up investigation and track down leads. They can do their level best to bring justice for the victim and when unable to do so, can let go in their minds of the unsuccessful conclusion with the satisfactory feeling that they did all that was possible under the constraints of the criminal justice system. And yes, there are unfortunately many legal constraints law enforcement Officers are confronted with each and every day. They do not agree with most of the constraints, but as sworn professionals, they grit their teeth and abide by them.

They are then able to, so to speak, let it go and move on. They have the mental ability to not take it home with them. They are confident that they did their best and to just say to themselves, not all cases will be cleared. This type of Investigator is not to be construed as uncaring or in any manner unprofessional. They are just totally aware of the limitations they face within the system. And, of course, working within the system is a matter for a completely different chapter in the investigations of such crimes.

Then, there is the other type of Investigator who becomes so involved with the Murder cases and many times with the victim's family and friends that the investigation becomes part of their everyday lives. They take it home with them and have the feeling that until a successful conclusion is reached, not only have they let the victim down, but also the victim's family and friends. These are the exceptional Investigators who never, ever, let it go. Unfortunately, in these instances, it greatly affects the personal lives of the Investigator.

Marquis and Young's first priority was to attend and witness the actual autopsy, a practice deemed to be routine in a Who-Dun-It Murder of this nature. While this was not considered to be a choice assignment, both were well aware of the importance of viewing first-hand the autopsy as it is performed, seeing up close the extent of the wounds. Further documentation of those wounds as to length and depth are necessary at this time.

Having been told of Holmes and Combs opinion as to this being a crime of passion, these professionals were careful to not go into the investigation with a pre-conceived opinion about the offense. However, after viewing and understanding this medical investigation of the offense, they noted that not only were there indeed seven stab wounds as earlier indicated, there was extensive bruising and scratching around the face of the complainant. This indicated that not only was the victim brutally and repeatedly stabbed, she had also suffered a severe beating. The defensive wounds were obvious to her hands and arms as Sherry had attempted to ward off the assaults. Then the doctor conducting the autopsy advised that the stab wounds were gaping as if the weapon was twisted as it was being removed and that the wounds were very deep, as deep as five-and-one-half inches. It was the Doctor's opinion further that the knife used in this offense was at least six inches in length. An examination of the victim's vagina indicated no sign of sexual assault or the presence of semen.

The obvious goal of this gruesome procedure is to not only determine the cause of death but also the manner in which this victim died. CAUSE AND MANNER. Wounds are very carefully charted and documented for not only the Medical Examiner's internal report, but also for the Investigators to record in their offense report. All of this detail is necessary to be hopefully used and presented in a future trial in a court of law. Detail, detail, detail. This cannot possibly be stressed enough. The possibility that this factual report could someday be part of a United States Supreme Court ruling is always there. Remote, yes, but always possible. The Investigators knew full well the importance of documenting every move they make as well as with each and every item of evidence recovered. Once such information is officially documented in the offense report, to waiver from that would strain their credibility, especially when it came time to testify in a court of law. An Investigator cannot testify on the witness stand other than on the information and facts that are documented in the official report. For an Investigator to say on the witness stand that this was not how I meant it to read is totally unacceptable. The official report becomes the law enforcement version of the Gospel, so to speak.

After the victim's remains arrived at the Morgue, more photographs are taken. Seasoned Patrol Investigator Nelson P. Foehner received this assignment on Tuesday morning. He took additional photos to those taken at the scene and also took a complete set of finger prints as well as palm prints of the victim. Those prints of the victim could be of much value in the elimination and determination of which prints recovered at the scene are friendly and which prints might possibly be connected to a stranger.

To any Homicide Investigator, these were alarm signals sounding off when the autopsy was performed. In addition to the overkill of seven stab wounds, there existed evidence of an accompanied assault as well as the wounds gaping. Gaping, to the doctors at the morgue as well as to the Homicide Investigators, usually meant some type of hatred or revenge on the part of the assailant. The initial assessment by Holmes and Combs that this was a crime of passion was showing to be more credible as time wore on.

In an effort to recover any and all evidence that might be of value at a later date, head and pubic hair samples were taken and tagged in the Police Crime Lab along with scrapings from the fingernails. The autopsy had also revealed the following regarding the stab wounds:

Sherry, being a lady of small physical stature, was recorded at the Morgue as being five feet, seven inches tall, weighing 118 pounds. The stab wounds inflicted reached a depth of five-and-one-half inches in several instances. The wounds damaged one lung, as well as her liver, pancreas, spleen, and also one kidney. This definitely appeared to the Pathologist and Investigators as a classic case of overkill. The suspect, whoever it was, seemingly left no opportunity for Sherry to survive these wounds and identify her assailant. At this point, after previously conferring with Holmes and Combs, all involved were in agreement that the perpetrator was someone who knew the victim and likely held some deep-seated negative feelings toward her.

When Holmes and Combs returned to duty that Tuesday afternoon at 4:00pm, once again they met and conferred with Marquis and Young. The results of the autopsy were reviewed and discussed at length with each other and also with Lieutenant Crittenden. The Lieutenant was nearly sixty years old at this time, with no immediate plans to retire to leave what he considered to be the dream job of supervising Murder investigations. His input was always not only welcome, but also very well respected.

The investigation would continue on two shifts, with two Supervisors fully apprised of the elements of this crime. The Detectives were experienced and planned among themselves on the continuing investigation.

They made lists for each pair to complete and also made plans to continue the person-to-person communication each day to share their findings as to any progress that had been made.

This initial plan with four Investigators was soon proven to be inadequate as there were a large number of leads to check out. More assistance was requested of Lieutenants Crittenden and Porter, and as they were prone to do, they immediately responded by assigning Detectives Ken DeFoor and Tommy Baker to assist. Their first assignment was to re-interview the reportee, Sherry's brother, David Dean. He had found his sister's body when he went to her trailer to check on her welfare. At the time of the discovery of this crime, David told a rather interesting story to the Homicide Detectives. He had a very plausible explanation for going to the trailer to check on his sister, but he then began to explain his suspicion about the ex-husband, Jerry, being responsible for his sister's death. He stated that Sherry had on numerous occasions indicated that she was in fear of her life. She had related to a number of people that Jerry had openly made statements to her that he was going to kill her in order that he could obtain full custody of the three-year-old son, Jon. It was later learned that Jerry had been very careful NOT to make these statements in the presence of other people. Sherry had shared her concerns with many of her family and close friends and there was no doubt among them that, based on some of Jerry's other actions and behavior, he in fact had threatened Sherry's life.

Then David dropped a bomb on the Detectives as he told them the following story several days after Sherry was found:

David stated that on the previous Saturday night, June 14, he had difficulty sleeping and at about 2:30am, he began worrying about Sherry due to the reports she had given him about Jerry wanting to kill her. David lived just a short distance from Sherry's trailer so he drove to the trailer park. Finding her car there and the trailer with no lights on, he drove past her trailer and parked several trailer lots away. He just sat there and watched her trailer for approximately 20 minutes. He was just about to leave when he saw a man climb over the wood fence at the rear of Sherry's trailer. This man was dressed in a white shirt and dark pants and David stated that he could tell from the man's build and his walk that it was Jerry Easley.

Further, that this man walked to the back door of the trailer and after fumbling with the door for a minute or so, entered the trailer. It appeared to David that this person had a key. He continued watching and about five minutes later, David saw Jerry exit the trailer and climb back over the fence. Not seeing any lights come on and not hearing any sounds from the trailer during that time, he just thought everything was all right and went on home. To any police officer, and more so to seasoned investigators, this story seemed rather far-fetched. Seeing a violence prone ex-husband enter his sister's house in the dead of night and just blowing it off and going home? What a story this was, they thought! However, then again, David seemed a bit strange to them and even though they felt his story was strange also, maybe, just maybe it could have been true. They also wondered among themselves as to why David held this information for several days.

There were other events that had occurred at the trailer while the scene detectives were conducting their initial investigation that further aroused their suspicions regarding Jerry. One such event that occurred while they were there was that Sherry's home phone rang and when Detectives answered, they learned that it was Jerry Easley's divorce attorney. He indicated that Easley had contacted him that date stating that he had attempted to contact Sherry on Sunday night regarding returning John to his Mother after the weekend visitation. Easley told the attorney that he was unable to contact Sherry and was now concerned that he would be held in Contempt of Court by not returning Jon at the appointed time. This, along with other suspicions regarding Jerry as a suspect, just added more to their thinking that Jerry might just possibly be "their man".

After hearing David's rather fantastic story about the happenings there early on Sunday morning, the initial response by Detectives was that this was almost "too good to be true". David was interviewed at length regarding the truthfulness of his information and maintained steadfastly that what he stated was in fact true. A written and sworn statement was taken from David, which he freely signed.

At this point, it would have seemed that with David's statement along with the time of death being ruled in approximation to the time David allegedly saw Jerry enter and exit the trailer that a Murder warrant would have been in order. However, to say that Detectives were skeptical about David's version of the events that night would have been a gross understatement. There is an old saying that goes like this: "If it seems too good to be true, it probably isn't".

The Detectives spoke among themselves regarding David's version of the events that night. The more this was discussed among themselves, the more questions were raised than answers found. If David was so concerned about the threats on Sherry, why did he not check on Sherry immediately knowing that Jerry had no business whatsoever to be there at anytime, much less in the middle of the night? David's story was perplexing to the Detectives, to say the least.

Prior to attempting to obtain a Murder warrant on Jerry Easley, Detectives decided to move cautiously. The decision was made to ask David Dean to take a polygraph test on the truth and veracity of his statement. Initially, David readily agreed to be "put on the box". The test was scheduled for Wednesday, June 18, 1969. However, David Dean failed to report to the Central Police Station where the test was to be administered. Of course, they knew full well that Wednesday was the day prior to Sherry's funeral and they understood that this date would be a difficult time for such an important phase of the investigation.

When Detectives located David again to ascertain the reason he had failed to show up for the test, he initially stated that he had forgotten about it and then stated that he would rather take it at a later date. He was then asked directly if had lied about seeing Jerry at which time he broke down and admitted that yes, he had lied. He reasoned that he and his entire family felt so strongly that Jerry was responsible for Sherry's death and it was his feeling that this version would cause Jerry to be arrested for the Murder. He fully admitted that this was his idea alone and that while everyone in his family felt Jerry was involved, no one else goaded him into telling this story. Several days in the crucial stages of this investigation were lost due to the Detectives having to absorb this fantastic lead and work it out. In Detective lingo, David's version needed to be proved or disproved in order for the investigation to move forward. Unfortunately, it was disproved and the Detectives were back to "square one".

Even though David Dean's fantastic story was determined to have been made up, Detectives focused on learning more about Jerry Easley. All of the Dean family members were interviewed. There was Sherry's Mother and Stepfather, her Dad, four sisters and two brothers. While none of them had ever directly heard Jerry threaten Sherry, she had told all of them of the various and numerous threats he had made to her. The common theme of these threats was of the nature that he would kill Sherry in order to obtain custody of Jon AND that he WOULD GET AWAY WITH IT. He also told her that he would have an ironclad alibi and that he would be in his home town of Elkhart, in East Texas.

Of course, Detectives realized the possibility that some of this information could be hyped up by the family, who, to a person, considered Jerry as the prime suspect. As more and more people were spoken to, Detectives realized that there was very likely a great deal of truth to these suspicions of Jerry being involved. Friends and co-workers of Sherry were interviewed and all related the same threats that Sherry had shared with them.

To the veteran Homicide Investigators involved, to say that Jerry Eugene Easley was a person of interest would have definitely been an understatement. The scene photos were reviewed over and over by these fine men as well as an up and coming expert in the newly emerging field of Profiling. The consummate opinion was that the suspect was someone with a great deal of anger towards Sherry Easley. There was no missing property and no forced entry and these facts lingered constantly in the minds of these Investigators.

A Fresh Pair of Eyes to Review
the Investigation (15)

IN LATE AUGUST, Detective E.D. (Sonny) Combs became seriously ill and was taken off of the case. Combs, a combat veteran of the Korean War, had been a Prisoner of War for some sixteen months and had contracted several serious health problems as a result of that brutal confinement. It had taken its toll finally and after August, 1969, his physical health was never the same. He was basically relieved from his Homicide Division duties and went on sick leave. Sonny never returned to duty. His partner and friend, Ira Holmes, was assigned unofficially to assist Sonny and his family with whatever was needed. Sonny Combs, a true patriot and excellent Homicide Detective, passed away in January, 1971 at a young age of 42. He was survived by his wife and four sons, all four under the age of 18.

As time passed from June through July and then into August, the six original Investigators began to "catch" additional cases to work on as leads in the Easley case slowed down. Everything up to date had been thoroughly reviewed with no positive results that would lead to a criminal charge.

There are occasions in lengthy, complicated investigations that the Investigators working the case reach a point that two fresh eyes to look over their work becomes necessary. This was the thought at the time. There were two Homicide Detectives that stood out consistently as Homicide "dicks" that were exceptional in their field and were dogged in their pursuit of justice for complainants. Homicide Detectives are proud that they stand up for those who cannot stand up and speak for themselves. This point is borne out repeatedly by the fact that victims of the crimes of Burglary, Robbery, Theft, Sexual Assaults, as well as other lesser crimes, can on most occasions stand up and testify against those who have assaulted them or stolen their property. Herein lies the exception for Murder complainants - SOMEONE has to speak up for these victims as they are not able to do so on their own behalf.

Paul Nix and Ed Horelica had been Homicide partners for nearly four years. They had come to be known as the "big boys" in the Homicide Division and while this term was somewhat resented by some of the other Detectives in the Division, there was also an adequate amount of respect for them. Their investigative abilities and case-clearing successes that accompanied that term spoke loudly for these two men.

Nix, in his early 40s at this time, was a twice divorced 16 year veteran of the Department. Paul was the father of two sons. He was known to possess a fondness for alcohol, occasionally to excess. However, he was devoted to his profession and was known to go the extra mile to solve a Murder case.

Horelica, in his late 30s, had also been divorced and had been on HPD for 13 years. He was now attempting to assist his current wife in the rearing of their blended families of six children, four daughters and two sons. On a Detective's salary, Ed was known to stop on many occasions at the day-old bakery on Washington Avenue near the Central Police Station to stock the family up on bread to go with the vast amounts of peanut butter and jelly his wife Annette had shopped for.

In 1967 and again in 1970, the Houston Police Department Homicide Division was confronted with two offenses that would trouble any Homicide Detective - that being the Capital Murder cases of Houston Police Officers. These cases, just as those brutal Murders of citizens in which the original scene pointed at no suspect in particular, were known as WHO-DUN-ITS. Also, in this same period of time, eight young females from the Houston-Harris County area had disappeared from the streets of Houston or from public bus stops. Most of these young innocent victims were later discovered Murdered and dumped in the then-rural areas of Fort Bend and Brazoria Counties south and south- west of Houston.

Nix and Horelica, along with a number of other dedicated Detectives in Houston and the surrounding counties, eventually developed information which led not only to the clearance of the two Officer Murders, but also in the instances of these young females who had been kidnapped, sexually assaulted, brutally Murdered, and dumped in fields for their young bodies to rot. In all of these mentioned cases, Nix and Horelica were recognized as the lead Investigators in these lengthy and complex investigations, not only by their HPD counterparts, but also by the large number of Investigators from outside agencies who assisted in the Murder investigations of these young teenage girls.

As a result of Sonny's deteriorating health, Detectives Paul Nix and Ed Horelica were assigned to work this case full-time until such occasion that they would have to be pulled off to begin a fresh investigation. Nix and Horelica, being the very thorough investigators they were, immediately began reviewing the existing case file to determine if there were not only any clues overlooked, but what else needed to be done on this investigation. One of the first items that jumped out at them was the whereabouts of Jerry Easley on the night of the Murder. Where was he? What was his alibi? And, if he actually had an alibi, was it solid?

Jerry Easley's Alibi (16)

T HERE WERE NUMEROUS indicators that these experienced Homicide Detectives recognized that would lead them to believe that Jerry Easley was someone that should be looked at very closely for this crime.

Through the years, there had been a distinction drawn from a "person of interest" as opposed to someone referred to as a "suspect". This was necessitated through years of facing questions from defense attorneys in a court of law. These defense attorneys would suggest in open court, many times unchallenged by the prosecution or the Judge, that if an individual had been declared a suspect that the Detectives had already made their mind up regarding the case and were close-minded regarding other possible motives for the commission of the crime as well as the exclusion of other individuals. This was ridiculous reasoning for sure, but just another one of the endless streams of questioning that an investigator was forced to endure on the witness stand when a defense attorney had nothing else to "hang his hat on". These were merely "smokescreens" thrown up to possibly confuse the jury with other possibilities for them to consider, thereby giving the jury an opportunity to bring the concept of reasonable doubt into play. And unbelievably so, these methods actually worked on occasion.

When Jerry Easley finally came in to speak with Homicide Detectives, he arrived on Monday, June 23, 1969 accompanied by two attorneys. His divorce attorney, Mr. Tom Babcox, and a criminal defense attorney, Mr. John Leggio, came to the Homicide Office with Jerry. Veteran Detectives Jimmy Marquis and Willie Young conducted the interview and requested of Jerry that he advise them of his whereabouts over the weekend his ex-wife was murdered. Jerry then began to relate the following, about which he spoke openly and freely. Detectives Marquis and Young both commented later that Jerry was very confident when he spoke of his whereabouts and never wavered once during his version of the weekend's activities. Their thoughts were that he was being very truthful OR he had rehearsed his act very well. The following is a summarization of Jerry Easley's verbal statement to the Homicide authorities:

On Saturday morning, he arrived at 8:00am at Sherry's trailer to pick up his son. Then, he went to the apartment of his girlfriend, Sharon Hammond. He picked her up, after which time they drove out west of Houston to a rural area to look at a pony for Jon. He and Sharon privately spoke about the pony and realized that Jon was rather young for this activity and also that it was not financially feasible with their situation at the time. While Sharon was still in an apartment of her own with a friend, they did not anticipate this arrangement continuing for very long in the future. After looking at the pony, they went to several other locations in Spring Branch basically running errands. After eating lunch, they drove to Buffalo, Texas, where they planned to do some camping over the weekend. It was later learned that neither Jerry nor Sharon owned any type of camping gear whatsoever nor were they known to be previously interested in camping. That was thought by the investigators to be rather odd.

Continuing, in Buffalo, they stopped at an old friend's house to say hello to Bob Cockerham and his wife. After an hour or so of visiting, they saw another acquaintance in Buffalo and stopped to visit a short time with him. Then, Jerry related that they went to a friend's pharmacy there in Buffalo. This pharmacy was owned and operated by Susan Mann, who was the sister of another of Jerry's friend, Larry Jackson, whom he had known since his earlier collegiate days at Sam Houston University. Further, that after the pharmacy visit, they located Larry Jackson who owned a cabin in the rural area north of Buffalo.

Jerry stated that he, Sharon, Jon, Larry Jackson and his wife, as well as Susan Mann and her husband John Mann, all spent the night at the cabin. The following morning, Jerry, Sharon, and Jon left Buffalo and after stopping at the Coushatta Indian Reservation near Livingston, they returned to Houston. From Sharon's apartment, Jerry called Sherry's trailer to see if she was home so he could return Jon to his Mom. After several failed attempts to contact Sherry, he also phoned Sherry's step-father, Mr. Kimes, in an attempt to determine Sherry's whereabouts. After Mr. Kimes stated that they had not seen or spoken to Sherry, Jerry went to bed and then called his attorney the following morning. He stated that he called his attorney as he was concerned about not being able to contact Sherry to return their son and that he might be held in contempt of court. This was basically all Jerry had to offer at this time and the interview was concluded.

It did seem that there was not any interrogation at this time as this was merely an informational interview. A common tactic in investigations was to gain the information that was given freely and then do extensive follow-up to determine whether the suspect or person of interest was being in any manner untruthful. If it was thought that a suspect or person of interest was being untruthful about small details, it could possibly be that he or she was being equally as untruthful regarding matters of much importance.

After the interview, Jerry's attorneys were asked about the possibility of Jerry taking a polygraph test regarding his alibi. This idea was quickly and totally rejected by both attorneys, a not at all unusual bit of advice from an experienced defense attorney. And of course, this decision was based on the legal advice of two attorneys and in all probability, had been discussed at length prior to arriving in the Homicide office for the obliga-tory initial interview. In this era of criminal investigations, the polygraph test was a very common tool for Investigators. It was a common practice to ask a person such as Easley to go "on the box". However, this refusal to cooperate with this examination raised yet another red flag regarding the involvement of Jerry Easley in Sherry's murder.

Detectives Marquis and Young then discussed at length the contents of this interview with the scene Detectives, Holmes and Combs. Several points from the interview were very interesting to the investigators. They could not forget the point that Sherry had related to her family and friends that Jerry said HE WOULD BE OUT OF TOWN IN ELKHART AND WOULD HAVE AN ALIBI WHEN SHERRY WAS KILLED. Elkhart, his hometown, was only 40 plus miles east of Buffalo, and approximately the same distance to Houston as was Buffalo. Also, that this alibi from Jerry involved a very large number of people who needed to be questioned regarding Jerry's story. The thought and idea then crossed the Detectives' minds if Jerry is lying, could that large a group of individuals be covering for Jerry? At the time, that seemed rather implausible.

However, the thought was not lost on these Detectives that Jerry Easley had, on the spur of the moment that Saturday afternoon, sought out these individuals and made contact with them. Could he have been skillfully setting up an alibi? Or, possibly it may not have been on the spur of the moment, but calculatingly done knowing full-well that Jon was with him and Sharon. Many possibilities ran through the Detectives' minds over this scenario. Also, the thought entered their mind that Jerry was fully aware that Susan Finch was going to be moving back to Houston and living with Sherry very shortly. Was he thinking that it was "now or never", knowing that Susan would be around Sherry and Jon almost constantly in the near future? Was he that thorough and devious in planning anything for that night? It appeared, on the surface, that Jerry Easley had deliberately sought out these God-fearing and respectable friends and in doing so, set up an alibi for himself for that weekend. The thinking among these seasoned Investigators was that if this alibi was pre-arranged as they were suspecting, they were dealing with a very unusually conniving individual.

Homicide Detectives Paul Nix and Ed Horelica undertook the task of proving or disproving Jerry Easley's story. Their first stop in Buffalo, Texas, was the pharmacy that Susan Mann and her brother, Larry Jackson, owned and operated. They learned here that Larry had been the first to get to know Jerry Easley at Sam Houston University and during Jerry and Sherry's marriage, the Easley couple had been up to the Buffalo area on a number of occasions. It was during these times that Jerry and Sherry had become acquainted with the extended family of Larry Jackson.

The word had been received by the Jackson/Mann family that Jerry had begun a new relationship very soon with a woman named Sharon. The entire Jackson and Mann family in Buffalo had grown fond of Sherry and were not comfortable at the prospect of Jerry bringing Sharon so soon into this mix. From the limited knowledge they were aware of regarding the dissolution of this marriage, it was their feeling that Sherry had been done wrong by Jerry and most also felt it best that this friendship with Jerry just be put on hold for now. This family of God-fearing Christians had, for several years, become exposed to Jerry's ways and were actually not that fond of this man. However, they to a person liked and respected Sherry and even though Jerry was the friend of Larry's that had brought them all together, they more or less tolerated to an extent Jerry's occasionally rather bizarre actions. They had spoken among themselves and all felt it best that they not pursue their friendship with Jerry, and more especially so, not with any new female in his life. These were their feelings on June 14, 1969, and they were obviously totally unprepared for the events that took place in Houston later that Saturday night.

When Jerry, Sharon, and Jon arrived at the pharmacy in Buffalo, Jerry struck up a conversation and over a short period of time, asked Susan what she and her husband John's plans were for that night. Sue said that she and her husband had actually planned to go out on a dinner date, but she was not sure as to how to tell this to Jerry. She felt this way as she knew Jerry to be a persuasive person, even to the point of being pushy at times. While she did not openly say so to Jerry, Susan further felt that she did not like the idea of Sharon being with them so soon after Jerry had divorced Sherry. However, basically Jerry was pushing the idea of being with the Jackson and Mann families that night. Finally, Susan, being the kind and considerate lady that she was, relented and told Jerry that they had no plans. Jerry, being the type of person that the Jacksons and Manns knew him to be, then raised the ante and just came out and told Susan that they would like to spend the night at the cabin with them.

Susan contacted her brother Larry and told him that since Jerry was actually his friend, that he, Larry, should be spending the night at the cabin also. Larry agreed, but he was also not at all comfortable with the idea of Sharon being there with Jerry. However, it was agreed upon that to just keep the peace for now, that all would spend the night together at this very small, cramped hunting cabin. While all of these fine East Texas Bible Belt Christians felt pretty much the same way about Jerry, they all went along with the situation for this June night at the cabin. To a person, later they all felt more than a small amount of guilt having been suckered into being alibi witnesses for Jerry.

After dark, Jerry began acting very strangely. Even at the time, the Jacksons and Manns had come to the strange realization and felt strongly that Jerry had actually pushed himself into this overnight cabin adventure. John Mann said that he assumed they would all stay up late, playing dominoes or other games, as they had done on a number of previous occasions. This had been the normal activities for this group previously when Sherry was in the picture. And usually, a good time was had by all in attendance unless on several occasions when Jerry exhibited rather strange behavior, that being he would suddenly become upset over seemingly minor issues. However, such was not to be on this occasion, as early on Jerry had indicated very adamantly that he just wanted to go to bed. That was thought by all at the time to be extremely odd since he had pushed the idea of being at the cabin from the initial contact that day.

This cabin in the woods was described as having only three rooms - kitchen, living room, and one bedroom. The Buffalo, Texas area in November and December is a prime hunting ground for white-tail deer and there are many such cabins in the Piney Woods of East Texas. As was the case in many such cabins, there was no indoor restroom. This type of structure is used year-around by many, usually by males who gather in the quiet country surroundings to play cards, dominos or other games of chance, and on many occasions, consume vast amounts of alcohol in a safe surrounding. Outdoor cookouts are common with such games as horseshoes, washer pitching, and target practice being common enjoyable occurrences.

While there were several ceiling and floor fans, there was no central air conditioning for this cabin. Mid summer nights in the East Texas

Piney Woods could be very humid and actually the heat becomes rather stifling at times, especially if there is no breeze blowing. The sleeping arrangements for this night were as follows: Jerry Easley and young Jon slept in the only bedroom. Sharon and Larry Jackson slept in separate beds in this bunkhouse type arrangement. Susan Mann and her young child slept in one bed located in the living room. John Mann slept on a pallet on the floor near the front door of the cabin. John Mann later recalled that Sharon had accidentally stepped on him sleeping on the floor pallet. Since there was no indoor restroom, John assumed at the time that Sharon was going outside to relieve herself in the natural surroundings.

These people were interviewed at length individually regarding the times they went to sleep that night. Prior to bedtime, John Mann and Jerry left the cabin to take the Jackson's teenage brother Jimmie back to Buffalo. John stated that when they returned, Jerry parked his Buick headed south down the road. They even sat in the car for a short time watching for rabbits and other small game crossing the road. Upon further questioning, it was learned that Jerry's Buick was facing west when everyone got up the next morning. This raised the possibility that in fact Jerry could have left the cabin during the night while everyone else was asleep. Susan felt that they were all in bed by 10:30pm, actually a very early time to end the evening as compared to similar such gatherings in the past. Everyone turned in early at the persuasive suggestion of Jerry Easley. Larry Jackson, however, had a date and arrived at the cabin shortly after midnight. Could Jerry Easley, with all of these people present in this small cabin, have gotten up during the night and driven to Houston's Spring Branch Campbell Road? That seemed to the investigators to be a rather far-fetched idea. However, the possibility of this intrigued them more and more as they considered it.

Follow-Up Investigation into the Alibi (17)

THE VETERAN DETECTIVES Paul Nix and Ed Horelica had been assigned full time to the case. Interstate 45 was a major highway leading both north and south out of Houston. This new interstate was part of a nation-wide system of highways to allow vehicular traffic to drive at speeds of 60 to 70 miles per hour. The even-numbered interstates were to be in basically an east-west direction while the odd-numbered interstates were to follow a near as possible north-south direction. In the instance of Interstate 45, it was designated to follow basically the route of the old U.S. Highway 75.

At this time in June, 1969, the interstate was completed only as far north as Centerville. From there, going further north would require a very short detour east to the old U.S. Highway 75, and then 15 miles north of Centerville to Buffalo, a small community comparable in size to Centerville. The cabin was nine miles further east of Buffalo out on U.S. Highway 79 and then one-and-seven-tenths miles south on a small dirt road.

After interviewing all of the individuals who were present that night at the cabin, Nix and Horelica then decided to time this route from the cabin to the scene of Sherry's murder on Campbell Road. They drove in excess of 75 miles per hour, realizing if Jerry Easley had made this trip, he likely would have been in a rush and would have driven at the maximum allowed speed limit. The ever-calculating Investigators found the distance to have been 137 miles, which they covered in one hour and fifty minutes. Twice that time would be figured as three hours and forty minutes. Of course, they also thought about the fact that if Jerry Easley had driven at that rate of speed, even though it was in the wee hours of the morning, he would have taken a chance of being stopped for speeding. Also, they meticulously factored into the equation as to how much time it would have taken for someone to do what was done to Sherry inside the trailer on Campbell Road. They were now convinced that it was a possibility, albeit a remote one, that Jerry had set up this elaborate alibi with these innocent friends having been used to cover him. Later, after having learned of all this from the Detectives, it was the feeling of the Manns and Jacksons that they had in fact been used by Jerry for his alibi.

Realizing that this trip was made in the early Sunday morning hours with little or no traffic, Nix and Horelica contacted each and every law enforcement agency between Buffalo and Houston, including the Texas Highway Patrol. Their thinking was that just possibly Jerry could have received a traffic citation en route to or from doing the dirty deed. Unfortunately, as good as this idea was worth checking out, the results were negative.

While Jerry was seemingly cool after having been interviewed by the Homicide Detectives, the Manns later advised Nix and Horelica that Jerry had made a trip to Buffalo to warn them that some Houston cops would likely be in town to question them. Basically, Jerry in his typical assuming manner went to great lengths to advise his alibi witnesses that they were in fact just that. Jerry was not content with just advising his friends of the forthcoming inquiry. In addition, it was also later ascertained that Jerry had also returned to Buffalo after the interviews and inquired as to what had transpired in the follow-up interviews. It would seem to the average individual that Jerry had something to hide and/or something to be concerned about. He had placed a number of his friends "on the spot", and was not one bit embarrassed in doing so. Again, the friends in Buffalo as well as these experienced Detectives felt that these inquiries by Jerry were just more fuel to add to their feeling that Jerry had in fact cleverly set up the entire overnight situation at the Buffalo cabin.

Nix and Horelica continued this investigation well into the month of August, 1969. The case was reviewed at length with Supervisors and Detectives familiar with the facts. It was clear to all concerned that this was a critical point in the investigation. There was no physical evidence to connect anyone, including Jerry Easley, to Sherry's Murder. The evidence collected at the scene - fingerprints, palm prints, blood and hair samples as well as the rubber glove finger tips did not prove to be beneficial to the investigation. There was the seemingly well-established alibi that had been checked out. It was the consensus of opinion that after speaking with the friends of Jerry in Buffalo, that this had been carefully orchestrated. Then, of course, there was what was believed to have been a strong motive for Jerry Easley to harm Sherry. However, at this juncture, there was no way to connect Jerry Easley. It was time to "make it or break it", and it was further decided to make an effort to charge Jerry Easley with the Murder of his ex-wife Sherry.

The thought process behind this decision was to hopefully arrest Jerry Easley with Sharon present, where she could then be questioned at length regarding the night at the Buffalo cabin. The case was presented to two top Assistant District Attorneys, both of whom were highly experienced in the intricacies of Murder investigations and who were always ready to assist law enforcement. Equally important was that they also had the authority to accept or decline charges. Information was received from someone in recent contact with Jerry Easley that he, Sharon, and Jon would be leaving on Saturday, August 30 for a trip to the Grand Canyon in Arizona for an extended vacation. Further, that Easley was, in fact, fleeing Texas as he felt that authorities were closing in on him.

After this information was determined to be reliable, it was the thinking of the D.A.'s Office as well as that of the Homicide Detectives that Easley should not be allowed to flee the state's jurisdictional bounds as this would make the investigation even much more legally complex. A Murder charge was filed on that day and a statewide pickup was placed on the vehicle Easley was believed to have been driving, a blue 1967 Buick. Later that afternoon, Travis County Sheriff deputies stopped this vehicle on the southwest edge of Austin, Texas. The Buick was occupied, as suspected, by Jerry Easley, Sharon, and Jon. Jerry Easley was then arrested, after which he advised Sharon in the presence of arresting Officers not to talk with the police.

Houston Homicide was immediately notified and arrangements were made for the Travis County authorities to transport Easley, Sharon, and Jon to La Grange, Texas, in two separate vehicles in order to keep Easley separated from Sharon. They were met in La Grange by Detectives Nix and Horelica as well as two Houston Juvenile Division Officers, who took custody of Sharon and Jon and returned them to Houston. Nix and Horelica took custody of Jerry Easley and returned him to Houston to face the Murder charge.

As was Jerry Easley's constitutional right, he was met in Houston by two defense attorneys in the Homicide Office. A lengthy conference was allowed with his two attorneys, both of whom had been involved with Easley either in the divorce from Sherry or the happenings leading up to and after the Murder. Jerry Easley invoked his Fifth Amendment right against self-incrimination and refused to answer any questions proffered to him. He also refused to take a polygraph test. He was placed in the City Jail on the Murder charge.

Sharon, prior to leaving Austin, had summoned her brother to the arrest scene. He volunteered to drive Easley's Buick back to Houston, which also gave him the opportunity to be with his sister upon their return to Houston. Back in Houston, Sharon was read her legal rights just as Jerry had been. She was then questioned at length by Nix and Horelica regarding her knowledge of the events of the weekend of June 15th.

At no time did Investigators suspect Sharon of having any direct involvement in Sherry's death. They were mainly concerned about her knowledge of the crime and anything she had learned after the crime. She denied knowing anything about the offense. Her Father, Mr. Hammond, also came to the Homicide Office and he and her brother Charles had a lengthy conference with Sharon, both imploring her to tell what she knew. She refused to say anything about Jerry, at one point yelling at her father saying, "They know that the only way they can get to Jerry is through me, and I am not going to help them". She also adamantly refused to take the polygraph exam. This anger toward her father was later thought of as just totally out of character for Sharon, who had always enjoyed a close relationship with her Dad.

She was released to her Father and brother later that night and arrangements were made for her to return the next afternoon to possibly take the exam. She returned as requested but refused to take the test. Jon had been released to the custody of the two attorneys.

The charges against Jerry Easley were dropped three days later and he was released. There was no physical evidence against him - only the circumstantial case as well as a very strong motive. The D.A.'s Office and the Homicide Investigators had played their hand and lost that round. Hindsight is always 20/20 but one can only wonder what would have been the outcome had Sharon cooperated with authorities and told not only what she knew, but also what she had suspected about that night in Buffalo when she awoke and discovered Jerry Easley and his car to have been gone in the middle of the night. She could have testified against Jerry at the time as they were not yet legally married. They did get married later on September 15, 1969. IF ONLY?

Houston newspaper
photo, 8/30/1969

Mrs. Sharon Easley, Goodrich
High School Faculty, 1980

Jerry Easley, Senior, Elkhart
High School, 1959

Jon Easley, Freshman,
Goodrich High School, 1980

Cruise Air motor home, Lake
Pleasant, Arizona, 1984

Cruise Air motor home, Montgomery
County, Texas, February, 1985

Jerry Easley, after his arrest, 10/1985

Sherry Ann Dean Easley's
grave marker, Woodlawn
Cemetery, Houston, Texas

Jerry Easley's grave marker, Strong's
Memorial Park, Slocum, Texas

Trash bag in Arizona containing body
parts of Sharon Easley, May, 1985

Jonathan Edward Easley, 2018

Dan Alton McAnulty Jr., 2018

Superintendent of Goodrich ISD (18)

GOODRICH, TEXAS, A small unincorporated community on U.S. Highway 59 some 70 miles north of Houston, was a quiet place that many from the city would have loved to call home. Of course, the main detriment to living in such a place is that the employment opportunities are extremely limited in small communities such as Goodrich, which was in Polk County, with the County seat being in nearby Livingston, Texas. In 1980, most of Polk County was greatly benefiting from the recent construction of the nearby Trinity River Authority's Lake Livingston.

Prior to the lake being completed in 1969, the tax base of this area, as well as the economy, was rather limited. There was very little industry and the Goodrich Independent School District tax base consisted of income from farming, ranching and timber. Due to a State of Texas law, property taxes were assessed very low on land used specifically for agricultural purposes, thus providing very liberal tax breaks on the majority of land encompassed by the School District. Thus, income was very limited for the purpose of educating the children in the area.

Lake Livingston was formed by the Trinity River Authority, a state-authorized agency. The lake quickly filled up from the monstrous Trinity River watershed which begins north of Dallas and Fort Worth. From there, the Trinity River flows some 200 miles in a winding course through the famed Piney Woods of East Texas.

The construction of the Lake Livingston Dam was precipitating an economic boom in that just seven miles west of Goodrich, a lengthy stretch of Lake Livingston shoreline was being consumed with large homes being constructed on the lake. Waterfront homes, with bulkheads and boat houses, were being rapidly constructed. This tax base was increasing, which now meant more income for the Goodrich Independent School District.

In the late 1970s, these growing pains created issues which had not previously existed within the small rural school district administration. These issues were many and varied and while not previously that important or recognizable, were now surfacing. The School Board recognized this and felt that the future would require more innovative and more professional educational leadership. Parents who had relocated their children to this area brought with them greater educational expectations. In a number of instances, the parents demanded change in the school system, and they wanted those changes NOW.

As a result of these needs, in the spring of 1980, Goodrich began actively pursuing a Superintendent to lead this rural education district into the decade of the 1980s. In the early summer of 1980, the locally elected seven-member School Board interviewed a number of applicants for this most important and prestigious position. Their choice was Jerry Eugene Easley, an educator who had most recently been employed in Houston. It is very likely, in hindsight, that the Board later realized that they may have been motivated to a greater extent by a time frame than they should have been for selecting the right man for the job. It is not clear how thoroughly they may have vetted the candidates, but be it as it may, Easley was their choice - a choice that would be later regretted by not only the Board, but also by many citizens.

In the latter part of the summer of 1980, the Goodrich Independent School District, which is governed by the seven-member Board of Trustees duty elected by the community, officially hired Jerry Eugene Easley. Easley was 38 years old and a veteran educator. He had worked for both the Cypress Fairbanks School District (northwestern suburb of Houston) as well as for the massive Houston School District, which consists of the greater portion of the City of Houston. Easley had also served as chairman of the Chemistry Department of the South Texas Junior College in Houston.

Easley came into the Goodrich district with high aspirations of improving the schools in the district. His philosophy was one that Goodrich needed a community school - one that would involve the citizens as well as the kids. He vowed to get the community involved through adult continuing education, among other programs. It was an admirable goal, one that later would prove very difficult to achieve. His hiring came too late in the summer to apply for a number of federal grants available for such purposes. However, his hopes were high that a number of his new and innovative programs could be staffed with volunteers from the community.

Easley had extensive plans to also improve the athletic programs as well as to provide career training for the older students who had neither the desire nor the ability to succeed in a traditional college program. He eagerly outlined plans to expand to a Junior Varsity athletic program in both football and basketball. These opportunities had not previously existed at that level. It was also his goal to expand the athletic programs to tennis as well as organizing several sorts of school competition, athletic and academic, for the local female students.

Jerry Easley had apparently sold himself to the Goodrich School Board, which was comprised of local residents of the community. Elected School Board members in Texas are usually upstanding members of the community; they serve voluntarily, and elect to run for those positions in local elections. Serving on the Board, especially in small rural communities, is a highly respected position as the trustees serve the entire community.

Easley's comment upon his entrance to the new job assignment was that this district would be one of the "showcases of the state" within two years. He turned out to be very prophetic, although it was very likely not the showcase he or anyone else on the School Board or the community had envisioned.

To say that the new Superintendent was enthusiastic regarding the challenges that lay in front of him would be very true in that he was also desiring to form career education programs in three areas - career awareness, career orientation, and career training. Easley was quoted in the *Polk County Enterprise* as saying "we have some good people on the board and in the community". Easley would be moving to Goodrich, where he, his wife Sharon, and their 14-year-old son Jon would be living in a residence owned by Goodrich ISD. This living arrangement was apparently part of the compensation package included in Easley's contract, as was the norm in many like-sized communities. The residence was not the most modern that the Easley family had been accustomed to, but was livable. Also, since there were no rental or mortgage payments to deal with each month, it was considered more than adequate. The structure itself was comparable to the parsonage of a very poor church congregation.

Easley was hopeful his program would begin on a volunteer basis since he claimed to have received numerous phone calls about his plans for the program. Individuals who feel qualified to teach continuing education classes or those who wished to participate as students were encouraged to come forward and provide their talents on a voluntary basis for the time being. However, as is the norm with community volunteers, very few actually came forward.

While Easley was not involved in selecting his top co-administrators, he was very complimentary of both James Ahern, recently hired as the new principal, and Tim McDonough who was also designated as a principal. McDonough had been with the Goodrich School District upon Easley's arrival while Ahern had just recently been hired from the nearby Splendora School District. Over and over again, Easley stated enthusiastically that in two years, "this district will be one of the showcases of the state".

Hindsight is 20/20, but it was thought later that with the seemingly rushed hiring of Easley, it was not a good practice to hire a new Superintendent who had not been allowed any input into the choices of his top administrators, namely Ahern and McDonough.

Superintendent Easley began work in Goodrich in late August, just prior to the beginning of the school year. Shortly after assuming his responsibilities, he discovered what he believed to be an irregularity in that an Education Aide, Ms. Trixie Pratt, had recently been promoted by the School Board to District Business Manager. This promotion was accompanied by a substantial salary increase.

This matter further caught Easley's attention when he learned that Ms. Pratt was a sister-in-law to Board Member William W. Pratt. In addition, she was also related to the Tax Appraisal District's Mr. J.D. Pratt. It was Easley's contention that Ms. Pratt's promotion and increase in salary was in violation of the Texas Nepotism Statute.

Easley's research of this Statute and the situation as it existed, further reinforced his opinion that this promotion was in violation of the Texas Nepotism Statute in that this employee's brother was School Board President while her brother-in-law also served on the Board of Trustees. As a result of this discovery, Mr. Easley took it upon himself to terminate Ms. Trixie Pratt's employment with the District. This matter was not discussed with any of the Board members in that Easley unilaterally made this decision.

The immediate attention paid to this personnel matter by Superintendent Easley was construed by some to be motivated by one of two reasons - (1) Was he paying due diligence to correcting problems within the district? OR (2) Was he challenging the previously approved policy that the Superintendent was not also the de facto business manager? Was it a power play on his part? His suspicion was that the Board had hurriedly taken this action after hiring him but prior to the actual date he assumed his duties as the Superintendent. That may or may not have been true. In Easley's ever-suspicious mind, it was no doubt true. However, the gauntlet had been thrown with his decision to terminate the employment of this lady who had been known to be very proficient in her duties over her many years of employment with the district.

After being terminated by the Superintendent, Ms. Pratt immediately filed for unemployment compensation. This angered Easley, as if he felt by this action of Ms. Pratt that his authority was being challenged. He then pushed the issue even harder and vowed to fight this effort on her part to obtain unemployment benefits through the Texas Employment Commission. He additionally filed a civil suit to recover the salary differential that Ms. Pratt had earned after her short-lived promotion. Easley also vowed, as a public service to the community, to release any other reports from time to time regarding alleged administrative discrepancies.

In Texas, the school Superintendent of a district such as Goodrich serves at the discretion of the elected Board of Trustees. These Trustees have a legal, moral, fiduciary and community responsibility to make decisions they feel best for the overall operation of the District. In very rare instances would a Superintendent have the broad power to dismiss at his will any District employee? Any such personnel decision would be for the Superintendent to discuss with the Board and make his case for whatever his recommendation would be. This would be the proper and prudent approach for any such personnel matters as this. However, Mr. Easley chose to deal with the matter in his own way, which turned out to not be very popular with the School Board or the community.

However, this is what Mr. Easley did almost immediately upon assuming his Superintendent duties. Of course, this did not set very well with the existing Board of Trustees who were accustomed to have matters such as this discussed with them for their approval or disapproval.

The nepotism issue was rightfully a possible point of contention to be considered. It was very likely one that Mr. Easley could have fought and if approached properly, he could have won the battle. While Easley was in a rare instance of being technically correct in his actions, relationships were not off to a very good start with the Board. However, Jerry Easley, being the autocrat that he was, did not seek support for his decision. He just unilaterally went ahead and took whatever action he deemed appropriate in this matter and others.

After this initial problem, Easley proceeded to improve the School District as he had promised to do. There were the usual disgruntled parents who came to the Board meetings complaining about the manner in which their "darling" children had been treated but this was considered to be part of the territory in the administration of any school district.

However, Easley then began a campaign to have a member of the Polk County Appraisal District removed from his job. This man was Mr. J.D. Pratt, the father of Board Member William Pratt and the father-in-law of previously terminated district employee, Ms. Trixie Pratt. The dissension was increasing by December, 1980, and attendance at the monthly Board meetings was increasing. Greater attendance meant lengthier meetings and the longer the meetings, more tension was noticed in the meetings. Also, the number of questions from disgruntled and confused citizens added to the contentiousness of the meetings.

While Superintendent Easley was making a large amount of waves with the elected Board over what he perceived to be nepotism within the District, it was realized that he made a rather hypocritical move upon immediately arriving and assuming his Superintendent duties. That move, however it was handled, included the hiring onto the Goodrich High School staff of his wife, Mrs. Sharon Easley. Sharon was very likely more than qualified for this position and was listed in the Goodrich Hornets 1981 yearbook as being on the High School Faculty as a Math Teacher. She also held other responsibilities as Faculty Sponsor of the 1981 Annual, which had not been published for several years. In East Texas terms for Jerry Easley, what was "good for the goose was not good for the gander".

Realizing he was having difficulties with his ideas of managing the school, Easley pursued another angle. Two of the seven School Board Trustees were minorities. Easley noticed that on most of the issues brought before the board for a vote, the two minority members supported him. He also observed that of the 20-member senior class, seven were minorities. These same ratios held to be nearly identical for the junior, sophomore, and freshman classes at the high school.

Even though there was no real racial tension at the school, Easley decided to appeal to the minority community to make friends and thereby gain support. He also felt that the two minority members were not totally comfortable with the long-held white majority that had existed for many years. To move his ideas forward, Easley began attending black churches - worshipping, mingling, and making friends and contacts each and every time. He was even rumored to be making it obvious when he would make a large contribution to the collection plate. This also did not sit well with the other Board members other than the two minority members, as they viewed this as far outside the realm of the responsibilities and duties of a school Superintendent. It was viewed as an obvious political move on Easley's part, thereby causing even more problems with the Board.

If the situation was not already progressing from bad to worse, Easley caused even more problems with the Board when he submitted an open letter to THE RESIDENTS OF GOODRICH ISD. This missive was published in one of the weekly community newspapers, *The Big Thicket Messenger*, on November 13, 1980. Excerpts from that letter are as follows:

"Citizens of Goodrich: Circumstances require that I call your attention to the forces of evil working within our community. Biblical history substantiates that what the devil cannot control, he attempts to destroy. I further submit to you that disciples of the devil are active in our community and since they no longer control, they are attempting to destroy. Their destruction is aimed at the Superintendent and the Christians sitting on the Board who have returned the school to the community, placed the student body above selfish concerns, and cast out the evil forces who once controlled the school. Should these devils succeed, they would destroy the school as it exists and return it to a prison run by the devil's taskmasters".

Easley went on to use the word "demons and criticized several petitions which had been circulated around the community, the object of the petitions being him, Jerry Easley. He also stated that in the war against Satan, you cannot be in the middle of the road, that you cannot sit on the fence and refuse to take sides. You are either a servant of the Lord or under the influence of the Devil".

In opposition to Easley's diatribe in the media, the rhetoric heated up even more against him when the following was published in the local Goodrich newspapers:

"Matthew 7: 15-Beware of false prophets, which come to you in sheep's clothing, but inwardly they are ravening wolves."

"Mark 3: 25-And if a house be divided against itself, that house cannot stand."

"Mark 13: 5-And Jesus answering them began to say, Take heed lest any man deceive you".

The same ad posed the question: "Is Mr. Easley truly qualified by his past professional and personal experiences for positions of authority such as school Superintendent?" After that question, came this advice; "Become informed - then decide. Whatever is in the best interest of our children's social environment; after all, they are our future caretakers."

The source of this ad was not the Goodrich ISD Board, but very likely from concerned citizens who had an insight into the situation created by Easley. It was probably supported by several members of the Board, who had wisely chosen to remain anonymous while gaining the support of citizens willing to come forward and speak their mind.

Needless to say, the open letter by the Superintendent to the community was later deemed as the beginning of the end for Superintendent Jerry Easley. In his mind, either you were for him, or if you were against him, you were working for the devil himself. For Jerry Easley, this was the pattern of his life that had been exhibited on many previous occasions. There was no middle ground, no area in which to discuss and possibly reach a compromise on whatever the problem may have been. It was "Jerry Easley's way or the highway".

For the School Board, for them to be referred to as devils, demons, evil forces, disciples of the devil, or under the influence of the devil, was definitely not something that would make for a good working relationship with the Superintendent. Things would soon be going downhill faster than the proverbial "snowball in hell".

The problems of November and December, 1980, continued on into the new year of 1981. Even the Holiday break had not calmed the waters. In reality, the problems had actually festered over the Holiday break.

On January 30, 1981, a special board meeting was called to order during which time a motion was passed to suspend Superintendent Easley. This action was later amended to include the phrase "Malfeasance of Office". Easley, at this time, still had several supporters on the Board. Their reasoning was to give this outsider a chance to place into action the policies he so assuredly stated he could and would. As a result of this support, this action by the Board to suspend Easley was taken by the narrow vote of four to three. The Board and the citizens in the community were divided in their opinion of the Superintendent as well as in their support of his policies. No matter what or how the Board was split, as far as the School District was concerned, this was not a good situation for the children. Just as with other people Jerry Easley had been involved with previously in his life or later, the WAR WAS ON.

Early in February, a large crowd gathered at the Board meeting to demand answers as to why Easley was terminated. Although the Board had been advised by legal counsel not to provide answers, some of the citizen's questions were answered in general terms. On the past Friday, many students boycotted classes and this even became somewhat of a racial issue. 184 students in the Goodrich District were classified as SICK on that date, a situation never experienced in Goodrich prior to this. While this was unacceptable from an academic aspect, it now became a serious financial matter for the District to deal with as absences directly affect the amount of State of Texas aid forthcoming to the District. When children are not in attendance at 10:00am of a scheduled school day, they are considered absent for the entire day. This was not a good day for the Goodrich ISD.

Amidst all of the turmoil, there was School Board business that required attention. By State Statute, there existed the necessity of a School Board Trustee election to be held in April, 1981. For the Goodrich

Independent School District, this would become one of the most critical elections in the history of this small East Texas educational jurisdiction. The election had become basically a one-issue debate involving the status of their former Superintendent. While there were several side issues that were of vital importance to the District, the public and voters were known to be viewing this election as not only a referendum on Jerry Easley, but also on the Board's very close decision to terminate his employment.

At that time, Easley had the support of three Board members, two of those being the minority members that Easley had courted over the past months. The election was promising to be a very heated one and sentiments were running high on both sides of the aisle. School board elections were historically considered very low-key campaigns. Occasionally, a Board member becomes "in over his head", so to speak, in that the matters before him or her that demand their total attention become too much for them to deal with. He or she may wish to give up and resign and then support some other well-meaning citizen challengers for that position. Those situations are rare, but rare indeed was the contentious upcoming School Board election.

Following the January Board decision to suspend Easley, on February 21, 1981, the Goodrich School Board, once again by the narrowest of margins, four to three, moved to terminate Superintendent Jerry Easley. In this vote, the same three trustees voted to retain Easley. A large community crowd had gathered for this impending vote, which brought ripples of applause through one side of the auditorium accompanied by roars of protest from the other side.

The Board President, Mr. Edward Larson, was concerned that there would be problems at this meeting. He requested the Polk County Sheriff, Ted Everitt, to be present. The Sheriff responded as requested with two of his deputies. When the uproar began, Sheriff Everitt took charge and advised the protesters to the Board action that he would adjourn the meeting and clear the auditorium if order was not restored. Whether it had been his true intent or not remained to be seen, but one thing was certain - Jerry Easley had totally succeeded in dividing this community.

After calm was restored, several questions were raised from the audience, most specifically what the justification for the firing would be. The School District's retained Attorney advised that this information would not be released to the public until the proper notification was made to Easley. Easley was served with his termination papers on February 25, 1981. These papers were basically an outline of the reasons for his termination.

Easley immediately responded by releasing the content of the papers to the news media, calling the accusations vague and unspecific. The reasons for termination were outlined in much detail in the termination papers. While they appeared to the average citizen as being rather thorough, Easley immediately launched his defense and again referred to these charges as vague and unspecific.

The allegations by the Board in supporting their decision to terminate were:

1. When Mr. Easley was interviewed for the superintendent's job, he denied ever having been arrested or being involved in any lawsuits. It was later learned that he had been arrested for Murder and on separate occasions, sued both the Spring Independent School District for termination of his contract and the City of Houston Police Department for his arrest on the Murder charge (which was later dismissed). Basically, this first allegation was that he had not been truthful in the employment interview. This was, in fact, true that he was not forthcoming regarding the questions presented to him at the interview.

2. When the Goodrich Independent School District found it necessary to hire an attorney to represent the District, Mr. Easley recommended an attorney from Houston, a Mr. Donald Perez. However, Mr. Easley failed to inform the Board that Mr. Perez had represented him on several previous occasions in both his civil and criminal problems. This allegation was that he had not been forthcoming and truthful to the Board with such obvious relevant information. Once again, he had not been.

3. Upon Mr. Easley's employment with the District, it was agreed that he would be allowed an expense account of $50.00 per month. Mr. Easley had subsequently, without authorization, begun charging the District $100.00 per month. This allegation was rather self-explanatory.

4. The original contract agreed upon by the Board and Mr. Easley authorized a $50.00 per month expense account. The amount of $100.00 per month was discovered to have been added to the original contract at a later date and on a different typewriter. A Questioned Document Examiner was hired to examine and confirmed the District's suspicions that Easley had tampered with the employment contract. This was an unlawful act in that he had tampered with a Government contract, considered to be a very serious violation of the Texas law.

5. Upon employment by the District, Mr. Easley was provided a home to live in which was owned by the District. This was with the expressed understanding that Mr. Easley would be responsible for his own utility expenses. Without Board authorization, Mr. Easley had the electric and gas companies switch the accounts over to the District. The District had already paid several months of these charges prior to this discovery. This allegation also was deemed to be self-explanatory.

6. Carrying a pistol on a School Campus - Prior to a School Board meeting in September, 1980, Superintendent Easley displayed to an elementary school principal a pistol which he took into the Board meeting with him. He indicated that he was doing this to handle any problems which may arise. This was deemed to be in direct violation of the Texas Penal Code as well as the Texas Education Code.

7. Posing as a Peace Officer in an attempt to justify his Carrying the Pistol - Mr. Easley later stated to the press, to the community, as well as to Board Trustees and other administrators that he was a licensed Peace Officer and being so, retained the legal right to do

this. Again, the fact that he could or could not have been licensed was not relevant to the situation. He was in violation of the Penal and Education Codes.

8. Mr. Easley instituted a curriculum change by adding a major course without submitting this for approval to the Board, a direct violation of District policy. In doing so, Mr. Easley caused problems for the physical plant as well as attempting to hire an instructor for this program, which caused the District to incur additional financial obligations not budgeted for nor approved by the Board. The Board clearly had statutory control over budgetary items.

9. Mr. Easley was found to have consistently overruled teachers in matters relating to discipline, and not only that, he did so in the presence of the students. This created not only additional discipline problems, but it also severely undermined faculty morale and authority.

10. Mr. Easley wrote a series of newspaper articles in such a manner which destroyed his ability to work effectively with the Board of Trustees and the faculty. In doing so, he brought embarrassment to the District and to the Board.

11. Mr. Easley had consistently neglected his duties as school superintendent by absenting himself from the District's premises during the school days and also by working on non-district matters while on the premises.

After being served with the termination papers which outlined these charges against him, Jerry Easley continued on the defensive with a reasonable explanation, according to him, for each and every allegation. Easley operated under the premise that the best defense is an aggressive offense. He did so in March, 1981, by filing a Federal lawsuit against the Goodrich School Board. This suit was not only against the Goodrich School Board as a whole, but more specifically named Board President Edward Larson and the three other Board members who voted to fire him.

According to the disciplinary requirements of the Texas Education Code, the Goodrich School Board was charged with holding a dismissal hearing on their firing of Superintendent Easley. Acting according to the law on advice of a newly-retained Board attorney, Mr. Miles Walton, they chose March 31 for this proceeding. However, immediately, Mr. Easley and his legal counsel, who had also filed a lawsuit against the Board seeking reinstatement, disagreed with this course of action. His lawsuit, which was filed in the United States District Court in Houston, was scheduled for an initial hearing. The School Board, with their duty to act according to statute, was proceeding with utmost caution on the advice of their legal counsel. They provided Mr. Easley the option of a public or closed hearing.

The legal maneuvering continued, with Easley and his attorney contending that the School Board, which fired him, was not the proper venue to decide this matter and requested a third party to hear the case. The U.S. District Court hearing was scheduled, but then postponed by Easley and his attorney as they were anticipating the School Board to back down and reinstate him as the School District Superintendent.

Not without irony, Easley had retained for his legal counsel none other than Mr. Donald Perez of Houston, who had previously represented him in the lawsuits against the Houston area school districts as well as against the City of Houston Police Department. This is also the same attorney that Easley, while Superintendent in Goodrich, had recommended to the Board to represent the District. Apparently, Easley thought there was no potential conflict of interest there, one of the items for which he was terminated.

Easley and Perez immediately sought to have a third-party hear the dispute and take action. They stated that the Board of Trustees were not impartial in their feelings and were not a proper body to hear the case. Later, the Texas Education Agency had scheduled a hearing in Austin for May 4, but Easley's attorney, Donald Perez requested a delay until May 13.

The April School Board election resulted in one of the anti-Easley Trustees being re-elected in a run-off. The election did not change the make-up of the Board at that time.

Goodrich Bomb Threat (19)

I F THE ENTIRE fiasco involving Superintendent Jerry Easley had not yet created enough conflict for the District and the students to contend with, there was more to follow. The following information came from newspaper excerpts in the days following Easley's ouster from the head position at Goodrich ISD:

Polk County Enterprise, April 23, 1981:

"JERRY EASLEY CHARGED WITH FELONY - Bomb Scare Evacuates Goodrich School. Easley free on $5,000 Personal Recognizance Bond after being charged with felony assault in connection with a bomb threat at Goodrich school. According to Justice of the Peace G.H. Galloway, the threat was made in a phone call at 8:25am at the Superintendent's office. Jenna Hicks, Goodrich school secretary, said she received the anonymous call from a man who said there is a bomb in the school. She identified the caller's voice as Easley's and added she was able to recognize the voice because she has talked with the defendant both in person and on the phone almost daily for the past four months."

Sheriff Ted Everitt said his office was notified of the threat shortly after 9:00 am and a subsequent search by his department and the Goodrich and Livingston Volunteer Fire Departments failed to locate any explosive device in the school. Acting Administrator Tim McDonough said students and faculty were evacuated. Easley was arrested Monday afternoon and was held at the Polk County jail long enough to be booked. Easley declined to comment, saying, "'I'm concerned about what you've been saying about me in the paper. I don't believe I've been treated fairly with what you've been putting in the paper". He further stated it was political and he was framed to take the blame for persons who oppose him.

D.A. James Keeshan of Conroe said he would take it to the Grand Jury for deliberation. This offense is legally defined as a Third degree felony punishable by 2-10 years and/or a $5,000 fine.

There were some citizens who openly complained that the election runoff was not even necessary. They were apparently unaware or unconcerned that it was required by law.

Polk County Enterprise, 5/24/81:

"Easley indicted on two counts of a misdemeanor bomb threat. Grand jury lowered the charge from the original felony based on a technicality as to whether or not a school was a public service."

Polk County Enterprise, 6/7/81:

"TEA HEARING, EASLEY DENIES CHARGES, TEA HEARING TO RESUME JULY 21".

A former board member, who was Secretary of the Board for several terms, testified about the procedure used when Jerry Easley was hired and interviewed.

Polk County Enterprise, 6/28/81:

"EASLEY OFF GISD PAYROLL - APPEAL PROMISED"

The GISD Board once again voted to fire Easley. Board President Edward Larson presided over a very lengthy meeting. On this occasion, the vote was five to none against Easley. The two minority members abstained.

The Goodrich community was thought by many people as being possibly occupied by a number of rednecks, commonly known in some circles as "BUBBAS". While that was very possibly an exaggeration of the quality of individuals serving on the Goodrich Board, election material distributed during this campaign noted two of the Board incumbents with nicknames as "Cooter" and "Poochie". Whatever conclusion that could be drawn from this is obviously left up to the reader, as those names seem to have been very endearing nicknames for the incumbents who honorably served on the Board prior to and throughout the Easley debacle. To their extra credit, both were willing to continue serving in order to place this matter behind the District and to continue to make decisions that were in the best interest of the children. Basically, they were honorable people and felt that since they had hired Jerry Easley, they needed to see this matter to a conclusion. "Cooter" and "Poochie" both had the welfare of the School District as well as the children in mind.

Easley vs. The Texas
Education Agency (20)

A s THE SCHOOL Board attorney prepared for the Texas Education Agency hearing, the original allegations against Easley were amended and clarified as more information surfaced regarding what Easley had been involved in both prior to his arrival in Goodrich and during his short time as Superintendent. As a result, the original set of allegations which had been submitted to the Texas Education Agency were stricken from their records and officially amended.

With the TEA hearing only a week away, the GISD board of trustees voted unanimously to replace the original allegations against Easley with new and more detailed items. This time the vote was unanimous and the hope was, after months of troubling and disturbing circumstances surrounding the operation of the Goodrich School District, that this entire disgusting matter with Jerry Easley could finally be brought to a conclusion.

Now, the legal battle was about to begin in Austin, Texas, the State Capital, where the Texas Education Agency was headquartered. Easley's attorney, Donald Perez of Houston, made the usual motions in an attempt to dismiss the original charges against his client. However, the hearing examiner allowed the hearing to continue and to allow the Goodrich School Board attorney Miles Walton, to present their case. The Hearing Officer was Bob Lewis, and an ex-board member was called by Perez to testify regarding his decisions while on the board. This man explained that back on January 30, 1981, he made the motion to suspend Easley with pay when the superintendent failed to answer a number of questions to his satisfaction.

The hearing began with a potential 19 witnesses scheduled to testify. Testimony and exhibits presented at the hearing were on the amended allegations.

Exhibit material at the time included information very likely not known by the Goodrich Board when Easley was hired, about the 1969 Murder charge, the federal lawsuit against the Houston Police Department as well as a lawsuit he filed against the Spring ISD in 1974. That lawsuit was later dismissed due to the lack of prosecution on the part of Easley. In this matter, Easley filed a lawsuit against the Spring ISD, but when it came time to prosecute the lawsuit, Easley made the decision to back off.

Also, a document examiner had determined that portions of Easley's contract were typed in at a different time and on a different typewriter.

Easley had been terminated on February 21, 1981 based on six allegations by the Goodrich Independent School Board, one of which was that he violated state law by bringing firearms onto the school campus. Easley, as usual, had what he believed in his mind to be a justifiable explanation for this, stating he was a peace officer having served as a deputy constable in Harris County (Houston) for the past 11 years and never resigned that commission. Of course, this came as a total surprise to the School Board. He expounded on his explanation by stating "If I do carry a pistol, it is within the realm of being a peace Officer and that I have never carried a weapon up there." At the time of Easley's supposed commissioning by Harris County Constable Walter Rankin, there were in fact a number of reserve commissions distributed on a favored-friend basis. This was a common practice, now discontinued, whereby elected officials could repay their supporters in a small way. However, the elected long-time and highly respected Constable immediately countered Easley's explanation by stating that Easley was given the document only to provide him a means of identification to be used on the school campus where he was employed at the time. Rankin further denied ever doing anything other than making Easley an "honorary" deputy.

Constable Rankin further indicated that Easley was never a certified law enforcement officer and that this identification was for use only on the Houston campuses and certainly not outside of Harris County. The Polk County Sheriff was contacted by Constable Rankin and asked to retrieve the identification from Easley. Of course, Mr. Easley had his explanation of the entire matter, which differed considerably from that of the Constable. The Texas Commission on Law Enforcement Officer's Standards and Education (TCLOESE) in Austin was contacted regarding the matter. They emphatically stated that Jerry Easley had never been certified in the State of Texas as a law enforcement Officer. Easley's response was that while unemployed from the School District, he would be seeking election for the position of Goodrich City Marshal, a position that requires that the holder of that job be a certified law enforcement Officer. This was totally new information to the Board, as this possibility had never been previously brought up by Easley.

Easley then countered that while he was never officially certified under rules established by TCLOESE, he was exempt in that he had been certified prior to that law being passed by the State of Texas Legislature. Basically, Easley was saying he was "grandfathered" in. Well, he was correct on one point in that TCLOESE never had a record of Easley in the State Capital of Austin of being a Peace Officer, certified or otherwise.

Easley's first action after being fired was to file a lawsuit in Federal Court, seeking immediate reinstatement as Superintendent and requesting $400,000 in damages. After a very contentious hearing, the Federal Judge declined to reinstate Easley, but further ruled that Easley be placed on a form of suspension pending a dismissal hearing before the Texas Education Agency. This was apparently the path that the law dictated such a matter would be eventually decided. The Judge also ruled that Easley would continue to draw his salary but would not be allowed to exercise any authority as Superintendent of Goodrich schools. The hearing by the Texas Education Agency was scheduled for May 4 in Austin, which would be after the April 4 election.

This controversy surrounding Jerry Easley had divided the community into three camps: One group favored Easley to return with the other two split somewhat, but with both strongly favoring his complete removal. Rumors had been running rampant about what had or had not occurred at the school district with Easley, and many citizens felt that they had not been candidly dealt with and were even disgusted to the point that they would not vote in the election. In summary, Goodrich had become a "showcase" school district but not in the manner it hoped to become. Also, no matter how far-fetched, Jerry Easley had an explanation formed in his mind that justified any and all allegations presented against him.

Childhood Days of
Jonathan Easley (21)

Jon began his early education in the first grade in the Aldine School District at the nearby Thompson Elementary School. His Dad was an educator in this school district and the family took up residence in the Greenridge North Subdivision on Chipman Drive. This home was a newly constructed brick veneer tract home equipped with a double-attached garage in addition to three bedrooms and one-and-a-half baths or two full baths. This young family resided here for nearly six years.

From this location, the Easley family moved to a residence at 15401 Old Humble Road in 1977, at which time Jon was 11 years old and just entering the sixth grade. Jerry Easley had purchased a plot of land at this location and this proved later to be a very lucrative investment. It was here that Jon attended school for several years through the eighth grade. The reason for the move from Aldine to Humble was a change in employment for Mr. Jerry Easley.

Life was not altogether easy growing up in the Easley household, one that Jerry Easley demanded total control over. This personality trait of Jerry's had carried over from his years of domineering behavior to Sherry. Next, Jon would fall victim to his Dad's dominance. Sharon, for whatever reason, went along with Jerry's controlling personality. There are many people who saw it for what it was, but none were able to become involved by quietly giving her advice. If she had complaints and expressed them, it had to be a private complaint. Unfortunately, no one stepped in and attempted an intervention into this totally domineering control that Jerry was practicing. As Jon became older, he bore the brunt of his Dad's irrational anger displayed to both he and Sharon.

Jerry was prone to become angry at the world around him, and who better to take that anger out on other than Jon. Jon seemed to never do anything right in his Dad's eyes. Jerry had a bad temper for just the smallest infraction of rules, and on many occasions for just being a boy, Jon would be punished by being told after supper to get ready for bed. Then, Jerry and Sharon would appear in Jon's room for the punishment phase for whatever act, many times very minor and insignificant, Jon had allegedly committed.

Jerry had a baseball bat which was "slimmed down to size"; likely meaning that one side of it had been shaved down to be flat. Jon would be forced to lie across the bed on his stomach, with Sharon sitting on Jon's hands. Jerry would then proceed to strike Jon's buttocks, hands, feet, fingers, anything he could strike. Jerry did this as a disciplinary action, whether or not Jon had done anything serious enough to deserve it. In nearly every occasion, it seemed this behavior surfaced because Jerry was mad at the world when he came home that evening. He was angered over the actions and behavior of other people that he had no control over. So, he vented those frustrations on those he had control over, his loved ones.

On one occasion, Jon and another student were admonished by a teacher for talking in class. Jon had told this student to quit talking to him during class, but this kid did so anyway. Both were sent to the school office. According to school policy, when any kid was sent to the office, it became necessary to notify the parents of the child. Jon was upset and distraught and emotional, as he knew full well what action awaited him at home that night. Jon begged the administrator not to call his home, but this was a policy that had to be followed.

When Jon got home that evening, his Dad told him "You're going to get the board tonight". And, he did get the board, just about as bad as ever.

The next morning, the school administrator had his turn to administer corporal punishment to Jon. The administrator asked Jon if he wanted to take his stuff out of his rear pockets to receive the whipping. Jon replied

"I guess so, but it doesn't really matter because it's going to really hurt anyway". The man asked Jon what he meant, and Jon told him what had occurred the night before. He asked Jon to pull down his pants, which Jon did. Jon was completely black and blue on his back side and the administrator told Jon that he was obligated to report this situation to the local authorities. Jon begged the administrator not to report it, that it would only be worse on him when he got home that night. This was one time that it should have been reported, but the administrator apparently felt sorry for Jon and disregarded the policy.

The required reporting of this matter to the proper authorities would have brought about some type of intervention, which was in fact sorely needed. However, it did not occur. The administrator meant well, but this was one of those occasions that following the proper protocol might have possibly triggered an investigation into the Easley home situation. Today, there likely would have been an intervention by Child Protective Services and even a criminal investigation would have been initiated.

Then, in the summer of 1980, the move was made to Goodrich, Texas. This move provided for Jon a completely new perspective on life, having been in crowded classrooms in Aldine and Humble, as well as having been surrounded by a melting pot of other children, many different from him. Jon did not really experience any problems getting along with this diverse group of children in Aldine and Humble, but Goodrich was a completely different experience and he began in the Goodrich schools as a Freshman, a ninth-grader. Goodrich at the time, just like many other schools in the area, had the traditional four classes at the high school level.

In the fall of 1980, Jon entered the Freshman class as a full-fledged Goodrich Hornet, the hornet being the official mascot of Goodrich High School. This was a happy time for Jon, as his Dad was THE Superintendent of Schools and his Mom Sharon was a newly- hired high school math teacher, in addition to being named the Faculty Sponsor of the high school annual, *THE HORNET*, the official yearbook for the school year of 1980-81. Jon's photo in that yearbook showed him to bear a striking resemblance to his Dad.

Just as Jon's beginning weeks and months began very well, his student life took a turn for the worst as his Dad's problems with the School Board became very much aware to the public. Kids will be kids, and as the level of rhetoric between his Dad and the School Board continued to escalate, Jon began receiving a large amount of undeserved flack from his fellow students. Fair or not, this was the case, and after the fall semester as the situation became worse between his Dad and the Board, as well as the public involvement, Superintendent Jerry Easley made the decision to move Jon from the school.

It was also just prior to this time that Jon became aware that Sharon was not his biological Mother. Openly, he had dealt with this in a very mature manner. Who could say how he was really dealing with this revelation? Now, he was experiencing unwarranted criticism and harassing statements from his classmates that he was hoping to become friends with.

Not many, maybe a few, high school kids can attest to the fact that their high school years were spent attending seven different high schools. Jon Easley could later recall the turmoil this must have caused within his inner self. For the completion of his Freshman year, which had began so promisingly, Jon was sent to Jacksonville High School in Jacksonville, Texas.

Jerry Easley had a college friend in that city and moved Jon to live there with these family friends. Things went as well as could be expected, and while Jon achieved good grades there at this larger school in deep East Texas, there must have been other issues involved as Jerry moved him back to the Goodrich area to finish the Freshman year, this time at nearby Livingston High School. Three high schools in less than nine months!!!

In the summer of 1981, the employment situation had deteriorated completely with Jerry Easley's employment in Goodrich. He had been publicly fired in early 1981, and the battle was on as he immediately obtained legal counsel. Basically, he was forced out of the district-owned housing he had been provided there and while his termination was being appealed in Austin, Texas, Jerry and Sharon took Jon and moved once again, this time back to the address in Humble, Texas. Jon's Sophomore year in high school began at Humble High School, but before the year was over he was enrolled at Aldine High School in the previously attended Aldine District. There were some redistricting issues in the Aldine District at the time and the Easley's residence was deemed to be in the Nimitz High School zone, also in the greater Aldine District.

It was at Nimitz that Jon began his Junior High School year and if that was not enough, to be moved from one school to another, he finished that school year at the Aldine Contemporary High School. If one would find it difficult to believe that a good student could nearly finish all of his high school credits in just over three school years while attending seven different high schools, it was accomplished by Jon Easley: Goodrich, Jacksonville, Livingston, Humble, Aldine, Nimitz, and the Contemporary High School. Even though Jon had not yet learned of the circumstances surrounding his biological Mother's death, the beatings by his Dad and the turmoil of his high school years had to take a toll on his persona. However, there was more to come for Jon to endure.

The Reeveston Garage (22)

FOLLOWING THE GOODRICH Independent School District disaster, Jerry Easley found himself without a means of support. He was not only unemployed, but most likely at this time "unemployable" by anyone in the education field, especially in the State of Texas. Word travels very fast around Austin, more specifically after the well-publicized Texas Education Agency hearings.

The hearings in Austin had created a massive amount of publicity, totally negative, surrounding his problems with the school district in Goodrich. This had given him a terrible reputation throughout the Houston area and probably throughout the state. The hearings had also brought up the bomb threat charges in Polk County and also the untruthfulness he had displayed on his original application to the Goodrich School District. Also surfacing was his propensity to file frivolous civil lawsuits on his employer or anyone else that he might have a disagreement with. One might have thought the economic outlook would have been rather bleak for this man, who was now 40 years old and at an age which is usually considered the prime earning years of a professional individual's life. However, whatever else Jerry Easley might have been described as or would be described as later, he WAS NOT a quitter.

Prior to moving to Goodrich, Jerry and Sharon had purchased some acreage on Old Humble Road where he, Sharon, and Jon resided for a short time. Upon returning from Goodrich, this area had experienced tremendous growth and as a result of this, the value of this acreage had gone up as well. This was a chance for Jerry to make a sizeable capital gain and he chose to cash in on this investment and sell the land for a profit. Jerry sold this property, nearly ten acres of commercial land, for a profit of $127,000.

This was surely more money than he had ever possessed in his life. Fortunately, he did not blow the money but instead, invested it wisely. The early 1980s were still a carryover of the high interest/high inflation era of the late 1970s and even Certificates of Deposit were earning double digit interest rates of return. Even with inflation soaring, this had been a very favorable time to have money invested in a safe place.

The automotive mechanic business was something that apparently appealed to Jerry and as a result of this windfall profit from the Humble property, Jerry chose to invest some of that money into a property on Reeveston Road. This property was held at the time by an individual who was experiencing financial difficulties himself, and Jerry, however he learned of this situation, stepped in and bought it. It was one of the few deals in Jerry Easley's life that he actually helped someone else by taking a major financial burden from them. It was a very lucrative deal for Easley also and he sorely needed a positive turn to rid the negative taste of the last several years in Goodrich. His ego as well as his pocketbook both sorely needed a boost.

The location was a good deal at the time for him also. This was in the Aldine area of North Houston, near to the Chipman address where the Easley family had previously lived. For many years, Aldine was a rural, unincorporated segment of Harris County that was home to many small Italian family-owned truck farmers. As the population of Houston moved to the northern suburbs, many of these farms were sold to provide land for additional housing. The property on Reeveston consisted of an older residence and a large metal building on several acres.

It was here at 13834 Reeveston Road that Jerry, Sharon, and Jon moved to in the fall of 1981 following the fiasco in Goodrich, Texas. Using an existing large metal building for a mechanic's shop, Jerry Easley formed a business named Easley Enterprises. While Jerry had no previous auto mechanic experience, he was confidently aware that he possessed an aptitude in that area of expertise, and so chose to go into this type of business. However, even with his confidence, he needed mechanics that had the actual experience he lacked so he advertised in the local newspapers for this type of employment. Jerry was not short on self-confidence and felt that in addition to his aptitude, he possessed the business acumen needed to make such an operation profitable.

In the early months of 1983, shortly after purchasing the Reeveston property, Jerry's newspaper advertisement for an experienced mechanic brought about an inquiry from a couple from Alabama, James and Judy Hollingsworth. They had recently moved to an apartment in Pasadena, Texas, while looking for employment. During this time period, Houston was going through a large economic boom. Businesses were thriving and it appeared to be the right move for the Hollingsworths. James presented himself to Jerry as an experienced mechanic and willing to work. Judy was to be a helper, a person who would retrieve the necessary tools and make trips to the automotive parts houses to procure the needed parts for James.

Judy's son from a previous relationship, Frankie Routt, was 16 years of age and came to Houston with his Mom and Stepdad. Judy would later be taught Jerry's system of bookkeeping for the business in addition to her other duties. This couple was searching for a manner in which to make a decent living for themselves, something they had not been able to achieve previously. In addition to young Frankie, the Hollingsworth family also included, at times, James's son from a previous relationship, James Jr., also known as Jimbo. To them, this appeared on the surface to be an excellent opportunity and both were willing to work hard in order to make the situation workable for both them and Easley.

Jerry Easley had numerous problems dealing with people. Throughout his life to this point, he seemed to make it his practice to surround himself with people whom he felt were less educated and therefore, in his mind, more amenable to go along with any practice he chose, whether it be legal or illegal, ethical or unethical. The Hollingsworths were hired initially as James being the mechanic Jerry needed. The Hollingsworths, by Jerry's way of thinking, were the type of people he preferred to deal with. Consequently, after James basically proved to Jerry that he had the necessary mechanical skills as well as the tools of the trade, the couple was then hired by Jerry to run the shop for him on some type of a promised share of the garage's profits.

James and Judy arrived on the scene in March, 1983, and for several months, lived there on the property in a trailer home that Easley owned. This working and living arrangement continued for five to six months, at which time Jerry advised James and Judy that he and Sharon were moving out of the house on the Reeveston property and would be going on an extended stay in their motor home in the Phoenix, Arizona area, specifically, north of Phoenix at Lake Pleasant State Park. This was a location at which Jerry and Sharon had previously spent some time and they were very anxious to return there. This move was also attractive to the Hollingsworths as they would now be able to move out of the cramped trailer home into the wood frame home that Jerry and Sharon had previously resided in.

"Promised" is a key word in this arrangement that Jerry set up with James Hollingsworth and his wife, Judy. They would ultimately become the first of a number of people over the next several years that Jerry hired to assist him in the actual mechanic work conducted at the garage.

The business thrived for a short time. The economy was booming in Houston at the time and Jerry had used his salesman abilities to sell his garage services to a number of service-related businesses to repair and provide maintenance on their fleets of vehicles. He had such arrangements with a local lumber yard, a nationally known lawn service operation, and a number of smaller operations such as those who provided electrical and plumbing related services. The larger companies did not present a cash-flow problem for Easley Enterprises as they seemed to have the ability to pay as they went. However, problems began to arise with some of the smaller individually-owned businesses as they seemed to constantly be experiencing cash flow problems.

When hired on by Easley, James performed well in the actual working operations of the garage while Judy did her part by being a runner, retrieving the necessary parts for the garage jobs. When Easley announced in September, 1983, of his plans to move to Arizona, a different working arrangement between the Hollingsworths and Easley became necessary. Judy explained to Easley that she was not capable or willing to take care of the books for the garage. Easley quickly quashed that idea of hers and sold her on the idea that he would train her to do the books, and if she did it his way, it would be just fine. Easley was quite a salesman in his presentation to Judy and she agreed to give it a try.

After learning Easley's bookkeeping system, it was during this time that she began to learn everything about the manner in which Easley handled his business and treated his customers. The more Judy learned about the bookkeeping end of this operation, the more skeptical they became with the manner in which Easley had been conducting his business. Sure, they were well aware of some of the major business-related problems Easley had experienced with a number of customers. However, they became very suspicious as to whether many of Easley's practices were ethical, if not illegal. In their mind, being unethical was one thing, but doing business illegally was entirely another matter. The Hollingsworths were not well-educated, but they were honest and hard-working. And, they knew right from wrong.

At this point, however, the overall situation had served them well, and without many other options for them with their limited education, they chose to go along with Easley's proposal for them to run the operation in his absence. Their main concern was whether or not they could continue to make the business profitable for themselves and Easley while operating it in an ethical and legal manner. Those concerns turned out later to be well-founded.

The Easley's left Houston and drove off in their motor home to see the world, at least the western portion of the United States. Work continued to be abundant and Easley would come back to Houston every month or so and would call and check in with them at least once a week as they did not have a permanent phone or address at which to be reached. Cell phones and computer communications were not the order of the day in the mid-1980s. As per their agreement, the Hollingsworths would send Jerry a check for his portion of the shop's profits. This appeared to work well for awhile until Jerry and Sharon seemingly tired of their daily routine at Lake Pleasant and decided to return to Houston in March of 1984.

Included in this decision may have been Easley's perception that the Hollingsworths' manner of doing business, not being the same as his, was not producing enough revenue or profit to satisfy his needs. Whatever the reason, Easley decided to return to Houston. Whether justified or not, Easley manufactured a major problem with the Hollingsworths and physically ran them off of the Reeveston property. They were able to leave with some personal belongings, but Easley confiscated many of James's tools of his trade, rendering him unable to easily find other employment in his chosen field. There were also a number of repair jobs on the books that James had performed but had not yet been paid for. Easley took these over for himself, and according to James and Judy, they left with just $35.00 in their pocket.

The only recourse the Hollingsworths had at this point was to file a civil action against Easley. Of course, these type of small claim actions rarely ever are settled by a Court of Law in a reasonable period of time. Unfortunately, many times the winner becomes the party or person that is best able to survive without a timely settlement. In this case, Easley was the most experienced party involved and he knew the legal system well enough that he and his attorney could stall any settlement. Also, he had financial resources to hold out and the Hollingsworths did not. They were basically out of luck even though in a fair hearing, they very likely would have prevailed.

Easley held on and absolutely nothing was gained by the filing of this action by the Hollingsworths who, in this case, did have what appeared to many to be a legitimate case against Easley. The case, after a number of resets and such, just basically went away.

It was June, 1984, and with the Hollingsworths out of the garage, Easley still needed someone to run the operation as he still had a number of clients who were relying on the business to keep their vehicles rolling. Shortly after the Hollingsworths were forced to leave the garage, Jerry once again ran a newspaper ad looking for a mechanic to run the shop. The ad was answered by a young ambitious mechanic named Jacky Clung. Clung was a hard-working young man, who was weary of working for other people and felt like he had the mechanical abilities as well as the business acumen needed to make such an operation successful. He was, however, rather naïve and in dealing with Easley for only a short time, got his "clock cleaned" financially by Easley.

Jacky Clung was married to a lady who was a school teacher with a modest, but regular income. She was also agreeable to assist her husband in investing money into the Reeveston garage and they entered into a legal agreement whereby Clung would invest money into the business, and since Easley owned the property and buildings, he would charge Clung $2,500.00 a month for his ownership equity. Also included in the agreement was the stipulation that Easley would also receive a portion of the profits from the daily operations.

In order for the Clungs agreeing to this deal, Easley presented to them his books for the previous years of operation. On paper, it looked real good and Mrs. Clung withdrew $25,000.00 from her teacher retirement funds to invest in the business. However, it did not take Clung long to realize that while Easley had presented the business to be profitable, profits from the legal and ethical operations were a different matter. Basically, there were two sets of books that Easley operated under. Clung very quickly realized that he too could make the agreement profitable, but only if he conducted his business in the manner that Easley did. Clung and his wife were not in any way amenable to do so and after putting such a large amount of money into the shop, realized that the monthly profit from running an honest operation was not going to be conducive to their agreement.

After several months of working long days to make the business work, Clung contacted Easley in Arizona and told him of his intentions of shutting down the business. Easley rather calmly told Clung that if that was what he wanted to do, that he would come to Houston to assist him in doing so. And, of course, Easley's definition of assist was likely completely different from what Clung and his college-educated spouse expected it to be.

Upon Easley arriving at the Reeveston garage and speaking to Clung a very short time about the predicament, Easley ordered Clung to remove himself from the premises. Clung protested this verbally but Easley insisted on him leaving or he would call the police. Clung had no desire to get into a violent situation with Easley, but was confronted with other issues here also. Not only had he and his wife placed this large amount of money into the business, Easley would not allow him to gather up the considerable amount of mechanic tools in the garage. He just basically ordered him off of the premises with no discussion on how to resolve this extremely sticky situation in a fair and equitable manner. Once again, it was "Jerry Easley's way or the highway".

In addition to the tools, Clung had purchased over $2,000 worth of generic automotive parts, such as air and oil filters, items that if purchased in quantity, afforded him a lower cost per item in addition to the savings he realized by not having to make as many trips to the auto parts store. And, then there were the bookkeeping assets that Clung had accumulated, those being unpaid invoices on work already performed but not yet collected. Clung was nearly ready to revolt against Easley when Easley physically ordered Clung to leave at gunpoint. This became a repeat of the ordeal, only worse than what the Hollingsworths had experienced.

Understandably so, Clung left but mentioned to Easley that he was being forced to take legal action against him. Easley's next move, after running Clung off at gunpoint, was to begin a legal eviction process against Clung, foreclosing on him. Once again, the system that Easley ranted and raved about as not working for him, was being used. Easley knew the ropes and even though Clung and his spouse were far from the uneducated type Easley was familiar in dealing with and shoving around, Easley knew that time was on his side even if a civil suit was filed. He would then just be in a situation where he could wait Clung out who had now lost his ability to work at his profession, being without the "tools of his trade".

Jerry Easley was a ruthless individual, with no empathy for anyone else's problems or plight in life. Clung and his wife had learned the hard way, just as the Hollingsworths had. Jerry was once again calling the shots, and in the driver's seat, so to speak.

Jerry Easley's Justice System (23)

JERRY EASLEY HAD told several people that the legal system just simply did not work well for him. Whether or not his propensity to file civil suits which were not of any substance was a true measure of his feelings, well, that could be debated. Jerry had a long history of attempting to use the system to his advantage. It could certainly be said that Jerry Easley, from the beginning of his adult life, attempted to resolve his issues with other people in the proper manner, in the courts. However, again, whether or not his litigations had merit is yet another subject. Obviously, in his mind, they definitely had merit when he felt he had been wronged.

A review of his civil litigation history revealed, other than his divorce from Sherry Ann Dean Easley in 1968, he was also involved in civil court matters over the years with South Texas Junior College as well as the bitterly contested firing from the Goodrich Independent School District in 1980 and 1981. That led then to the well-publicized hearings in Austin, Texas, with the Texas Education Agency in 1981.

Elmer Price was an electrical contractor who always seemed to be in financial difficulties. Easley and Price seemed to have a natural dislike for each other and Easley's inability to get along with people led to civil suits with Price associates such as Cable Electric, Able Electric, Barb Farrell, Albert Wilsom, Wilford Sacky, as well as with Price himself. The business operations at Easley Enterprises, also known as General Auto Repair, led also to civil disagreements with James and Judy Hollingsworth, Jacky Clung, Jane Riley, and Jack Powell, all of whom at one time were in business relationships with Easley at the Reeveston Garage.

While Easley fared somewhat well in the minor disputes, he came out on the wrong end of the litigations with the South Texas Junior College and the Goodrich I.S.D. matter. The negative result for Easley in those instances was likely due to the organizations he was challenging, them being with adequate funds for counsel to deal with his complaints. Still, Jerry Easley truly was of the opinion that the system did not work well for him and he mentioned to several people, including his son Jon that he needed to take it upon himself to settle these problems out of court. If anyone did him wrong, he would deal with it on his own terms. If it meant repossessing (stealing) his problem customer's vehicles in the dark of night, so be it. If some forging of vehicle titles needed to be done, so be it. He had even gone so far as mentioning to others around him that some of the people he was dealing with probably just needed to be done away with. Jerry Easley had plans and aspirations to win at any cost.

History has proven time and again that on any occasion where a "hit" has been carried out, the person arranging the actual hit has as much, if not more, to lose should problems arise. It has also been common practice through the years that a person does not approach someone to do such a job for them unless there exists a strong bond of loyalty or a certain amount of trust between the parties. To approach someone and make a proposal to kill someone makes that person very vulnerable in the criminal justice system, whether he is turned down or not

At that point, the person who was approached is in the driver's seat as he knows more than enough to make life difficult for the person who wanted the hit carried out. He knows who the boss wants hit and he probably has been provided useful and adequate personal information as to why the deal needs to be done. The person approached has very likely been provided very pertinent information about the hit's activities, habits, and whereabouts. Again, the prospective hit man, should he decide not to do the deal, has information that could be utilized against the person who approached him.

This possible vulnerability apparently did not bother Jerry Easley. Numerous people, over the period of several years, were approached by

Easley to carry out such proposals. Any one of them could have just simply gone to the authorities and warned them of Easley's requests. A sting could have then been set up and Easley could have been trapped, not entrapped, and charged with a very serious criminal offense -SOLICITATION OF CAPITAL MURDER.

Many large jurisdictions, such as Houston and Harris County, have undercover Officers who are skilled in dealing with such individuals as Jerry Easley. Unfortunately, it never came to that. As many enemies as Jerry Easley had accumulated in his everyday, rotten business dealings, and as many different individuals that he approached to do jobs for him, apparently no one ever came forward. He was not one bit bashful regarding making his true feelings known to just about anyone, stranger or not. Were they just scared of Easley or were they aware that their own lifestyle did not leave them with much credibility to begin making accusations? Several of these reasons as well as others not mentioned could have played into the equation. No matter what the reasons, it is not believed that anyone ever reported Easley's desires of physical violence to his purported business associates to the proper authorities. This is almost unbelievable, as the type of people Easley approached all had skeletons in their closet and would have been able to "cut a deal" with prosecutors for their own benefit. But, again, it apparently never happened.

There was yet another man in and around the Reeveston Garage that had raised Jerry's ire. This was a young man named Milt Roch, who had worked for Easley as a mechanic. Roch did a major repair job for one of Easley's customers and Easley found out later that the job was for a much larger amount of money than Milt Roch had reported to Easley. Under whatever oral agreement that existed between Easley and Roch on such a repair job, Easley felt that he was shorted on the deal by Milt Roch. Easley took offense to this and confronted Roch about his share of the extra mechanic work. This was not settled to Easley's satisfaction. Apparently, in Jerry's way of thinking, Roch owed him a substantial amount of money and refused to discuss it with Easley. And, you just do not do this to Jerry Easley.

After Milt Roch and Easley had their major disagreement, Roch bailed out of his agreement to run Easley's garage. This business should well have had a swinging type saloon door installed as there were so many mechanics in and out of the business. He left town and moved back to Missouri where he had hailed from originally. This perturbed Easley even more and he hired another flunky-thief, Jim Milton, who worked off and on for him, to drive with him to Missouri and take care of Roch. Easley and Milton left Houston during the summer of 1984 and went on a scouting mission to determine where Roch had moved to in Missouri. Sharon was working a full-time job at the time and must not have thought too much to inquire where Jerry had gone for several days. They did find where Roch had moved to but for some reason, the rest of the mission was not completed. It was probably due to the fact that while Easley talked up a big game about taking care of these people, it was not really something that he wanted to do himself or actually wished to even be present when his proposals were carried out. Again, legally speaking, he would not have had to be present when the act was carried out. He would have been legally culpable for merely proposing the deed.

Jim Milton was in the know about what Jerry wanted done to Milt Roch, but he too was out of the picture quickly. Next to be propositioned by Easley was yet another young man from the shop, Ricky Peters. Easley hired Peters and another kid named Johnny Holton to go to Missouri to do the deal, based on the location information which had been learned by him and Milton on their scouting mission. Easley provided Ricky and Holton a 1973 Gremlin, a shotgun, and $1,500 cash money to go and take care of Roch. It had never been determined how much money Roch had cheated Easley out of, but there was obviously a tremendous amount of bitterness and revenge involved in Easley's strong-felt need for revenge against Roch. In Easley's mind, he had been done wrong and he was obsessed with the idea of righting that wrong.

Peters and Holton left Houston telling Easley they were going to go and take care of Roch. However, they eventually thought better of this idea and stayed gone for a week, at least from Easley. It was never determined how far out of Houston they went on this alleged mission, but they never really went to Missouri. They had quite a good time partying on Easley's money and upon their return to Houston, Peters was drunk and told Easley they could not find Roch. Ricky Peters was very likely on Easley's bad list after this failed caper. Now what was Easley to do, find a hit man to take care of an agreeable hit man who had done him wrong? Actually, in his mind, that may not have sounded like too bad an idea to Easley at the time.

All of these people, beginning with Donny Harold and Jimmie Jackson and then later including Jim Milton, Ricky Peters, and Johnny Holton, knew about Easley's business that he had so openly put "on the streets". Normal people, that is if you can refer to someone who wants someone else killed as normal, would have been totally paranoid regarding so many unaccountable individuals knowing what he wanted done. If Jerry Easley was not paranoid, it could have been possible that with the rampant narcissism that worked inside him, he just merely felt that he was above the law and immune from the consequences of his actions. If he had been truly responsible for Sherry's death and getting away with it, could this have given him a false sense of security?

The Elmer Price Caper (24)

ONE SUCH COMPANY Easley was doing regular business for, maintaining their fleet of trucks, was an electrical service business owned and operated by a man named Elmer Price. Price was a few years older than Jerry Easley and had experienced his share of hardships and business setbacks. To say he was a grizzled veteran of bankruptcies would be an understatement. He had declared bankruptcy on several occasions, which necessitated him changing the names of the business titles he operated under. He had done business at various times under the names of Able Electric and also Accurate Electric. At one point, he was completely broke, but resumed doing electrical work under the name of a business set up as being owned and operated by his daughter. On this occasion, he began operating under the business named Cable Electric. All of these name changes were directly due to the bankruptcies, which necessitated him disposing of assets and settling his liabilities. Price was operating on a shoestring, very likely dodging creditors each and every day.

Having some assets, most of which were run-down and mechanically unsound trucks, allowed him to pick up small electrical jobs here and there. Of course, since his vehicles were in the terrible shape they were, he needed someone to maintain these older vehicles. It was through a stepson, Cliff Bartley, also in the electrical business, that he learned of the Easley Enterprises garage on Reeveston Road.

One of the "business practices" that Jerry Easley had learned in the mechanic business was to take a job into his shop with a quoted estimate of repairs to the owner. After he had gained physical custody of the vehicle and began the repairs (agreed upon or not) which rendered the vehicle unsuited for being moved from the shop, much more was found to be wrong with the vehicle. He would then perform those questionable repairs without the owner's consent. After having done so, he would then present to the vehicle owner a much higher repair bill than the owner could have ever even imagined. Most of the time, the owner was caught completely off guard and in a terrible situation. They were "up the creek without a paddle", as the old saying goes. They were now without the needed vehicle and with a repair bill they had no means or desire to pay.

In the State of Texas, there exists a civil remedy for such a situation for the mechanic, be it mechanical work or extending to other service industries such as electrical, plumbing, or air conditioning repair work. This civil remedy was commonly referred to as a Mechanics Lien. The only remedy open to the owner of the vehicle in such a case was to file a civil lawsuit against the shop owner, which required a lengthy path through the civil court system.

Easley was well aware of this law and used it repeatedly to obtain a new title of ownership on the repaired vehicle. He then would own the vehicle somewhat lawfully and sell it in order to reclaim his repair bill. This obviously created a large number of irate customers whose only recourse was to file a claim in civil court. If a person does not have the means to pay the repair bill to begin with, they usually would not have the wherewithal to take legal action. Many of these people in such situations were basically just completely out of luck.

To further pursue this questionable business practice, Jerry needed someone well-versed in the acquisition and transfers of vehicle titles with the State of Texas. He found an equally unscrupulous individual named Albie Waltmon, who operated a vehicle title service and was also a notary public, which assisted in the title transfers. Albie was very experienced in the nuances of title transfers, both legal and illegal. Once again, Jerry Easley had located someone with the same business scruples as he himself possessed.

When Elmer Price began to have his vehicles repaired at Easley Enterprises, all went well for a short time. However, there came a time when he was unable to pay the repair bill immediately as he needed to use the repaired vehicle to service his customers and then gain payment from them. Life was continuing to be tough for Price. Easley was not comfortable with any type of fee arrangement other than cash with anyone, much less Elmer Price. It seemed that while they were able to conduct business for a short time, this arrangement did not last long. It appeared to all who were aware of the situation that there existed severe personality problems between Easley and Price. Their tremendous dislike for each other was showing openly and those around the situation actually feared (and maybe even hoped for) a physical confrontation. One flunky of Easley's, having himself been taken advantage of, even commented to others that he would pay good money to watch the fight.

This rocky-road business arrangement between Easley and Price rocked on for several months, both just barely being able to tolerate each other's manner of doing business. It could have been that both recognized each other as possessing the same character traits. There are occasions where people are attracted to other people with the same likes and dislikes. However, in this instance, the similar business practices that Easley and Price shared soon reached the boiling point. There were numerous disagreements over the repaired vehicles. On one occasion, Price managed to pay Easley for a major repair job on one of the vehicles. After leaving the shop with the truck, Price was only able to drive 17 miles before the vehicle malfunctioned with the identical problems it had before it had been "repaired" by Easley. One can only imagine how that discussion must have gone between the two of them.

Following that problem, there arose a situation that seemed destined for big trouble. As he was prone to do with most anyone, Easley now went after a "bigger fish" and "padded" a repair bill on one of Price's trucks. It was almost as if Easley was playing a game, upping the ante as in a poker game. Price, being the fly-by-night operator that he himself was, couldn't cover the bill. He strongly suspected that he was being had by Easley, but at this point, he was also very aware that he needed the truck for an upcoming electrical job. This job, according to Price's reasoning, was the one he needed to get his financial situation straightened out once and for all. In Price's world, he was only that one big job away from success.

He had no choice so he relented to Easley and paid the repair bill with a company check. He took the truck away but he now had another problem in that he had insufficient funds to cover the check he wrote for the inflated amount of the bill. Price had previously experienced problems with checks written for insufficient funds. Those instruments are also commonly referred to as worthless checks or "hot" checks. So, now in somewhat of a precarious situation, he went directly to his bank that same day and authorized a stop payment on his check. Either way, he was in a bad situation and he was very much aware that it was unlawful for him to do so in the case of authorized repairs. Being in the electrical contracting business, he had undoubtedly used this law to his advantage on more than one occasion. However, he desperately needed the truck in question. There was very likely another factor he considered when making the bad decision he had chosen. That was, in addition to needing the truck, he also had a deep underlying desire to spar with Easley. Some who knew both Easley and Price had commented while they observed the ongoing proceedings that they were "two peas in a pod".

Shortly after Easley opened the mechanics garage, he became aware of the need for a tow truck. This allowed him to tow a disabled customer's vehicle to his garage and also allowed him to tack on a towing fee to the eventual repair bill. This tow truck allowed him to increase his business and was actually a good investment, even though the tow truck, or wrecker as they are commonly known in Texas, was a well-used vehicle. However, this was a good investment Easley Enterprises had made as it had paid dividends in several areas of the business.

In order to make all of the midnight tow truck runs and to benefit from the illegal recovery of repaired vehicles, Easley utilized the services of Albie Waltmon for the title work. It was later discovered that Waltmon had done 37 such title transfers for Easley. It was also later noted that Easley was very careful to not place these questionable vehicles in his name. He usually had them placed in Sharon's name or his Mother in Elkhart. He was using his own Mother to perpetuate these scams. It is probable that neither his Mom nor Sharon were aware that they were being used in this manner.

Shortly after Easley released the truck in question to Price, he went immediately to Price's bank to cash the check. One can only wonder how Price and Easley avoided being in the bank at the same time. That confrontation would have been interesting and very well could have turned into a violent encounter. When Easley learned that the stop payment order had been issued on the check, he became irate in the presence of a number of bank employees, even to the point of threatening Price publicly and also vowing that this was not the end of this rotten deal. Easley had basically been "called out" by Price, something that was not taken lightly by someone with the over-inflated intelligence that Jerry Easley believed himself to possess.

Price had played his hand, even though he was in violation of the law by ordering the stop payment. Easley, had he possessed any ability to exercise patience in this matter, could have eventually prevailed in a court of law over Price and could have likely also completely ruined Price financially. This was beginning to take on the nature of a poker game, each one raising the bet to bluff the other one out of the game and break him. Initially, it was thought that this match went to Price - at this time, anyway.

On another occasion, Price had purchased a two-ton truck from Easley, who claimed it had a rebuilt engine. Price paid with a company check, a good one this time, for $4,000. Shortly thereafter, the truck broke down. Of course, Price was upset and called Easley on the phone. They had words over the situation and Easley told Price he would "take care of it". Easley made some repairs on the truck and when Price sent one of his workers to pick up the truck, Easley wanted another $2,100 or he would not release the truck. This upset Price even more and in a subsequent phone conversation, he told Easley that he was going to come and get the truck. Easley's response was to the effect that "if you come over here, I'm going to blow your damn brains out". Price never got the truck and after this, he had no more dealings with Easley. This match, in this ever-increasing volatile situation, went to Easley.

Easley had previously, on several occasions to different individuals, explained his philosophy on such matters. To those who had come to know him well, they believed that he actually felt that the system did not work well for him, as he had the experience of losing civil court battles in his lawsuits against both the Spring and Goodrich School Districts as well as in his appeal to the State of Texas Education Agency. His conclusion was to just take the matter in his own hands and handle it his way.

Even though Easley had matched up well against Price on most of these situations, he was now ready to go in "for the kill". Easley's reasoning was that just because an enemy is mostly down and out as Price was at the time, there was no reason whatsoever to let him have a chance to get back up and continue to fight. At this point, showing a complete lack of patience as well as a burning desire for revenge, Easley took one of the shop workers and set out to wreak havoc on Price's business operations. Easley put the tow truck to use in yet another manner. He would just locate Price's vehicles, beginning with the truck involved in the dispute, and "repossess" it under the cover of darkness.

This was actually a crime of Auto Theft, but in Easley's mind, it was completely justified. Price would likely suspicion Easley, but Easley had yet another plan as he had obtained a warehouse at a different location from the shop where he could take the vehicle and secrete it. Price would not have any idea of its location. Easley did not cease his revenge with just this one vehicle, as with the assistance of one of his dim-witted minions, "repossessed" two more of Price's vehicles the same night, hiding them in his newly-rented secret facility. These vehicles, operated by Price, were not free and clear as Price was making payments on the mortgaged vehicles. Easley was actually seizing mortgaged vehicles. Basically, Easley committed Theft in these types of actions. However, repossession, while it is often done under the cover of darkness and secrecy, can be considered a legal move when done properly after obtaining a court order to seize any such mortgaged property.

Easley was prone to drive the wrecker on his repossession runs, but if he thought the situation might get rather sticky, he would use one of his shop workers to do his dirty work for him. One of these was a young man from Alabama named Norman Donny Harold, who was known to everyone around the shop as Donny. Donny was only nineteen and was easily swayed to do things that he probably should not have done. Donny was working for Easley during this on-going months-long dispute between his boss and Price. Donny would do Easley's bidding with the tow truck, many times on his own during the night hours. Consequently, while not considered the brightest of young men, Donny learned a lot about Easley and his rotten business dealings with other people. Ironically, Donny had previously worked for Price and had a major falling out with him. This might have entered into Donny's justification for going along with Easley's plan as it gave him some sense of satisfaction by getting back at Price. Donny was the perfect stooge for Easley in his war with Price. Most of the time, Donny went along with whatever Easley told him to do. Most of the time, but fortunately, not always. Donny had the common sense and morality to turn Easley down on several proposals, which ironically angered Jerry Easley, who was not one to be turned down without repercussions.

If the war was not on previously, it was on now between these two totally unscrupulous operators who had a serious dislike for each other. Price's only move at this time was to report the vehicles as stolen, in the hope that they would turn up and he could recoup his losses. He made numerous efforts to file charges on Easley, all of which were turned down due to the never-ending civil matters between him and Easley. Prosecutors are basically reluctant to file criminal Theft charges against someone involved in an on-going civil dispute. Charges of a violent nature are the exception, but fortunately this volatile situation had not yet escalated to that point. This was an extremely frustrating time for Price, as he sensed at every failure that he was not only losing this game, if that's what it was, but more importantly, his fading livelihood. His previous business related difficulties, many of which resulted in bankruptcies, lessened his credibility when attempting to file charges on Easley. One crook filing charges on another crook was not something the Harris County District Attorney's office wanted to clog up the court system with.

James and Judy Hollingsworth, the first of a number of operators Jerry Easley hired at his Reeveston garage, were aware of Easley's manner of doing business. It would not have seemed to be a good idea for Easley to put his rotten business dealings out in the open, especially after he had cut the Hollingsworth portion of the shop's profits every chance he got. Just like Donny Harold, the Hollingsworth couple knew way too much and after being shafted by Easley repeatedly, they sought out Elmer Price to inform him what they knew regarding his trucks. Most of these events occurred in 1984. By way of this collaboration, Price learned about where a large amount of his electrical material went after his trucks were taken in the darkness of night. Not only did Price lose the use of his trucks, he was also out a significant amount of supplies that he had purchased for his current electrical jobs. He also was able to learn where the trucks had been taken, one of which was driven to Arizona and sold.

Like the Hollingsworth couple, many of the people who became disenchanted and weary of Easley's business tactics were all of the same ilk: They were basically good people, but mostly with very little education and with no business experience. They were, however, very wise in the ways of the world as most had experienced a number of difficulties in their lives. Some were without the ability to understand how they were being used over a period of time by Easley. Some learned rather quickly, and with others, it took them a longer time to realize what was occurring.

One of Easley's common methods of compensating the mechanics for work done was when he would review their time sheets with each employee; he would berate them by saying that this particular job, whether it be a transmission job or radiator replacement, should not have taken that amount of time. He would then reduce the mechanic's paid hours to an amount he felt the job should have taken. They had no recourse other than to quit, which occurred on a regular basis after the Hollingsworth family had enough and bailed out. Some of the other individuals that went to work for Jerry on a percentage basis were Gene Daniel Pyle, Jacky Clung, and Johnny Robinson. All experienced the same type of shady dealings with Easley and all left for basically the same reason. Apparently, no matter how much they knew that could harm him, Easley was shrewd enough that he had information on them and some of the questionable practices they had participated in with Easley. They were all reluctant to go to the authorities after they were shafted by Easley. Marty Vail was another of the young, inexperienced mechanics who was drawn in by Easley and Marty actually made several trips to Arizona in late 1984 or early 1985 with Jerry Easley.

Easley also used an older male friend of his, Paul Pryor of Pasadena, Texas, to transfer some of these forged vehicle titles. Mr. Pryor was somewhat of a mentor to Jerry, even though it was difficult to understand this close relationship that existed between the two. Paul was a part-time minister, very much a spiritual man and his thoughts and opinions were well regarded by Easley. To make these transfers work to the point of them at least appearing to be legal, there had to be a number of forgeries committed. Easley was nothing other than a sophisticated class of auto thief.

As a result of all of these business dealings, Price filed a civil suit against Jerry Easley, which was still pending at the time Jerry and Sharon began spending the majority of their time in Arizona at Lake Pleasant. Again, Easley won another poker hand, so to speak, from Price.

Norman Donny Harold (25)

NORMAN DONNY HAROLD, who was known to all while growing up as Donny, was born in Mobile, Alabama, on September 20, 1960. Donny lived in Mobile during his early years, leaving there after his Freshman year in high school when his Mother's job took her to Hawaii. His parents had divorced several years prior to this and his Dad remained in Alabama.

Both of Donny's parents had done well in their respective careers, his Mom being a Civil Service employee of the United States Navy, while his Dad was a Vice-President of a major American railroad company. Much was expected of Donny as he grew up, but Donny struggled in school. While in Hawaii, he continued to struggle with his academics and even though he received much encouragement from his Mom, he dropped out of high school.

At the age of 18, somewhat lost as to what direction his life was taking, Donny returned to the main continent and wound up in New Orleans, where he joined the United States Army National Guard. He was required to finish high school and obtained his G.E.D. while serving on active duty in the Guard. Donny was trained at Fort Jackson, South Carolina, and felt he had found his niche when he completed advanced training in vehicle maintenance, specifically power generation and wheel vehicle mechanics.

After Donny's active duty requirements in the Guard were completed, he eventually returned to Mobile, Alabama, where he became employed at a clock manufacturing company servicing machines in their plant. He was laid off from that job, which greatly distressed his Mom regarding his overall progress in life and his future. Their relationship continued to become even more strained and after not being able to find gainful employment there in Mobile, Donny moved to Houston, Texas. He was hoping for a fresh start and this was actually a bold move on his part as he had no real contacts in Houston other than a childhood friend of his named Jimmie. It was very likely that he also wanted to remove himself from the constant stress of succeeding in life as both of his parents had done and as they desired him to do.

In Houston, he reconnected with Jimmie and moved in with him in an apartment in the Greenspoint area of extreme far North Houston. Through Jimmie, he began working for an electrical contractor named Elmer Price. Price was not the most successful businessman and was constantly having trouble not only paying his suppliers, but also his employees. Donny and Jimmie had moved into a ratty apartment owned by Price which at the very least provided them with a roof over their head even though they were not being compensated at times by Price.

Donny had a telephone installed at this apartment and a disagreement arose with Price over the phone bill. This led to Donny cutting the phone wires in retaliation for Price garnishing some of Donny's wages for the installation of this phone line. This then led to Price running both Donny and Jimmie off of his property.

During Donny's short employment with Price, he became acquainted with Jerry Easley, who at that time in 1983, owned and operated the vehicle mechanic garage. Donny was well aware of the business problems that Easley and Price had experienced.

Meanwhile, Donny, who had fallen out with Price over the phone line, was now working for Easley in the mechanic's shop. Donny apparently had difficulty dealing with employers, or possibly it was that he was merely gullible and easily taken advantage of. Just as with Price, Donny was working for whatever money Easley would give him occasionally.

Then one day, Easley contacted Donny and Jimmie and asked them to take a ride with him. Easley buttered them up some by taking them to a restaurant and picked up the tab for lunch. For Jerry Easley, this was very unusual. Suddenly, Easley came right out and asked Donny and Jimmie what they would charge him "to feed Price to the fishes". Neither Donny nor Jimmie was considered the sharpest knife in the drawer, but they both had seen the movie *The Godfather* and realized what Easley was asking of them. Even stranger yet about this offer was the fact that Jimmie was still working for Price at the time even though Price had run him off of his property previously.

Easley further explained to Donny and Jimmie that Price had written him a postdated check for $4,000 and then stopped payment on the check when he decided he was not pleased with the work Easley had done on this one particular truck. Easley had even a more detailed plan yet for this act, explaining to Donny and Jimmie that he had a .25 caliber pistol and that it would be very easy to go in Price's house and shoot him in the head while he was asleep. With a .25 caliber pistol, one of the smallest caliber pistols ever made? Even Donny and Jimmie had to wonder how this would work out. Shortly after this proposal to commit Capital Murder was tendered to Donny and Jimmie, Easley even gave Donny a .25 caliber pistol and a sawed-off pump shotgun.

Donny later stated that after this proposal was presented to them, both he and Jimmie became very quiet and never actually accepted or denied the request "to feed Price to the fishes". It turned out to be a very uncomfortable moment and then Easley changed the subject just as suddenly as he had brought it up originally. Nothing more was said for a time and then Easley let them out of his truck and went on his way.

Donny and Jimmie had heard Easley speak about and berate Elmer Price regarding anything and everything. He was actually just preaching to the choir as both well knew Price's manner of treating them and others. They knew that at the end of their work week, when they were working for him, Price would review their work slips and adjust the hours accordingly to his thinking. He would say to them that just because it took you four hours to do a certain job, it was actually only a two-hour job. He would use his assessment of the task and then only pay them for the two hours that he thought was appropriate. Price was constantly in trouble with his clients and being sued on a regular basis by people who had allowed him to do electrical work for them. Because of this, he had a number of fiscal liens registered against him and basically was not able to openly run his company under his own name anymore. Of course, he was just crafty and devious enough to work around that and at one point in time, was operating the same business but under his daughter's name.

After recovering from the shock of being offered the job of "feeding Price to the fishes", Donny and Jimmie actually had a laugh about the complaints and accusations Easley had about Price. The old saying crossed their minds, "talk about the pot calling the kettle black". Both, especially Donny, were well aware that Easley treated his employees, or his flunkies, the same manner in which Price did. They even discussed the idea of how many people Easley and Price together, if they combined forces, could cheat.

A few days later, Easley once again contacted Donny and this time, brought up the same subject but indicated to Donny that he did not want Jimmie involved since he did not feel he could be trusted, especially due to the fact that he was still working for Price. He stated this to Donny even though Donny had never even remotely or openly indicated that he was even considering taking Easley up on this offer. To Donny, it was almost as if Easley expected him to do whatever he asked, no matter how far-fetched and illegal it seemed to be. Here, once again, Easley had placed himself in a very vulnerable position had either one of these two young men gone to the authorities with this proposal. But, unfortunately, they did not.

Several weeks passed with no more discussion of doing the job on Price. After contacting Donny once again, Easley drove him to Goodrich, Texas. Donny was totally unfamiliar with Easley's previous problems at the Goodrich Independent School District. Easley went on to tell Donny that there were three individuals in Goodrich who had done him wrong and he wanted them taken care of. Easley was not shy about "spilling his guts" and reflecting his true feelings about people who, in his mind, had done him wrong. It seems that everyone he had any contact with at any time had done him wrong in one manner or another. Easley went on to explain, probably in an effort that would convince Donny to agree with him, what these individuals had done to him. He stated that these people had accused him of setting up a bomb threat at the school and that if anyone had ever done him wrong, it was these three individuals. Jerry Easley had definitely accumulated more than his share of enemies in his lifetime. And, there were more to come.

Jerry continued by driving by the alleged home of one of these people and telling Donny that this man is up early every morning jogging around his neighborhood and how easy it would be to take this shotgun, showing it to Donny just prior to this, and taking care of this guy when he was jogging. Jerry told Donny that this guy was a lawyer. This could have been a member of the Goodrich School Board, a Mr. Arnie McDonald, who was previously the Polk County Attorney and now in private practice. Mr. McDonald's connection to the school district fiasco was not made clear to Donny.

After taking Donny to this location, Easley then proceeded to take Donny on a further "grand tour" of Goodrich. He drove him to a location where a female lived, explaining that this woman had been a receptionist at the school when the alleged bomb threat had been called in and had later identified Easley's voice as the person making the call. This would have been Mrs. Jenny Hicks.

That was two of the three, after which time Easley drove Donny past a local real estate office, indicating to Donny that this real estate salesman had wanted Easley's Superintendent's job and while on the Goodrich School Board, had consistently voted against any item he had brought before the Board. Easley even had a plan for Donny to accomplish this matter, suggesting that Donny could pose as a prospective home buyer at one of this man's properties and then take care of business when the salesman arrived for the showing. This would have been Mr. Edward Larson.

Following this "grand tour" of Goodrich, Donny had not spoken much or even commented about the requests made by Easley. Finally, after moments of silence, Easley did not ask for a yes or no answer from Donny. Instead, in true Jerry Easley fashion, he merely came right out and asked Donny how much money he wanted to do the jobs. After Donny replied that he was not certain about anything like this, Easley again was not to be denied and told Donny that times were tough, that there was not much work for him right now and that he was willing to pay $500 to Donny for each person he took care of. $500 per hit? $500 for a Capital Murder offense? Even Donny, who was very much naïve and inexperienced in the world, especially the world of Capital Murder, thought later how ridiculous Easley's proposals were.

Needless to say, according to Donny, it was a very long and quiet ride that evening from Goodrich back to Aldine. In a further attempt to justify to Donny the importance of having this done, Easley explained to Donny that the legal system just does not work well for him. However, it is his goal to defeat this legal system and that if anyone ever does anything to him or gets in his way, they "ought not to have done it". He stressed this in a very authoritative manner and on several occasions on this trip, reminded Donny of the manner in which he had been treated by Price over the phone situation and that he should remember this as to the type of person they were dealing with. Once again, Easley had placed himself in a very vulnerable position. And, once again, Donny did not go to the authorities regarding these "hits" that Easley wanted done.

Donny went back to work for Easley, doing odd jobs around the garage. The compensation remained about the same - not much. Donny never gave Easley an answer one way or the other regarding the offers on Price or "the Goodrich Three". Easley did, after the trip to Goodrich, tell Donny not to say anything to Jimmie about any of this.

Shortly after the Goodrich trip, while Donny was extremely uncomfortable with the situation with Easley, he was told out of the clear blue by a third party that Easley was desiring to help Donny and send him off to college. Jon Easley had been known to Donny from being around the shop as Jerry Easley's son, and even though they were not the best of friends, they got along in the work situation at the shop. Another garage flunky of Easley's, a teenage kid named Franky Routt, called Donny to the side one day and advised Donny of Easley's plan to send both he and Jon off to a Bible College in East Texas. Franky's Mom and Stepfather, the

Hollingsworths, had worked for Jerry Easley for a time and had actually run the garage business during some of Easley's frequent absences.

Finally, one day shortly thereafter, Easley proposed this idea to Donny, buttering him up and saying it was his wish to help him and that he would make all of the arrangements as he had contacts with the upper echelon at the school and that it would be possible for him and Jon to even room together in an apartment.

While Donny was not the brightest young man, he felt that Easley wanted him out of the way since he had basically turned him down on two separate occasions to commit Capital Murder. Donny felt like this could be a way out of the difficult situation he had found himself in. And, more importantly, he thought it just might be his chance to get away from Jerry Easley. Of course, with the generous offers Easley had given him to assist him with college, Donny should have known that this was too good to be true. However, there were not many other options open to him at this time and he decided to take Easley up on these offers.

In September of that year, 1983, Donny left for Jacksonville Bible College in the small East Texas town of Jacksonville. Donny had never been involved in the college admission process and was told by Easley that arrangements had been made. To his amazement, he found that Easley was right. The road was greased completely for him. The admission and finances had been arranged with the College Dean, Mr. Roland Gotham, an old acquaintance of Easley's. Room and board was arranged also and Donny was placed in a three-student apartment with Jon Easley and a young man named Scott Henning. Jerry Easley even left three vehicles at the apartment and indicated that one of those vehicles, a Chevy Nova, was for Donny's use. With what Donny knew about Easley's business dealing with vehicles, he could only wonder which one or if all were of a questionable title background. He wondered to the extent that he was reluctant to drive any of the three.

Donny settled in for the fall semester of 1983 and surprisingly, developed a strong work ethic on his academic schedule. He realized that this could be the opportunity of a lifetime if he was mature enough at the age of 23 to take full advantage of it.

All was going surprisingly well and even though Donny and Jon got along with each other, it was not a very close friendship nor was it ever going to be. The third roommate, Scott, was amicable enough but did not spend very much time around Donny and Jon as he had developed a close relationship with a female student at the college and this mostly occupied his time. Then, just prior to Thanksgiving, an unknown male came to the college looking for Donny. It was discovered that this person was paid by Elmer Price to locate Donny and attempt to obtain his testimony in his ongoing civil lawsuit against Jerry Easley. Donny made no commitment to do so and shortly thereafter, Easley came to the college apartment to talk to Donny about Price looking for him. Donny told Easley that he just wanted to be left alone by everyone about the entire situation. He had no desire to become more involved in either Price's or Easley's shady dealings.

Jon, who had no desire either to be involved in his Dad's business, was told to tell Donny that his Dad wanted to take Donny hunting over the Thanksgiving school break. Donny's suspicions were definitely aroused by this information. For as long as he knew Easley, he had never once known Easley to go hunting or even talk about hunting. Thanksgiving is prime deer hunting season in Texas and when Donny turned down the offer, it must have angered Easley. Donny was adamant that he was not "going to be the fox in the hunt", so to speak. Fortunately for Donny, his naivety was fading away at a rapid pace.

In retaliation, Easley came to Jacksonville and took all three of the vehicles back to Houston. Why would he take Jon's vehicle also? Jon was not surprised by this action on his Dad's part as this was a pattern of behavior that he had witnessed his entire life. While there was no indication that Jerry Easley had any American Indian blood in this ancestry, Jerry truly fit the term "Indian Giver". He did not give gifts out of generosity or out of the kindness of his heart. Gifts were given for a reason and that was usually to butter someone up to do what he wanted. If that idea fell through, he thought nothing of just taking the "gift" back just as suddenly as he had given it in the first place. Jon Easley had not only personally experienced that type of action by his father, he had also previously observed it being done to other individuals.

Thanksgiving came and went. During the fall semester, Donny had applied himself to his studies. While most of the financial aspects of his college experience had been taken care of, Donny needed extra money as do all students. He certainly did not intend to ask Jerry Easley for any other assistance. He was in college and hoping to major in Sociology. He then began working part-time at a nearby convenience store there close to the college in Jacksonville. He was doing well in school, and for the first time in his somewhat troubled life, he felt he was accomplishing something, something also that would make his Mom proud. However, the threat or problem that was Jerry Easley was never far from his mind.

Assault at the Bible College, Jacksonvillle, Texas (26)

December 1, 1983

LIFE WAS GOING on at the college in Jacksonville. However, Donny was having difficulties concentrating on his studies and was constantly haunted by the propositions that Jerry Easley had proffered to him in recent months. While he never once thought of agreeing to Easley's proposals, he could not help but think about what Easley was now thinking. Was Easley regretting making those offers for him to commit Capital Murder on four different people? Was Easley currently actively recruiting someone else to do the dirty deeds for him? Had Easley been successful in lining someone up to go along with this sick scheme of his? And another question that actually haunted Donny was this: Was he himself on Easley's list of enemies? Further, the offer to go hunting with Easley at Thanksgiving bothered him just as much as anything about this strange situation.

Donny and Jon Easley, while not being the best of friends originally, were becoming better friends, maybe partially due to the fact that they both knew they needed to make this situation work for as long as possible. They were getting along, basically learning how to tolerate each other and do the best they could. However, with Jon being ever-present, it was even more difficult for Donny to eliminate from his mind those constant questions about Jerry Easley. Even though he and Jon were relating better than ever to each other, it was just not possible to discuss his fears with Jon. Jon may or may not have known, probably did not, of all of his Dad's activities even though he was well aware of the continued business problems that his Dad had with other people in and around the mechanic shop.

Then, late in the night of Thursday, December 1, 1983, actually just shortly after midnight, Donny was in bed already as was Jon. They were in single military type beds in the same bedroom in this two bedroom apartment. There was a knock on the door and Donny answered the door. The late night visitor was none other than Franky Emory Routt, who Donny and Jon both knew from the garage on Reeveston.

Franky was only 16 years old, and was not progressing very well in life, sort of following in the pattern of the other flunkies that Easley seemed to recruit for menial jobs around the shop. The Hollingsworth couple, both from rural parts of Alabama, were somewhat drifters in life, from one job to another. They were also typical of the caliber of people that Jerry would surround himself with, to him the type he could easily control and manipulate for whatever purposes suited him at the time. Of course, they were also very street smart and life savvy and eventually also saw through Easley.

This was the same Franky Routt who had originally told Donny of Easley's plans to help him and send him to college with Jon. This was also the same Franky Routt who told Donny that Easley wanted Donny out of sight as he "knew too much". And, yes, Donny knew that he certainly did know too much. He knew way more than he was comfortable knowing. But now what, he thought, is Franky doing visiting him literally in the middle of the night?

This was truly a strange visit from Franky, who Donny had not seen for several months. Franky told Donny he was in town to visit a sick aunt and was just dropping by to say hello. Arriving at midnight to visit an ailing aunt? Donny was suspicious of this, not believing it for a minute. This brought not only a suspicious feeling on the part of Donny, but also a very eerie feeling. Donny was apprehensive, but was also thinking "Am I being too paranoid"? Donny was as polite as possible trying to get rid of Franky, as all he wanted to do was to get to sleep in preparation for the next day's classes as this was a school night. Even stranger yet to Donny and Jon was that they knew Franky to be a known thief and liar and seemed to revel in starting arguments and fights around the garage. Neither cared much for Franky and yet here he was, in the middle of the night visiting them.

Donny's suspicions were further aroused when he asked Franky where his aunt lived in Jacksonville. Franky replied that she lived down by the railroad tracks. Donny knew that there were two sets of railroad tracks running through the town, and when he asked Franky which tracks, Franky stated he did not know. Donny eventually reluctantly invited Franky inside. After about 20 minutes of idle conversation, Donny was telling Franky that he needed to get to sleep. Then, Franky asked him to come outside, that they would walk down the street to the nearby convenience store and get a Coke.

During this time, Jon had gotten out of bed after hearing the conversation and realizing who it was talking to Donny. While Jon had entered the conversation, Franky did not ask Jon to go with him to get a Coke, just Donny. Donny remained persistent that he did not want to go get a Coke, that he just wanted to go to bed as he had classes in the morning at 8:00am. To be able to do this, he even told Franky that if he wanted to spend the night, he was free to sleep on the sofa in the living room.

Franky went into the restroom and then came out shouting to Donny that there is someone outside and he needed to go see who it was. Now, Donny's suspicion feelers were becoming stronger and felt like something very strange was occurring. He kept telling Donny that someone was out there, to go see who it is. Finally, Jon spoke up and said I will go look, that it might be a friend of his who he was always exchanging childish pranks with. Jon went outside, and Donny, now becoming very sleepy, told Franky that he was going to bed.

Donny tried to go to sleep, but was also very anxious that something very serious was happening here. Jon came back in shortly and had a very surprised and concerned look on his face. Jon laid down in his bed and Donny in his, but they were having face-to-face contact from only three to four feet away. Donny saw that Jon was not the same as usual, that he appeared to be very concerned about something he had seen outside.

Donny was dozing in and out of sleep even though he was disturbed by all of this. The next thing he knew he felt a tremendous blow to the back of his head. He later stated that it felt like someone had discharged a shotgun inside his head. It was like a loud roar and he then jumped up out of bed and saw someone running out the front door.

Donny felt his head and felt a gash in the back of the head and quickly became covered with blood. His initial response was to tell Jon to get him some help. Jon replied that he couldn't do that because his Dad was outside and had come to take Donny back with him and Franky to Houston.

Donny, now more scared than ever, grabbed a wooden clothes bar from a nearby closet and started to go outside after Franky. Jon told Donny to stop, even pulling a 16-inch Jim Bowie knife out from under his bed and telling Donny that you are not going anywhere. Donny, not knowing it at the time, was actually being somewhat protected by Jon. Donny finally told John to put the knife down or he was going to take his head off with the clothes bar. Jon, not being a fighter, put the knife down and Donny ran outside, armed with the wooden bar.

Outside, he ran through the apartment courtyard in the direction of the parking lot. He then heard Franky say to someone, "Here he comes, here he comes". Franky then was heard saying "Come here, Donny, come over here". Donny then saw Franky's car parked underneath a security light and even though he did not see Franky, he saw Jerry Easley standing outside of the vehicle holding what appeared to be a rifle. Easley then threw the rifle across the top of the car, aiming it directly at Donny. The wooden clothes bar no longer appeared to be an adequate defensive measure to Donny and he ran to a neighbor's apartment. Not even knocking on the door, he just grabbed the unlocked door knob and hurried in shouting to the three guys he knew to be living there.

Donny ran into Jack Fitzpatrick's bedroom and shouted that Jerry Easley was trying to kill him. Danny Conner, another occupant of this apartment, heard the commotion and when he came in the bedroom,

Donny told him the same thing. Danny went to his car and got his .30/06 rifle and he, Donny, and Jack went out looking for Jerry and Franky, but they and the vehicle were gone.

Jack called the Dean of Students, Jerry Easley's friend, Mr. Roland Gotham. When he arrived, he was confronted with a very confused group of young men, especially Donny and Jon. Both were reluctant to tell the story about what had occurred and Mr. Gotham recalled later that it was like "pulling teeth" to get at any sense of the truth from either one of them. Eventually, he did learn from Donny some semblance of what could have been the whole story about Easley and Franky coming over there to kidnap him and about being struck in the head.

Mr. Gotham then went over to talk to Jon Easley, and Jon attempted at the time to cover for his Dad and told Mr. Gotham that Donny had slipped and fallen, which made no sense at all to anyone. Jon then broke down completely, crying that he was told by his Dad outside earlier that they were there merely to take Donny back to Houston because he had stolen some things from his previous roommate Jimmie. That story even made less sense than Jon's original version and of course, to Mr. Gotham this aroused his further suspicions about the truth and veracity of anything Jon was relating to him.

At this point, Jon Easley was a very emotionally distraught young man of only 17 years of age. Now, in the dead of night, in his first semester of college, his Dad and a friend had conspired to kidnap and murder his college roommate. Jon was nearly to the point of a mental collapse and actually did so when he added up all of the above chain of events.

After further questioning by Dean Gotham, Jon told part of the truth, saying that his Dad told him they were going to take Donny to a motel near Palestine. Eventually, Dean Gotham came to the conclusion that Donny was telling the truth about the entire matter.

It appeared to both Jon and Donny at this point that Dean Gotham was either not taking this as a serious matter or he was just not believing their version of the incident. While this made no sense at all to Jon, he was further told by Dean Gotham that he would be allowed to leave the school quietly providing he assisted in convincing Donny to not pursue charges. Jon could not help but wonder about this statement. Why would he have to leave the school when he had not done anything but witness this assault? However, at that point, the Dean was more concerned about the reputation of the College than he was worried about Donny's injury or Jon's education and future. It seemed as if the Dean was wanting this situation to just go away.

Damage Control for the College (27)

S UDDENLY, THE ALL-IMPORTANT concept of damage control, all important to the college, that is, reared its very ugly head. The Dean pointed
out to Donny that if he reported the incident to the authorities, that it
would ruin his and the school's image in the eyes of the public. He even
cautioned Donny about going to receive medical attention as it would be
required that the authorities be notified at that time also.

Donny was very upset at this time. First, he could not believe that all
of this had happened and now, even after the truth had come out, he was
being advised not to report it to the police or even receive medical attention. Being basically in shock at this time, he reluctantly went along with
Dean Gotham's advice but also told him that based on how he felt the next
day, he was probably going to the hospital to have the large gash on his
head treated.

Donny did go for treatment the next day and for whatever reason,
the police were not notified of the incident. It's probable that the admission clerk was not aware that such an injury was always required to
be, by law, reported to the local law enforcement authorities. When
he returned to school the next day, he found that the story had been
made known to almost everyone in the student body. The incident was
the talk of the school. Some of his friends, who were missionary students, came to him and told Donny that they were not satisfied with the
manner in which Dean Gotham and the school's administration had
responded to the severity of the situation. Little did the powers-that-be
know that since the true story was all over the school, it was not possible

to keep the lid on the story as they were so embarrassingly desperate to accomplish.

This group of students, including Donny and Jon's roommate, Scott Henning, talked Donny into going to the next step in the school hierarchy, the President of the college. Scott Henning had not been present during this incident, but learned of it quickly after arriving at the apartment after visiting with his girlfriend. Of course, by the next day, Mr. Gotham had covered himself and had already spoken with the President and informed him of the entire incident. One could not imagine that the two had not discussed the important aspect of damage control. A cover-up had been arranged, the object being to keep this felony assault on campus as low-key as possible. Above all, the school's reputation and image was at stake here with little or no concern for Donny's injury or justice prevailing.

Mr. Gotham's appeal to Donny to not go forth with a formal complaint or medical attention had not actually done the trick. Now the President was faced with providing cover for the rather nasty situation he and Mr. Gotham had already attempted to put the quietus on. Faced with a small group of upset students over the handling of the problem, he lowered the reputation of the college even more by making a further appeal to Donny. He politely explained to Donny that if reported further, it might sling a little mud on the college, but the important point Donny needed to remember was that the Administration and even some students might feel that Donny was just being rebellious and unappreciative toward the school. He also pointed out to Donny that he might be able to stay at the school if this was not reported to the authorities. Donny thought long and hard about what these words meant. If I do report it, I will not be able to stay at this school? The only college opportunity Donny felt he would ever experience was now being dangled in front of him and possibly taken away?

The President advised Donny of this in the presence of six young idealistic Bible College Missionary students. Basically threatening Donny in front of this number of students was not at all a smart move.

These young men and women knew right from wrong and encouraged Donny to stand his ground on this matter. Surely, the President did not think that this matter, really no fault of the school's, would go away quietly when so many young students knew of their stance on the matter. Donny, however, was apparently swayed by the President's assessment and advice.

Marital Problems in Arizona (28)

JERRY EASLEY WOULD easily become restless, never satisfied with the current status in life, whether good or bad. He had accumulated a significant amount of cash from the Humble real estate deal and after running the Reeveston Garage for several years, the manner in which he did business proved to be very profitable. With his massive ego, his thinking was that other profitable ventures were certainly awaiting him. He and Sharon had previously visited a location in the mountains of Arizona, north of Phoenix, Lake Pleasant. The climate was tolerable year-round and after arrangements were made initially to lease the garage business out to other individuals, Jerry and Sharon set out for the western United States and eventually, to stay at Lake Pleasant. Their business and personal plans were to derive income from the garage lease and enjoy life at the lake.

The marriage of Sharon and Jerry had been on very shaky ground for some time. Jerry had become even more domineering over Sharon as time passed. Sharon had been forbidden by Jerry to have contact with her family, but Sharon was secretly contacting her Mother by phone and also on several occasions, in person. At one point when Jerry and Sharon began their travels, Sharon's Mother, Marguerite Hammond, accompanied them. However, after witnessing Jerry's rants and raves at Sharon for seemingly minor issues, she ceased traveling with them.

Sharon confided to her Mom that the situation was very volatile, and she was "sitting on a powder keg". Further, she was going to have to fight Jerry or flee from him because he wanted total submission and obedience from her along with total isolation from any of her family or friends. Her actual words to her Mom were "fight or flight". She wanted neither, but she was fearful that the situation was coming to the point in the relationship that one would be necessary.

She recalled to her Mom also that she was not only fearful of him physically, but also remembered what he did to his son Jon several years ago at the Reeveston garage. Jon had made him angry over some seemingly trivial matter so Jerry took a shovel and large garbage can to Jon's room. He loaded up all of Jon's clothes and property, including a stereo system, took the items out on the back property and set them on fire. Sharon could just see Jerry doing that to her belongings in one of his fits of anger. Sharon was actually becoming very fearful of Jerry physically, but felt the need to not share those feelings with her Mom, who was concerned enough already. Sharon, while really needing to share her problems with someone, was also attempting, in her own way, to keep the severity of the situation away from her widowed Mother, who was experiencing many physical problems of her own.

Sharon complained to her Mom that Jerry watched her very closely and wanted 24 hours a day accounting for her every activity. Sharon was a volunteer at the Park Ranger Station at Lake Pleasant State Park where they resided in their motor home. While Sharon's job was that of a volunteer, she thoroughly enjoyed the contact with other people, relationships being something she was not allowed by Jerry to have many of. This volunteer assignment had its other perks, the main ones being that she and Jerry received free parking privileges at the park as well as free electricity for their motor home.

Of course, Jerry was comfortable with this at the beginning for the obvious financial benefits. However, Jerry was offered the opportunity to participate also, but he was basically anti-social with even their neighbors in the park and would not participate in this volunteer work. Sharon thought that Jerry felt that "volunteering" was beneath him.

Part of Sharon's duties at the Park was working in the aid station helping the full-time paid Park Rangers in minor duties such as collecting fees from campers and doing other odd jobs as well as secretarial duties. Sharon loved this job as it not only allowed her some social interaction with others, but also provided her the opportunity to escape somewhat from Jerry's increasingly large thumb. There were both male and female Park Rangers at this location and Jerry was constantly badgering Sharon about working around other men. He was extremely jealous and had on many occasions, without any grounds, accused Sharon of having affairs with the men Rangers. The dress code for Park employees and volunteers was usually western, meaning jeans and western shirts and with some people, cowboy boots. After all, why not, this was in Arizona cowboy country with horses and cattle in abundance throughout the mountainous countryside. However, Jerry would not allow Sharon to wear her "cowgirl" clothes because in his mind, that's what a "whore" wears.

On one occasion while Sharon was on duty at the Ranger Station, Jerry dropped by, probably to check on her to see what she was doing other than her job. When he did so, Sharon was among four or five other Park personnel, male and female, all of which were discussing the day's activities while having a cup of coffee. Jerry made a scene regarding this and in front of Sharon's co-workers and friends, forbid her to drink coffee. He was against the use of coffee, yet he was known to drink soft drinks, mainly Coca Colas, throughout his day and was rarely if ever without an open container of his favorite soft drink. Jerry did not use alcohol, which was not a problem with Sharon as she did not drink either. It was explained at one point that someone in Jerry's family had been a heavy drinker of alcohol at one time and it was for that reason he was against its use altogether. Needless to say, this incident was a very embarrassing one for Sharon, but then again, she was somewhat used to some of his tirades and felt obligated to apologize to her friends for his behavior. Through the years, she had been placed in such a situation on more than one occasion where he had embarrassed her in front of friends and on very rare occasions, with her family.

Some of Jerry's other idiosyncrasies were that he liked to sleep late in the morning. Further, he had no use for clocks and said on many occasions that he did not wish to be controlled by time. Sharon, on the other hand, was an early riser and enjoyed getting up early in the morning and go for a jog around the park. This area north of Phoenix was a great place for outdoor activities, nearly year-round. Jerry did not like Sharon doing this, even refusing to allow her this enjoyable physical activity. On one occasion when she got up and went jogging anyway, he pouted and stayed in bed all day. This seemed like mere jealousy on his part, but it was actually just another form of manipulative control that he attempted to utilize over Sharon.

Another example of his irrational behavior was shown that while he knew Sharon liked to get up early in the morning, he expected her to stay in bed with him until he wanted to get up. Then, amazingly, he would be upset with her because she did not have breakfast ready for him.

Jerry was also somewhat of a hypochondriac, always complaining about some real or imaginary ailment. He actually told Sharon at one point that he considered her to exist for his comfort. He would wake Sharon up during the night, complaining to her that she did not keep him covered up in bed or move over close to him in order that he could stay warm and comfortable. His body seemed to produce heat, but he constantly complained of being cold. Sharon, with her knowledge of chemistry, felt that there could have been something seriously out-of-sync with Jerry's metabolism, something that with the proper treatment, could be successfully dealt with. But, Jerry would have no part of her hints at doing so little as seeking a diagnosis. And, all she could do was hint. To do more, would create yet even more havoc between Jerry and her.

These mood swings of Jerry's very much bothered Sharon and she had, very carefully, suggested for him to consult a physician to determine if there could be a medical problem causing him to act as he frequently did. However, he would not see a doctor. On one occasion, Sharon had made arrangements with a nurse friend of hers to draw blood from Jerry to have it tested. That would necessitate Jerry's finger to be pricked with a needle, but that idea was nixed because he faints at the mere sight of blood.

Was this idiosyncrasy of Jerry's regarding the sight of blood pertaining only to his blood, or also to that of others? Recalling that Sherry Dean

Easley was brutally and repeatedly stabbed with a knife, thereby creating an extremely bloody crime scene, this was a rather strange feeling that Jerry possessed regarding the mere sight of blood. Or was it just another part of his hypochondria coming in to play in order to avoid any treatment?

All of these issues in attempting to please Jerry, or at the very least, getting along with him, was taking a terrible toll on Sharon. Her physical health was suffering from the constant tension. She was taking Maalox for her stomach problems, was coughing up blood, and her menstrual cycle was in turmoil. In summary, she was a walking physical and mental wreck, on the verge of a total mental breakdown as well as likely dealing with a peptic ulcer. She was walking on eggshells around Jerry, afraid to make a move that she knew she needed to make such as leave him. The explosive situation was becoming more volatile each and every day.

Sharon discussed with her Mom the three alternatives she had thought of: Jerry may have a brain disease and eventually she would be caring for someone in a vegetative state of mind OR he will change for the better OR God will take him. Of course, none of these were short term solutions to a continuous long term problem. Deep down, her thought that he would change was just wishful thinking.

After being isolated for so long from her family, Sharon began to rely more and more on her Mother for support and guidance. Of course, Mrs. Hammond would have been hard-pressed to say much positive about Jerry as he had been the one who had insisted on Sharon's estrangement from her family. However, Mrs. Hammond was also very careful not to be overly negative toward Jerry, but just attempted mainly to be supportive of her daughter in an advisory capacity. Sharon opened the door about counseling and her Mom totally supported that idea. It was through Mrs. Hammond's minister in Houston that Sharon was connected with a counselor in the Phoenix area.

Throughout these rough times in the marriage, Sharon had an ally in Jon and they had become very close as both had experienced the increasingly difficult behavior of Jerry. Sharon had always been very spiritual and had taught her step-son the same beliefs. She and Jon could speak to each other about this situation and Sharon, through the church that she and Jon attended regularly, had sought the assistance of a professional counselor. Of course, this had to be done on the sly as this would surely set Jerry off had he known. As paranoid as he was becoming, this would have been taken by Jerry as Sharon talking to a stranger about their problems.

These counseling sessions were somewhat helpful to Sharon as she was able to learn more about the behavior she was dealing with. Sharon was encouraged to continue with her spiritual life in that this was felt to be the only way she could deal with Jerry. She also became aware that unless Jerry himself seeks help, he was not going to change unless something very drastic occurred in his life. This counseling was similar to what family members are told in the Al-Anon program of Alcoholics Anonymous and that if Jerry does not change, an intervention might become necessary in which Sharon and Jon would present a united front to Jerry. An ultimatum of sorts - if he did not change or at least express a willingness to change, then both Sharon's and Jon's emotional support should be removed from Jerry. Sharon, deep down, knew this to be true, but being the ever-devoted Christian wife that she was, found this approach very difficult to seriously consider and even more importantly, go through with.

While Jerry and Sharon had enough of their own marital issues, one that stood out above others was Jerry's jealousy. The jealous behavior exhibited by Jerry previously at the Ranger station continued in even a more aggravated manner. He did not treat Sharon very well in a number of areas and at the same time, was very jealous of situations that brought her into any type of contact with other males. This was a very large problem in and around the Lake Pleasant Ranger Station and one which frequently thrust Sharon into a very embarrassing situation. On one occasion, after Jerry warned Sharon not to go on driving patrol around the park, he learned that she had left the Ranger Station with a female Ranger on a five-minute trip. Again, he made his proverbial mountain-out-of-a-mole-hill over that occurrence, just totally embarrassing Sharon in front of her co-workers.

Jerry was the one with the jealousy problem, but he was also the one who on occasions placed Sharon in a difficult position. One such time that stood out was on one of their many trips across the desert from Houston to Lake Pleasant. On this occasion, Jerry was transporting vehicles to Arizona for whatever reason he thought necessary at the time. Jerry had become associated through the Reeveston Garage with yet another usually unemployed mechanic by the name of Stephen Farris. Farris and Jerry had completed several successful repair jobs jointly and it was mutually decided to move to Arizona, open up a vehicle repair service there and supplement that operation with a tow truck for a wrecker service.

This ill-fated business venture began in June, 1984 and it was on this trip to Arizona that Jerry teamed up as driving partners his wife Sharon and Stephen Farris. Easley was driving along towing a trailer with another vehicle. Stephen Farris was 27 years old at the time while Sharon was 42 years of age. There was no attraction from Sharon to Stephen Farris, but the important thing to Jerry was that he imagined such an attraction. This was thrown up to Sharon on a number of occasions by Jerry and this just totally exacerbated an already volatile marital problem.

During the planning and set-up stages of this proposed business venture, Farris was working on some of Easley's vehicles. He had his own tools, as most mechanics are required and expected to have. With Jerry's jealousy raising its ugly head each and every day, the business venture wound up on the back burner and Farris decided that it was not going to work out at all. He advised Easley that he was going back to Houston and that he wanted to be paid for the work he had performed for Easley while there in Arizona.

Farris had driven his personal vehicle, a 1975 Chevrolet truck, to Arizona and also towed a work trailer with some personal belongings and more importantly, the mechanic "tools of his trade". Easley's response to Farris in regards to money owed him was that it was actually Farris that owed Easley. At that point, things became rather heated between the two of them, resulting in a major blow-up. A friend of Stephen's, Timmy

Goslin, had come to Arizona and was to be a part of the business venture as an employee of both Easley and Farris.

Easley then ordered Farris and Goslin off of his rented Lake Pleasant trailer spot and physically prevented Farris from access to his truck, trailer, and tools. This was a volatile situation that could very well have escalated into a serious physical and violent confrontation. Easley seemed to hold all of the cards in the game at this time. Whether Easley was motivated by his jealous suspicions or by his somewhat usual shady business practices, Farris was just basically out of luck.

Then, to further aggravate the situation, Easley had the truck, trailer, and tools as well as some other of Farris's other personal belongings moved to a public storage facility in nearby Phoenix, Arizona. That facility, which had been rented by Easley, would not allow Stephen Farris access to his belongings. Again, Farris was young and somewhat naïve as most of Easley's business partners were. Easley knew Farris's options were limited, but Farris did have the foresight to hire an attorney to represent him.

Jerry had then openly accused Sharon of having an affair with Stephen Farris, claiming to her that she began it on the motor trip from Houston to Arizona, a situation that he himself had thrust her into. Her knowledge of the business problems was limited and even though she suspected that Jerry was wrong in his dealing with Farris and his tools, could not utter a word to Jerry regarding her opinion.

Jon was beginning to realize how difficult his Dad was becoming towards Sharon, who confided with Jon about the marriage difficulties. At this time, Jon was living just behind Sharon and Jerry in the park in a separate motor home, a Winnebago, and was attending a junior college nearby, attempting to continue his education after the Bible College incident in Jacksonville. Jon's Dad provided this motor home for Jon.

He was privy to many of their problems and while he knew he could not openly take sides, he was drawn into the problems whether he wanted to be involved or not. On January 15, 1985, Sharon decided that she had enough of Jerry and was going to leave him. Prior to this, way back in 1973 when they lived on Chipman Street in Aldine, Sharon had left Jerry for a short period of time but returned. At the time, Jerry demanded that if she ever was going to leave him, that she tell him prior to doing so. For whatever reason imaginable, Sharon agreed to this demand. Sharon, being the honorable and truthful individual she was, vowed to keep her promise about telling him when she was going to leave.

Now, in late January of 1985, she told Jerry about her plans to leave and he became, as expected, very upset and violent. He became physical and violent with Sharon, even pinning her up against the trailer wall, refusing to let her go. There existed an intercom system between their motor home and that of Jon's, and this communication system actually turned out to be somewhat of a lifesaver for Sharon as she was able to let Jon know what was going on. Jon rushed over and was able to get Jerry to release Sharon.

Jon, whether he wanted to be involved or not, was involved, and right in the middle of this worsening marital discord between his Dad and Sharon. Jon assisted Sharon in loading some of her belongings in her truck while Jerry began crying and begging Sharon not to go, repeatedly promising her that he would change. Of course, Sharon, who had heard all of this previously, insisted that she had to separate for the sake of her sanity as well as her safety. Jerry then agreed to leave and go to Houston for a few days to give Sharon time to gather her thoughts about this ever-increasing volatile situation.

When Jerry returned five days later, he found a note from Sharon advising him that she had left him and for him not to attempt to find her. At this point, Sharon had gathered her thoughts and had come to the realization that she needed to get away from Jerry, that he was not going to change. Too many promises had been made by Jerry regarding his ways, and she could not take much more. Sharon had, as usual, confided in Jon her whereabouts. Jon was aware of where she had gone to stay with some church friends there in Arizona.

After finding the note, Jerry rightfully assumed that Jon probably knew of Sharon's whereabouts. Jerry was actually very jealous of the close-friend relationship that existed between Sharon and Jon. Jerry immediately rushed over to Jon's motor home and a large emotional scene took place as Jerry, in his usual demanding demeanor, insisted that Jon tell him where Sharon had gone. Jon held his ground, as he had promised Sharon that he would not tell his Dad of her location. However, Jerry being the persuasive person he was, convinced Jon to contact Sharon so he could talk to her. Jerry and Sharon spoke on the phone and Sharon, as she had done a number of times previously, gave in somewhat and agreed to meet with him at Sharon's church. The plan was to meet with their minister for a serious marriage counseling session.

It was at this time that Jerry had his "come to Jesus meeting", promising Sharon the moon. While Sharon was somewhat skeptical of Jerry's promises, she was hoping and praying that Jerry had been "truly reborn".

Over the next week or so, Jerry and Sharon made a road trip to Houston driving a vehicle that had some engine problems. They drove this vehicle to the Reeveston Street mechanic shop that Jerry still owned but was leasing it to yet another mechanic who operated the business, thereby providing Jerry with some source of income. They contacted Mrs. Freddis Hammond, Sharon's mother, who picked them up from the garage and drove them to Hobby Airport in Houston, where they then flew back to Arizona. This was also the first time that Mrs. Hammond had seen her son-in-law in twelve years. At this time Jerry hugged her and was somewhat cordial to her. If this twelve-year assertion was true, this would have meant that Jerry Easley had not been present for his father-in-law's funeral.

While the marriage was not going that great, the conversation one day turned to horses. Jerry was actually the one initiating this idea, probably in an attempt to make up with Sharon for all the previous problems he had caused. Again, in an effort to curry favor with Sharon, Jerry suggested that they could drive over to California to look at some Paso Fina horses, the breed that she was very fond of and loved to work with. Sharon loved horses and at one point in Texas, owned a Paso Fina horse. However, it disappeared under a very strange set of circumstances. It was later learned that Jerry, in a rage of anger, had arranged for someone to pick up the horse. He would later report it as stolen. Sharon never knew the truth about the horse's disappearance.

Jerry had actually offered Sharon's horse for sale to a law enforcement Officer that had vehicle repairs done by Jerry at his shop. This Officer told Jerry that he really had no reason to buy another horse at that time. Jerry then made the statement that if he did not buy the horse, he was going to kill it. The Officer, who at one time rode on the Houston Mounted Patrol, liked to ride horses. He then told Jerry he would take the horse just to keep it from being killed but wanted a bill of sale to prove he had not stolen the horse. Jerry agreed to this arrangement and sold the horse for one dollar. This Officer, who is known, but prefers to remain anonymous, had another Officer friend of his witness that transaction. As far as Sharon knew, she believed that the Paso Fina had been stolen just as Jerry had told her. Whether it be Jon's personal belongings or Sharon's beloved horse, nothing was out-of-bounds for Jerry to vent his anger over.

Since the confession and counseling session with their minister, Jerry had not been totally truthful about changing his domineering ways. Sharon had confided this to several friends at the Ranger Station. But Sharon, being the ever trusting soul that she was, told these friends that she was going to give him a chance even though she really did not want to go to either California to look at horses or to Texas with Jerry. With Jerry's anger growing each day, along with their ever-mounting marital problems, horses were definitely not high on Sharon's agenda.

Sharon and Jerry Leave Arizona for Houston (30)

SHARON AND JERRY Easley left Lake Pleasant, Arizona, on the morning of Monday, February 4, 1985. Lake Pleasant was about thirty miles north of Phoenix. The plan was to drive over into California, to an unknown location, for Sharon to look at some Paso Fina horses. While Sharon very much enjoyed horses, this was not her idea as the ongoing and increasingly worsening marital problems dampened her spirits about horse ownership at this crucial time of her life. Jerry seemed to be using horses to appease her and trying to make up for the past problems he had caused.

They were in the infamous Cruise Air motor home, and were also towing a flat-bed trailer on which was loaded a Dodge truck; the final destination was to be the Reeveston garage in Houston. It was strange that Jerry, who needed to tow the Dodge back to the Reeveston garage for major repairs, would elect to tow the loaded trailer through California looking at horses. In addition, Sharon had told her friends at the Ranger Station that she planned to be back at the lake on Friday, February 8, in order that she could work her regular volunteer shift.

On that same day, Jerry purchased gasoline in Picacho Peak, Arizona, some 60-70 miles east of the Lake Pleasant departing point. This location was right on Interstate 10 and approximately halfway between Phoenix and Tucson. Interstate 10 East would have been the logical route from

Lake Pleasant to any part of Texas and this was the trip that Jerry and Sharon made many times together. The time of day that this purchase was made is not known, but it would appear unlikely that any trip to California was not made as the nearest border crossing into California would have been 150 miles to the west of Lake Pleasant. Picacho Peak was well on the way east towards New Mexico and Texas when Jerry charged the gasoline, 48 gallons, on his Exxon gas card. At that time, Sharon was probably aware that the horse excursion to California had only been a ruse by Jerry to entice her away from Lake Pleasant. She was likely not in a good mood after this realization. It is unknown as to what exactly may have occurred after the gas stop in Picacho Peak.

However, on February 16, 1985, Jon injured his knee while playing intramural sports at Glendale College. He needed medical attention and asked a lady friend of Sharon's at Lake Pleasant to contact his grandmother, Mrs. Hammond, in order to make contact with Sharon and his Dad. Mrs. Hammond indicated that she had not heard from them. Jon also contacted his other grandmother, Mrs. Cora Easley, in Elkhart, Texas. She advised that while she had seen her son, Jerry, she had not seen or spoken with Sharon.

Jon thought that to be rather strange and several days later, on Thursday, February 21, 1985, his Dad appeared at Lake Pleasant in the now-repaired and previously towed Dodge. With Jerry, at this time, was a mechanic from Houston, Marty Vail. They were not in the Cruise Air motor home. Jon asked his Dad about his Mom and Jerry told him that Sharon had gone in the motor home to Georgia with some friends to look at some Paso Finas. Further, that he had given her some money to make a down payment on one should she find one suitable for her taste.

After taking Jon to a doctor about his knee, Jerry and Marty were making plans to return to Houston. Marty, one of the many fly-by-night, loser-type mechanics that Jerry seemed to attract, had come to Arizona with Jerry on his most recent jaunt across the desert from Houston, a distance of some 1,200 miles. Driving straight through with no overnight stays, this was nearly a 22 hour drive. Jerry, who made these trips like he was driving across town, said he planned to take Sharon's horse trailer with him when he left.

Prior to leaving, Jon asked Jerry once again about Sharon's whereabouts. Jerry told him that Sharon would not tell him who was going with her and that Sharon had made the comment to him that it was not any of his business. At this time, Jerry inquired of Jon regarding his financial situation for the rest of the semester. Jon told him that he would probably need about $1,000, which Jerry gave him. Jerry also voluntarily shared with Jon that he had taken in $3,000 from a repair job and had given Sharon $1,500 of it when she left on her trip to Georgia.

Jon thought this "none of his business" comment to be very strange, as it just seemed to him completely out of character for his Mom to make such a statement. Jon, while only being 18 years old, was not a "man of the world", but he felt strongly that something was amiss about this situation. Even being well aware of the many problems that existed in his Dad's marriage to Sharon, he still could not imagine Sharon becoming that calloused towards Jerry.

While Jerry had told Jon and several other people different stories about when he last saw Sharon, he told Jon on this occasion that it was on Aldine Bender Road when Sharon was driving away from a gasoline station that was very near to the Reeveston Road shop.

Jerry and Marty left Arizona on the night of February 21, 1985, leaving a Honda for Jon. They were driving Sharon's Dodge truck, towing her horse trailer.

At that time, neither Jon nor Mrs. Hammond nor Mrs. Cora Easley knew of the whereabouts of Sharon.

On Saturday night, February 23, 1985, at approximately 11:30pm, the Cruise Air motor home was discovered completely engulfed in flames in southern Montgomery County, which is just north of Houston and in the area of Spring, Texas. This location was in a rural area under the jurisdiction of the County of Montgomery as well as the Montgomery County Fire Marshall. Volunteers attempted to squelch the blaze, but the motor home was basically a total loss. Closer examination revealed that appliances such as the generator, air conditioning and heating unit, refrigerator, as well some of the furniture, had been stripped out of it prior to it catching fire.

The Investigative Connection (29)

To backtrack and list the time line of several major dates and events, these can be summarized as follows:

June 15, 1969 - The body of Sherry Ann Dean Easley was discovered in Houston, Texas, brutally murdered in her trailer home. In this lengthy investigation into the Murder of Sherry Easley, there were a number of strange circumstances which had come to the attention of law enforcement authorities. Sherry's ex-husband, Jerry, was definitely investigated as a "person of interest". However, nothing could be proven without a reasonable doubt and the Murder remained unsolved.

February 4, 1985 - Patricia Sharon Hammond Easley left Arizona with Jerry Easley, never to be seen again.

February 23, 1985 - The Cruise Air motor home which Sharon was last seen in was found burned in Montgomery County, Texas. To say the least, the reporting of the circumstances surrounding this vehicle was very strange indeed.

Now, no one in law enforcement can emphatically deny that on a number of occasions, inability to connect all of the dots and make something of a series of events is all too often an occurrence. This unfortunately occurs, especially when there are numerous law enforcement agencies involved and due to a lack of communication, the information each has is not shared with any other agency.

Unfortunately, in 2016, it has proven to have been a major issue with several Federal investigative agencies not sharing information with each other, either by accident or on purpose. This had led to such embarrassing situations where suspects such as the Boston Marathon terrorist bombers were not properly vetted, even though they had appeared on the "radar screens" of several agencies.

However, in 1985, there was a Houston Police Department Homicide Detective assigned to the Special Crimes Division of the Harris County District Attorney's Office. This man, Dan McAnulty, was a veteran Investigator, having worked the streets of Houston as a Police Officer on the night shift in the Third Ward, working out of the Central Police Station. Dan had joined HPD in Academy Class #40, graduating to the streets of Houston in April of 1969. He had proven himself as an out-standing investigator, having been assigned to the Juvenile Division as a Patrolman Investigator. After his promotion to Detective in 1974, his first assignment was to the Homicide Division. After ably working Murder cases for five or six years, he was transferred to the Internal Affairs Division, whose task is investigating the alleged or real wrongdoings of other Police Officers.

This was definitely not a sought-after position and only the best investigators with a clear and proven track record are chosen for this assignment. The Officers chosen for this undesirable assignment are also squeaky-clean (or perceived to be so) in their personal and professional lives. The old adage which definitely applies here is that "no good deed goes unpunished". That attitude holds true today in HPD as well as many other major agencies in the country.

Following that tour of duty, he returned to the Homicide Division. The norm at the time was that you would be rewarded for your Internal Affairs service with usually, within reason, your choice of departmental assignments. Dan chose to return to the Homicide Division once again investigating Murders and also working on the prestigious Officer-Involved-Shooting Team. His investigative talents had become widely recognized not only throughout HPD, but also at the Harris County District Attorney's Office.

There existed at that time an opening for an HPD Detective assign-ment in the Special Crimes Section of the D.A.'s office. Don Stricklin, who was the Special Crimes Chief Prosecutor, contacted Homicide Captain Bobby Adams and asked him if he would be willing to approve Detective McAnulty's transfer to their office. Captain Adams would have preferred not to lose this efficient Investigator, but at the same time, he did not wish to hold someone back for a seemingly better position. Captain Adams approved this move.

Dan McAnulty was well aware of the Sherry Dean Easley Murder case from 1969 as his Homicide training partner was none other than Detective Ed Horelica. Although Paul Nix had retired from the Department in 1973, he frequently returned to visit in Homicide and he and Ed talked a great deal about the Easley case, as both strongly believed they knew WHO-DUN-IT, but just were not able to prove it and make a case to take to trial. Through Ed, Dan became very good friends with Paul. These are the types of cases that really rankle Investigators, as they frequently relive these types of investigations and wonder in the back of their mind, "What did we miss"?

Ed Horelica, specifically, and to a lesser extent Paul Nix, became unofficial mentors of this bright young man, Dan McAnulty. They were mentors to a number of other young Detectives, who respected their knowledge and methods. This author was fortunate to have been one who gained knowledge from both of these fine men. They had a wealth of experience to share and were not ashamed to share their investigations, both successful and unsuccessful. Both did so willingly with Dan.

Dan had read the lengthy case file on Sherry Easley's brutal Murder and was convinced that Ed and Paul had been on the right track in their investigation. He not only read it, but studied every aspect of their case file and knew about the family dynamics of the Dean family. It was through a quirk of fate that he had occasion to meet someone familiar with the Easley family in East Texas. This chance meeting was not in any manner connected to law enforcement. It was one of those weird encounters that happen very infrequently. As a result of this acquaintance, he learned of the Hammond family, whose daughter Sharon had become married to Jerry Easley. It is truly a small world at times and this quirk of fate meeting was truly a God-send to all.

Dan, as many outstanding and successful investigators are prone to do, developed a friendship with Sharon Hammond Easley's family, specifically Mrs. Freddis Hammond and Sharon's two brothers, James and Charles. Mr. A.E. Hammond had passed away in 1977. An Aunt of Sharon's was also a contact that Dan had made, and he nurtured his relationship with her and respected her thoughts and feelings on this niece that she loved very dearly.

Dan's further involvement was initiated after he learned not only of Sharon's disappearance but also of the fact that the Cruise Air motor home had been found burned in Montgomery County. In early February, 1985, Dan's phone began ringing with the news of the latest tragic news involving women known by Jerry Easley. These developments were obviously of extreme interest to Dan and he was anxious to begin exploring further. However, his assignment was such that while still on HPD, he reported directly to the Assistant District Attorney in the Special Crimes Division. Dan was a hard worker and regularly worked more than his 40 hours, some hours for which he was compensated for, but much of it just donated to whatever cause or case they were dealing with at the time. Dan was definitely a "company man". Some would even say that Dan was "married to his job". Unfortunately, later in his career, his family life suffered and he became divorced.

To Dan, the Easley capers were "Special Crimes", and he was able to convince his supervisors at both HPD and the D.A.'s office that this situation deserved much further investigation. One of the capers was a Houston-Harris County Murder and this must have been enough for his superiors to agree to his request. Thus, while not having complete free rein, he re-opened the Sherry Dean Easley Murder case and began investigating the disappearance of Sharon Hammond Easley. This was approved by his superiors with the strict understanding that his normal caseload would not suffer. Dan was well aware of his obligations and jumped in with both feet. He was determined that if "Lady Justice" needed assistance in getting to the truth of these matters, he would do his utmost to succeed in that endeavor.

While making inquiries into the disappearance of Sharon, Dan was able to make even more contacts with a number of other area law enforcement agencies. He had contacted HPD Homicide Lieutenant Nelson Zoch, who at the time was the evening shift supervisor in Homicide. Dan and Nelson had known each other since 1969 when Dan arrived on the night shift central patrol where Nelson had been assigned for the last year. Nelson, just barely a rookie himself, had graduated from Class #37. They had ridden a few times together on the night shift and both later promoted to Detective and were assigned to the Homicide Division.

Back at that time in 1969, Dan was a baby-faced, tall and thin rookie just off his probationary period after he had completed Academy Class #40. Nelson and his cohorts commented on numerous occasions how much Dan reminded them of the rookie cop Malloy, on the then popular television police show Adam 12.

Nelson, at Dan's request, assigned Detective John Burmester to lend assistance to Dan on the Easley investigation. McAnulty had informed both Zoch and Burmester that he was subpoenaing Jerry Easley's credit card records to determine if and where he had purchased gasoline along the route. Burmester began making phone calls to law enforcement agencies along Interstate 10 between Arizona and Texas. It was through Detective Burmester's efforts that he learned of human body parts which had been discovered off of I-10 in Arizona. All sorts of bells were going off in the mind of this veteran Investigator. Prior to learning of these discoveries, the worst case scenario in his head was that the remains of Sharon would be found in the motor home, or actually even worse yet, that she had been inside and destroyed beyond detection. At least there now existed some hope that some identifiable evidence had been located.

It was through this chain of events and contacts that brought HPD Detective Dan McAnulty into this very complicated investigation. And, it would only become more involved as Dan dug even deeper into the mystery.

What is Arson? (31)

Arson is described as:
The malicious burning or exploding of the dwelling house of another, or the burning of a building within the cartilage, the immediate surrounding space, of the dwelling of another. This definition, by statute extends to vehicles with the specific intent to defraud or prejudice the property insurer. Further, a death resulting from the act of Arson is Murder.

The Penal Code of the State of Texas described in Title 7, Section 28.02, which was the applicable law in 1985, listed Arson as such:

(a) A person commits an offense if he starts a fire or causes an explosion with intent to destroy or damage any building, habitation, or vehicle.
   (1) knowing that it is within the limits of an incorporated city or town;
   (2) knowing that it is insured against damage or destruction;
   (3) knowing that it is subject to a mortgage or other security interest;
   (4) knowing that it is located on property belonging to another;
   (5) knowing that it was located on property belonging to another; or
   (6) when he is reckless about whether the burning or explosion will endanger the life of some other individual or the safety of the property of another.

(b) It is a defense to prosecution under Subsection (a) (1) of this section that prior to starting the fire or explosion, the suspect obtained a permit or other written authorization granted in accordance with a city ordinance, if any, regulating fires and explosion.

(c) An offense under this section is a Felony of the Second Degree, unless bodily injury or death is suffered by any person by reason of the commission of the offense, in which event it is a Felony of the First Degree.

The reasons for anyone to commit the act of Arson are many and varied. There is the pyromaniac who derives pleasure from seeing things go up into flames. Many such arsonists are actually arrested due to the weird mania of theirs in returning to or remaining near the scene of the fire and watching the excitement surrounding the blaze. In the instance of the burnt-out motor home in Montgomery County, such was not the case.

The act of Arson is a serious crime as noted above and there are occasions in which the act of Arson is used to cover up previously committed criminal acts. Arson is on many occasions used to destroy physical evidence, such as human remains. The odds of determining the cause of death of a Murder victim are much less if a corpse has been reduced to ashes, with nothing remaining but bone fragments. Arson can also be used to destroy fingerprints. Although modern technology has advanced tremendously in this area of investigation, again the odds of recovering valuable evidence of any sort are greatly diminished if a blaze has completely or partially destroyed such items.

In the matter of the Georgy Boy motor home being found completely engulfed in flames in a rural area, the immediate suspicion would be that this is very likely a case of Arson. The probability of someone camping or residing in this motor home in such an isolated, desolate location and an accidental fire starting would indeed be very remote.

Other common reasons for an act of Arson being committed is for insurance purposes. Individuals sometime find themselves in a financial bind, whether it be on payments on a mortgage or on a loan on a vehicle.

If the asset is destroyed by fire, the individual has a possibility of escaping from the responsibility for payment of said loan. Of course, if an individual purposely destroys a mortgaged asset and it is proven that it was such, that person not only remains liable for the mortgage/loan, but then would find themselves more deeply involved, having becoming culpable in a serious criminal offense.

Arson in Montgomery County, Texas (32)

THEN, AS THEY say, the plot thickened. On Saturday night, February 23, 1985, in the rural area of South Montgomery County, an emergency call was made regarding a large vehicle on fire on a deserted dead- end road. Fire Department resources responded to this call and found what appeared to be a motor home completely engulfed in flames. This being a rural area, no water source was available to combat the flames other than the water carried on the pumper trucks. The water supply likely would not have mattered anyway as the vehicle was totally aflame and out of control when the first pumper truck arrived.

A vehicle such as this is usually constructed of a light wooden frame-work surrounded by thin sheet metal or aluminum siding. The loss appeared to be a total one, and the only action available to this volunteer force was that of containing the blaze away from the surrounding wooded areas and the sparsely developed homes in the immediate neighborhood.

South Montgomery County Volunteer Fire Department, after responding and doing their best to douse the completely engulfed vehicle, followed up the next day by taking photographs of the loss and also mak-ing preparations in removing the remains from the scene. This area, off of Rayford Road and Riley Fussell Road, was just across I-45 Freeway and east of the burgeoning development in South Montgomery County now known as The Woodlands, a high-dollar multi-use area of quality homes and apartments, as well as commercial businesses and offices.

By State law, the Volunteer Fire Department was required to submit a report to the State of Texas regarding any such fire of this nature. This was obviously a necessary law that needed to be adhered to, as in such a case as this where there was total destruction. There always loomed the possibility of human remains or other such important criminal evidence being in the scarred shell. Also, local volunteer departments rarely, if ever, have an expert at their disposal that might investigate the fire and determine the origin and the ignition of the blaze. This report to the State of Texas allowed the Montgomery County Fire Marshall to enter the investigation and to make a full, professional inquiry into the cause of the fire. This report was filed in the next several days as required by statute. Also, reports were made available to any inquiries from insured parties of the ownership of this vehicle.

Tracing the Motor
Home's History (33)

T HE MONTGOMERY COUNTY Fire Marshal, Mr. Ed Robinson, took control of this investigation. It was determined that the registered owner
of the Cruise Air motor home was Mrs. Cora Easley, of Elkhart, Texas,
Jerry Easley's Mother. When contacted by investigators, she referred
them to her son Jerry Easley as the actual owner who had control of the
motor home. It was never determined why Jerry had the title registered in
his Mom's name, but so it was. And, strangely enough, he did it without
her knowledge. He had secretly involved his Mom in such a manner.

Mr. Robinson determined that the motor home was insured, but the
circumstances surrounding the coverage seemed suspicious, to say the
least. The previous policy covering the motor home had been lapsed for
some time, actually expiring on September 28, 1984. This would have
been in violation of the loan agreement with the financial institution that
held a lien on the motor home. But again, so it was.

After the policy had been lapsed for over four months, on February 8,
1985, Jerry Easley arrived at the insurance office in Houston to renew the
policy. He renewed the insurance in the coverage amount of $10,000 and
provided an initial payment of $213.00. After the proper paperwork was
prepared and the check for the premium cleared the bank, the insurance
went into effect ten days later on February 18, 1985. There was a waiting
period required here and this company policy was strictly adhered to in
order to satisfy the company's underwriting guidelines.

In tracing the ownership of the burnt motor home, it was ascertained that this vehicle had a very interesting and confusing history. The first record of this unit indicated that it had been sold from a recreational vehicle dealer in southeast Houston. This business was involved in sales and service of this type of unit in addition to also leasing such units. A Mr. Ray Flagstaff was listed as the owner/operator of this business and was involved in selling and trading all types of recreational vehicles. Unfortunately, he was not a very successful businessman and was constantly in arrears on his financial obligations. These issues forced him to eventually file for bankruptcy.

This particular motor home was originally financed by a Mr. Thompson, who was the owner of yet another motor home sales lot. After Mr. Thompson made the required payments for nearly a year, he struck a deal with a business associate of his, Mr. Ray Flagstaff, whereby he would assume the indebtedness with Reagan State Bank in the Heights section of northwest Houston. Reagan Bank approved Mr. Flagstaff and as would be the norm, Reagan Bank held the original title as the vehicle was considered to be collateral on the $12,000-plus loan. Mr. Flagstaff made payments on the note for a very short time and then, probably due to his ongoing financial difficulties, sought to cut his losses.

To do so, Flagstaff leased the unit to Mr. Cliff Bartley, who was later learned to be a step-son of Elmer Price, the financially beleaguered electrician who had experienced ongoing business difficulties with Jerry Easley. Flagstaff was not legally able to convey title to the vehicle since he still owed money to the bank. This agreement was not made known to Reagan Bank and likely would not have been approved had they been made aware of this arrangement. These were a strange set of circumstances surrounding this vehicle, but as it came to be fully known later, these were the type of individuals that Jerry Easley thrived on conducting business with. The term "birds of a feather flock together" was one such thought that later came to one's mind.

Shortly after Bartley recommended to his step-dad that he use Easley for his mechanic work, Bartley himself learned more about Easley's business practices. After Bartley took possession, he became aware of some mechanical problems with this motor home and had discussed the repairs with Easley. They had not agreed to anything and one day Bartley came home and the motor home was gone. He was told by his family that Easley came and got the motor home. It was learned later that Easley had really admired this motor home and he took it to his shop and began extensive repairs, basically tying up the motor home where it could not be moved.

The lengthy itemized repair bill became much larger than Bartley had paid for the motor home, which resulted in a major dispute between the two. This was very likely planned out by Jerry Easley. This caught Mr. Bartley completely by surprise as no agreement had ever been reached nor had he authorized Easley to tow the motor home to his shop, much less to perform the work that had been casually discussed. Mr. Bartley was not only surprised at this course of events, he was also unable to pay the repair bill. Obviously, Elmer Price had not adequately warned Bartley about the unscrupulous dealings he had experienced with Easley.

Easley won out and wound up with the motor home. Whether it be a woman or a motor home, Jerry Easley seemed to be of the mind-set that if he wanted it, he would just take it, permission or not.

As was his normal "modus operandi", once again Easley filed a mechanic's lien on the motor home, not aware that the vehicle was collateral on a bank loan. Of course, Easley had in his corner Mr. Albie Waltmon, the handyman vehicle title expert. It was later determined that Easley, when he began the mechanic's lien process, replaced the vehicle identification number (VIN) located on the body of the vehicle with another number plate. He also changed the license plate. These actions were totally against the law in Texas. When this matter was thoroughly investigated at a later time, it was learned that the State of Texas Motor Vehicle records had two title histories on file regarding this vehicle.

Mr. Bartley's involvement with the ownership/custody of the motor home was very hazy, to say the least. He had taken custody of the unit but did not have access to the title. Although he knew Easley was wrong in what he had done, in actuality, there was not a thing that he could legally protest about the situation. It was sort of like one thief stealing stolen property from another thief. Therefore, the history of this motor home's ownership continued in a very unorthodox fashion, with Reagan Bank seemingly being the loser in this transaction. However, Mr. Ray Flagstaff was eventually left holding the bag, so to speak, as he was debtor of record with Reagan Bank and legally responsible for the loan, which had now grown to over $13,000 from the unpaid interest on the loan. Reagan bank, being experienced in such matters, eventually recovered most of their losses from Mr. Flagstaff, who in a roundabout way, suffered financially and Easley gained. Of course, from the other side of the coin, Flagstaff possessed a bit of larceny in his heart when he made the deal with Bartley without Reagan Bank having knowledge of it.

And, of course now the motor home was completely destroyed by arson in Montgomery County. It had apparently served some sort of purpose for Mr. Jerry Easley, whatever that might have been.

A Missing Person Report
is Filed (34)

O F COURSE, WHILE it was obviously not known at the time the policy was being renewed, Jerry and Sharon Easley had departed Lake Pleasant in Arizona on February 4, 1985. Also unknown at this time was that Sharon had not been seen by any credible source since that date. Then, on February 23, 1985, the motor home was discovered burning in Montgomery County, Texas. As Fire Marshall Robinson continued this inquiry, more questions were arising than answers were forthcoming.

In Houston, Texas, it was now mid-February, 1985. Jon Easley had spoken to his Dad after his return from Arizona, the trip of which Sharon was to be riding with him in the Cruise Air motor home. Of course, as usual, Mrs. Hammond was out of the loop as to any communications. Jerry had made a token effort to mend the terrible relationship he had cultivated with the Hammond family over the years, but Jerry soon apparently forgot his tearful promises to mend his ways. Mrs. Hammond and Jon had been in regular communication with Sharon prior to this and both were equally concerned about Sharon's well-being.

Shortly after this chain of events, Jerry had made another of his seemingly always hurried cross-country trips from Houston to and from Lake Pleasant. Jon had been asking questions of his Dad about Sharon and had recently returned from Arizona to Texas. Just prior to this, with no information forthcoming from her daughter, Mrs. Freddis Hammond and Mr.

Charles Hammond, Sharon's brother, drove to the Montgomery County Sheriff's Department to report Sharon as a Missing Person. An official report was filed on March 5, 1985. They had decided to report her as missing in that jurisdiction due to the motor home having been discovered there.

After returning to Texas with his Dad, Jon was communicating daily with the Hammond family about Sharon. Detective McAnulty also set out to interview Jon in detail about the marital problems of Jerry and Sharon that he had witnessed in Arizona. Dan undertook the task of an extensive debriefing of Jon. With his deliberate and calm questioning of Jon, Dan learned much more from Jon and also verified some of his previous suspicions. Jon resolved to cooperate with the Detective in any manner necessary.

Dan knew at this point receiving the full cooperation of Jon was to be a touchy situation. How much could he expect Jon to assist in the investigation against his own Dad? While Jon had many suspicions about his Dad's dealing with other people, either at the Reeveston garage or in Goodrich at the school district, this was still his Dad. His Mom had been murdered, his step-mom Sharon was missing, but this was still his Dad. Jon agreed to fully cooperate but it would have been strange if he did not harbor some misgivings also.

Jon's knowledge of his Dad's crooked dealings with customers, employees, and business partners at the Reeveston garage was laid open to Dan. Dan requested that Jon begin recording all of his phone conversation with his Dad from this point forward. Dan formed a number of questions to be posed by Jon to his Dad in regards to Sharon's whereabouts. Jon was more than willing to cooperate in the investigation.

On March 12, Jon went to the Montgomery County Sheriff's Department to report what knowledge he had of his missing Mother. There, he spoke to Detective Carolyn Frost of that agency. Detective Frost immediately made contact with Jerry Easley, who at this time had not reported any information on his missing wife. When Detective Frost contacted Jerry, he was at a law library in Houston with his attorney. It was unknown as to what Jerry was researching at the library but he advised Detective Frost that he would be in later that week to speak with her on Friday, March 15.

On that Friday, Jerry Easley and his attorney and close friend, Mr. Jack Terry, arrived in Conroe, Texas. Jerry seemed totally unconcerned about his wife and told Detective Frost that he had been with Sharon up until February 15, 1985, a totally different story than those versions he had related to his son Jon. Easley further stated that his wife was driving the motor home the last time he saw it or her. In Detective Frost's opinion, Easley was primarily concerned about the paperwork that the insurance company required for a claim to be filed. He also appeared to Detective Frost to be in very much of a rush. Any questions the authorities had regarding Sharon's whereabouts were shrugged off and in several instances, not answered at all.

Jon, who over the years had become not only increasingly suspicious of his Dad, but more specifically, he had become very much aware of his Dad's untruthfulness. Jon had learned to pick up on the things that his Dad told him, many of which did not ring true to Jon. Also, Jon had experienced more than his share of difficulties with his Dad and had somewhat resigned himself to accept his Dad's ways.

However, this time, Jon was more concerned than ever. There was something about his Dad's comments regarding Sharon's whereabouts that he found very suspicious. There was actually much more than suspicion, especially after what he had witnessed out in Arizona, specifically the violent outbursts that he observed his Dad display towards Sharon. Additionally, Jerry's stories about when he last saw Sharon had changed somewhat, another thing that deeply concerned Jon.

Probably the most lingering concern or suspicion that Jon had was this: Sharon was very close to him and her Mother, Mrs. Hammond, and as far as Jon was concerned, Sharon would not have gone off to Georgia to look at horses WITHOUT speaking to either him or Mrs. Hammond. Jon felt without a doubt that Sharon would have contacted at least one of them and told them of her plans. To Jon, this was just not like the Mom he had known. She had told Jon that if Jerry wasn't doing what he said when they left Arizona, she would get away and fly back to Phoenix and call him.

In the period of several weeks following their departure from Arizona in the 1977 Cruise Air motor home, the present whereabouts of Sharon was a total mystery to Jon Easley as well as to the extended Hammond family - Mrs. Freddis Hammond and Sharon's two brothers, Charles and James.

Gruesome Discoveries in the Arizona Desert (35)

WHATEVER PROBLEMS SHARON and Jerry were having, things seemed to have come unraveled very quickly on this trip to California, or Houston, or wherever. Sharon seemingly would have been in either an agitated or frightened mode, or both, at this time when she realized California and horses were not the trip's destination.

It was later learned, much later actually, that on February 6, 1985, a citizen reported the finding of four four-inch pieces of blood-soaked foam rubber mattress pieces on the side of Old Highway 90. This location, which was approximately 100 miles east from the gasoline purchase, was now in Cochise County, Arizona, a very sparsely populated area of the Arizona desert. These items were recovered and taken into evidentiary custody by the Cochise County Sheriff's Department, the law enforcement agency responsible for this vast area of unincorporated desert. This discovery was documented to be just one-tenth of a mile south of Interstate 10, which would have been the normal route for anyone to take from Arizona with a Texas destination.

Then, just three months later, on May 5, 1985, two human femurs were discovered in the desert on the side of Old Highway 90, a mere five miles from where the mattresses items were recovered. These femurs, described as from the knees to the hip joint, were found inside a large black plastic garbage sack. Again, these valuable evidentiary items were recovered by the Cochise County, Arizona Sheriff's Department. While such discoveries such as these in the desert were not uncommon, both discoveries in the same vicinity raised investigative eyebrows within the department.

More suspicion on the part of authorities rose when on May 23, 1985, another gory discovery was made, this time on Highway 82, some 15-20 miles from the location of the femurs. Wrapped in clear plastic and then placed in several garbage bags was a female torso. This appeared to have been carried in a brown hooded house robe, "Harcourt" label. Prior to this torso being professionally examined by a duly-licensed and trained Medical Examiner, it was originally thought to be that of a White female from the age range of 28-34. At the time, Sharon was 42 years of age, but the investigative agency had no knowledge of Sharon Hammond Easley at the time.

The desert area of Arizona, not just in Cochise County, has been known for many years as a "dumping ground" for evidence of human remains and other items someone would not have any further use for. Items taken further off of the highway would stand a very good chance of not being discovered for even longer periods of time. However, these three discoveries were all found basically in the ditch or just past the ditch where a curiosity seeker with time on their hands could easily see the garbage bags and take notice. The dumped items being so close to the road would appear to have been done by someone alone and in a rush to not be seen, even though this road was very lightly traveled. Of course, even back then, this was mere speculation on the part of the Investigators.

In June, 1985, a woman's skull was discovered 25 miles north of Tucson. The area of the first three findings was in a closely related area approximately 50 miles southeast of Tucson. The skull was in Pima County and while the first three discoveries were thought strongly to be related, the skull was not felt to be connected as such findings were all too common in both areas.

The femurs and torso were examined by Guery Flores, M.D., Medical Examiner of Cochise County, Arizona, headquartered in Bisbee, Arizona, the county seat. Cochise County Sheriff's Department Investigator Eugene M. Kellogg, located in the small city of Sierra Vista, Arizona, was assigned as the lead Investigator for that agency.

After examination of the femurs discovered on May 5, Dr. Flores ruled that due to the lack of the rest of the body, the CAUSE of death could not be determined but he also ruled that the MANNER of death was Homicide. This autopsy was conducted on May 6. In elaborating further on his findings, Dr. Flores stated:

> "the right thigh shows the posterior femur almost completely skel-etonized and the anterior is covered by decomposed soft tissue and skin. The right femur shows at the level of the head of the femur multiple oblique cut incisions. No fractures were observed. The left thigh shows at the level of the femoral head incision of the fovea and the cartilage is superficially sectioned. The right and left kneecaps are present and almost completely skeletonized".

It was Dr. Flores' opinion that the femurs were that of a White person, probably female, with an estimated stature of 5 feet, four and one-eighth inches, plus or minus an inch. With the discovery of the torso on May 23, 1985, Dr. Flores had more evidence to work with than previously. He conducted this autopsy on May 24, 1985. His examinations were of the follow evidence:

> "1. A torso with decapitation at the level of the base of the neck and
> 2. Upper extremities with dismemberment of the right and left wrist and right and left hip."

It became very obvious to the Doctor and the Investigators that whoever was responsible for this dismemberment, did not wish to have any identification of the remains aided by fingerprints. Dr. Flores' findings from this post mortem were:

"This body was markedly decomposed and had been dismembered at the level of the hips and at the base of the neck. The neck was sectioned at the level of the base leaving an irregular wound. The chest was symmetrical and the breasts showed no alteration. The abdomen showed no scars. The upper extremities are sectioned at the level of the wrists."

In other words, there were no finger or hand prints to examine as well as no feet. Also, at this time, no skull to possibly conduct any type of dental examination.

The thoracic cavity was intact and the abdominal cavity showed the organs to be intact. The organs included the heart, lungs, intestines, kidneys, and uterus. Dr. Flores, probably working under the strong possibility that the torso and femurs were of the same person, felt that the torso was of an individual female of the same size he previously ruled, five feet, four and one-eighth inches tall. Of course, he had no knowledge of the existence of Sharon Hammond Easley at the time. However, she was known to be of that size.

Easley is Indicted in
Cherokee County (36)

WHILE THE ARSON investigation in Montgomery County was continuing, Detective McAnulty was actively pursuing the investigation in the Jacksonville Bible College incident of December, 1983. He had contacted not only Donny Harold, but also the witnesses to all or portions of that offense. The Jacksonville city authorities were contacted and now were assisting also as the Statute of Limitations on this offense were of concern to Dan. More importantly, the Cherokee County District Attorney's Office became actively involved and a conclusion was reached on this serious offense of several years ago. As a result, Jerry Easley was indicted in late 1985 for the felony crime of Conspiracy to Commit Capital Murder.

Jon Easley's cooperation was instrumental in assisting this investigation as it progressed through the justice system. The debriefing of Jon by McAnulty had painted a picture to the Investigator and the Cherokee County District Attorney of pathological and dangerous criminal behavior in which he was believed to have not only committed the offense in 1983, but also to have murdered two wives. His danger to anyone who crosses him was obvious to all.

One can only wonder what was crossing Jon's mind as he cooperated with McAnulty against his Dad. This had to have been a trying time for him. However, he easily recalled not only the personal treatment from his Dad, physically and mentally, but also the manner in which his Dad had constantly treated those whom were attempting to transact business with him. And then, December 1, 1983 happened.

Jon not only assisted McAnulty with the background information he possessed, but also with accompanying Dan to the East Texas town of Elkhart. They spent countless hours together as Dan, with Jon's assistance, was able to piece together other "pieces of the pie" that this investigation was placing together for the prosecution.

Detective McAnulty recalled those earlier discussions he had with Detectives Nix and Horelica. McAnulty was surprised at the time, but after investigating Easley over a number of years, he came to understand the comment that Paul Nix had made on more than one occasion, that Easley was such a dangerous man that if he saw him anywhere around his house or neighborhood, he would "just have to kill him"!

The Arrest of Jerry Easley (37)

BEING ASSIGNED TO the Harris County D.A.'s Special Crimes, Detective McAnulty had worked closely with prosecutors who were considered by law enforcement Officers as the elite. These prosecutors had worked their way up from Misdemeanor Courts to Felony Courts, where they proved themselves to be effective courtroom warriors. A next step for the exceptional was the Special Crimes Division. Dan had the ear of these prosecutors and had been working on the Easley case with the prosecutors in Cherokee County, who had agreed there was sufficient probable cause to warrant taking the evidence to a Grand Jury in that jurisdiction.

One such prosecutor in Special Crimes was John Cossum. McAnulty and Cossum had conferred with Cherokee County prosecutors and a plan was devised to not only facilitate the arrest, but to do so in such a manner to not only obtain additional evidence legally but also to spring a surprise on Easley. This plan was to subpoena Easley to a Harris County Grand Jury under the guise of investigating Albie Waltmon for his shady and possibly illegal transferring of vehicle titles. It was well established that Easley had used Waltmon's Texas Title Company for the transferring of titles on vehicles that Easley had filed mechanics liens on after the unsuspecting owners were confronted with inflated repair bills on vehicles brought in for repair at the Reeveston garage.

An unsuspecting Easley testified about his experience with Waltmon stating that he was supportive of Waltmon and respected his title work. A.D.A. Cossum focused on how many vehicles Easley had obtained through dealing with Waltmon. Cossum then focused on the Cruise Air motor home, asking Easley where that vehicle was located at that time. This carefully designed question led to further inquiries of Easley as to the whereabouts of Sharon Easley at that time.

This question just totally blindsided Easley, leaving him visibly shaken. After leaving the ninth floor Grand Jury room at 201 Fannin, Easley was exiting the building. McAnulty had arranged for Texas Ranger Joe Haralson to assist in arresting Easley in an effort to "re-create" Easley's 1969 arrest by the Rangers on the criminal charge of the Murder of Sherry Dean Easley. The arrest was carefully designed as a legal opportunity to search Easley's briefcase and vehicle pursuant to his lawful arrest.

Ranger Haralson and McAnulty then took Easley to the HPD Homicide Division and obtained an investigative "Hold" on him and booked him into the same City Jail in which he had been locked up in 1969 for the Murder of Sherry Easley. McAnulty had designed this to create a "déjà vu" moment for Easley in the hope that he might make incriminating statements regarding the Cherokee County case and more importantly, the whereabouts of Sharon Easley.

Although clearly rattled, Easley was experienced enough by that time to invoke his Fifth Amendment privilege to remain silent and avoid making any incriminating statements.

Easley's Pre-Trial Legal Moves (38)

FOLLOWING HIS INDICTMENT and subsequent arrest, Easley began his legal pursuit of those he felt were responsible for his troubles. On November 13, 1985, he filed his original pro se_complaint in the U.S. District Court for the Eastern District of Texas, alleging violations of his constitutional rights and seeking monetary and injunctive relief. This action was officially filed under Civil Action #TY-85-447-CA. Dan A. McAnulty was listed as the only Defendant. At this point, Easley had only been indicted and the name of Mr. Charles Holcomb was unknown to him at this time. It appears that Easley's plan of action was to immediately go on the offensive, thereby thinking he was going to be able to somewhat control his destiny. This strategy was not unlike those he had previously used, when he was quick to file a lawsuit or take illegal actions against any-one he felt had wronged him. He was likely thinking that a good offense would be of assistance in his defense?

In the original filing of this motion, Easley stated that he had been subject to police harassment by McAnulty committing the following acts in violation of his civil rights: Grand Jury tampering and abuse, illegal searches and seizures of property, taking of photographs, illegal telephone wire-tapping, making threats against his person, libel, slander, and alien-ation of affection of family and friends. All of these acts by McAnulty had resulted in the Plaintiff suffering great mental and emotional anguish which prevented him from properly benefiting from his status as a citizen of the United States. According to this filing, this Detective McAnulty had been very active in making the Plaintiff's life miserable with an uncertain future.

Easley was requesting of the Court a restraining order against any future such abuse, that any and all seized property be returned to him, as well as actual and punitive damages from McAnulty and any such future defendants.

In his first amended petition in February, 1986, Easley added allegations that McAnulty had conspired with District Attorney Charles Holcomb to "deliberately mislead the Grand Jury, suppress evidence favorable to him, using shoddy evidence before the Grand Jury, and using undue influence in coercing the Grand Jury vote". Mr. Holcomb officially entered the proceedings as a Defendant along with McAnulty. Easley further added that Holcomb and McAnulty had drafted a contradictory indictment which on its face "reeks of malice and malicious intent, vindictive prosecution, abuse of discretion in charges, and demagogic prosecution".

The Plaintiff was most definitely going on the offensive prior to proceeding to a trial date. At this point, he did not have an Attorney of Record. Even prior to conviction, Easley must have felt uneasy about his future as he began to file Motions for Discovery prior to trial. The legal maneuvers he filed in late 1985 and early 1986 were not successful. All were denied and in May, 1986, he went to trial.

From the date of his indictment forward, Easley had become extremely concerned that this indictment could actually come to trial. He had eluded the authorities on some criminal matters as well as a number of civil cases brought against him. He had always been successful but this time, he was very worried about this young Detective McAnulty who was seemingly prying into every aspect of his life. Working with his attorney as a defense was being built, Easley went the extra mile in an attempt to learn more about what Jon's testimony might be.

Easley and his attorney had carefully constructed what was meant to be a trap for Jon. Jon was contacted by a relative, who was obviously being coached in the questions and discussions he initiated about the Jacksonville case. Jon was ridiculed about the pending case by being told that the case was hinging on the testimony of a previously convicted felony offender (Franky) and a pathological liar (Donny). It was even brought up that if

Jon's Dad bought him a new car that maybe all of this could just go away. Actually not, in that Jon was not the complaining party in this attempted kidnapping but was a witness. The prosecution could have gone forward without Jon's testimony even though it would have been a much more difficult case to prove. It was becoming apparent to Dan, Jon, and the Cherokee County D.A.'s Office that the defense felt they were in a more precarious position than previously thought.

The Cherokee County Trial (39)

In what has been described as a bizarre case of a "hit man" being hired to kill a previously solicited "hit man", Jerry Easley, the former Goodrich ISD School Superintendent, went on trial in Rusk, Texas, the County Seat of Cherokee County, Texas. Easley had been indicted on five counts last October, including charges of Aggravated Kidnapping and Conspiracy to Commit Capital Murder.

Rusk is a very small community in comparison to Jacksonville, Texas where the offense occurred. The trial was scheduled to begin on Tuesday, April 29, 1986 at 9:00am. Norman Donny Harold was represented at this trial by the State of Texas and Mr. Charles Holcomb was the prosecutor. He was assisted by his Investigator, Mr. Jerry C. Jones. A jury had been selected the previous week on April 25.

Jerry Easley was on trial for Conspiracy to Commit Capital Murder, to wit planning the kidnapping and Murder of Donny Harold back on December 1, 1983. Easley was accused of hiring and transporting 16-year old Franky Routt to disable Donny and bring him to Easley's waiting vehicle.

Jerry Easley was represented by Attorneys Larue Dixon as well as local Jacksonville attorney, Dave Sorrell. A local private Investigator, Mr. Tim Taylor, was hired by Easley's attorneys to assist them in any matters they might need to be further investigated or clarified during the trial. In a matter going forth to trial, both sides, the prosecution and the defense, will have questions which need further clarification. These questions usually arise as testimony is given. When a person's liberty is at stake, no stone should be left unturned.

The first witness was Houston Police Department Detective Dan A. McAnulty. Even though McAnulty had extensive knowledge of other crimes and potential law violations committed by Jerry Easley, he could only testify in the Guilt or Innocence phase of the trial as to the elements of the crime Easley was on trial for. As is common in many criminal prosecutions, in order to prove a crime has been committed, it is on occasion necessary to involve a principal of the crime to testify for the prosecution. This, in law enforcement terms, is referred to as convincing the principal to "rollover" on the primary threat of the offense. In this case, Jerry Easley was the individual who wanted to have this crime committed.

Franky Emery Routt was one such individual that Jerry Easley was known to have frequently surrounded himself with. While Franky was not believed to be totally stupid, he was extremely naïve about life in general. Being only 16 years old at the time this offense was concocted, the prosecution's lengthy and thorough investigation deemed him to be someone, even though he had willfully participated in Easley's plan, who was potentially able to become a good citizen of our society. Thus, an offer had been made to young Franky Routt that if he testified at the trial of Easley as to what Easley desired to accomplish that December night in Jacksonville, he would be granted leniency or the possibility of avoiding prosecution completely.

A juvenile in the State of Texas could be tried as an adult at the age of 16 depending on various circumstances as well as the severity of the offense. This likely was not a difficult decision for Routt and his defense attorneys to make and to convince him to take. Any defense attorney worth his salt would have jumped at this opportunity for Routt to extricate himself from the responsibility of being in any manner involved with Jerry Easley. Franky Routt and his attorney took advantage of this chance and agreed that he would testify for the State of Texas against Jerry Easley. After the testimony of Detective McAnulty setting up the crime scene and the entire scenario surrounding the plan of Easley, Franky Routt took the witness stand and testified as to what had occurred at the Bible College that night.

The testimony of Franky Routt greatly interested the jury as he told of being recruited, at the young age of 16, to participate in this potentially deadly offense. It is certain, that on cross-examination, the defense attempted to rip this young man's story to shreds but he held his ground on his testimony of the events of that night.

If the jury was very much spellbound by Franky Routt's testimony, when Norman Donny Harold took the stand, they were equally as amazed by the victim's account. The third occupant of that dorm apartment, Jonathan Fitzgerald, now living in Dallas, was called to the stand. Jonathan was a Bible studies student at the time of the offense and was now a Youth Minister. He testified as to what he was aware of that happened that night.

Jonathan, being a Christian as he was, was adamant in his account of that nearly tragic night. His story was very weakly challenged by the defense, but they were apparently well aware of their limits to have this witness perjure himself. The four prosecution witnesses, McAnulty, Routt, Harold, and Fitzgerald, filled up a complete day of testimony. Court was then adjourned for the night.

The prosecution continued the following morning with their case against Easley. It was very likely an unsettling night of rest for Jerry Easley, even though he was out on Bond and living with a new girlfriend who was a former TDCJ prison guard he had met. He had to feel that his weird world was becoming totally unraveled. If he thought that, the previous day's testimony was nothing compared to what he would hear on Wednesday, April 30, 1986.

The first witness of the day was none other than Jerry Easley's old nemesis, Elmer Price. The prosecution seemed to take a chance by subpoenaing this man, who was nearly as unscrupulous as Jerry himself. Price, just like Easley, always operated on the edge when dealing with his customers. It was said at one time that Easley had met his match when he attempted to con Price out of his business vehicles after Easley had performed mechanical work and then presented Price with totally concocted and outrageous repair bills. However, Price, being the consummate con-man himself, was able to stand up to the personal attacks the defense presented him with.

The next witness after Price was one that must have totally destroyed Jerry Easley's hope to extricate himself from this crime. Not only that, but the total embarrassment in front of his family and friends was the testimony that his son gave against his Dad. Surely, Easley and his attorney must have anticipated his own natural son testifying for the State of Texas. However, it was the extent of the damaging testimony that the jury not only heard, but considered and believed. The jury must have observed the pain in Jon Easley's words as he testified against his Dad. The jury had to have considered what it must have taken for Jon to sit on the stand and speak out against his Dad. Then again, they also had to have seen that Jon's painful testimony against his Dad completely corroborated the testimony of Franky Routt and Donny Harold.

Richard Gott, who was the Dean of Students at the Bible College, was subpoenaed to testify, but did not as Jon Easley completely covered the events of that night. Gott, who was more than willing to just allow this crime to have happened without any prosecution, did his utmost to do so all for the good of the school. Of course, he was an old friend of Jerry Easley which may possibly have been part of his motive also in keeping this quiet. However. at this stage of their lives, Gott had apparently realized that his career still held much potential and that he would benefit himself by dropping this college friend from any future relationships. Also, the school's reputation was at risk here if the truth came out, that being that he was willing to not report this offense at all. He was saved as he did not have to testify.

The prosecution rested after the second day and the defense then had their turn. Their main defensive strategy seemed to be to attack the credibility of the State's witnesses. These witnesses were Dwight and Louise Moore, Curtis Carroll, Teresa Dawson, Leasa Ray, Paul Marchand, and Paul Priddy, all of whom were friends of Jerry Easley. Also testifying were a U.S. Coast Guard Officer as well as a handwriting expert.

While the testimony of Dwight Moore was not reviewed for this research, he was noted on several occasions, when commenting on Jerry Easley, as saying that he "had no use whatsoever" for him. Moore also said that Easley was the most vindictive person he had ever known and that he liked to sue people and hold grudges. And, that no one on Reeveston Road liked Easley.

It was evident in the Court Room that a number of Easley family members were present. Jerry Easley had a Mother and at least a sister and two brothers in the courtroom to hear what other people had to say about their loved one. It is interesting to note than none testified for their brother. Of course, the possibility exists that Easley chose to not involve his family in his problems. If so, it could be said that at least he did something honorable throughout this 17-year ordeal since his first wife, Sherry, was found Murdered. The defendant Jerry Easley was not required to testify in his own behalf but was allowed that opportunity to do so. He chose to not testify.

Final arguments were held at 1:00pm on Thursday, May 1, 1986. The jury received the charge at 2:30pm and deliberated until 4:30pm. At that time, they returned with a verdict of GUILTY OF CONSPIRACY TO COMMIT CAPITAL MURDER.

In the great State of Texas, as is the instance in most states, there are two phases in a criminal trial. The first one concerns the Guilt/Innocence phase. The Rules of Evidence as well as the Code of Criminal Procedures are applicable here. If a defendant is found GUILTY, then the admissibility of evidence is relaxed. It is here where a defendant's prior conviction and his character in general can be presented in testimony before a jury. After the jury found Jerry Easley Guilty as charged, he remained in the custody of the Rusk County Sheriff. The Judge then recessed the court for five days for the punishment phase to begin, this being the second phase of this criminal trial.

The proceedings continued on Tuesday, May 6, 1986 and the following individuals were subpoenaed by the prosecution to testify that Jerry Easley had a bad reputation for not being a peaceful and law-abiding citizen: James Hammond, brother of the missing wife Sharon Easley; Mrs. Freddis Hammond, Mother of the missing wife Sharon Easley; Sheriff Ted Everett and Deputy Darrell Longinot of the Polk County Sheriff's

Department, who investigated Jerry Easley in the Goodrich School District bomb scare; HPD Lieutenant Earl Musick and Assistant D.A. Joe Bailey, both of the Harris County District Attorney's Special Crimes Division; and Detective Debbie McKnight and Chief of Police Floyd Stiefer, both of the Jacksonville, Texas Police Department.

Final arguments on the punishment phase concluded and the jury received the case at 10:50am. The jury deliberated just over two hours and at 2:00pm, they returned with a sentence of 60 years in the Texas Department of Corrections. The charge the jury was given by the Judge required under State Law that Easley serve a minimum of 20 years due to the fact that a Deadly Weapon was used in the commission of this offense.

Easley's lawyers immediately filed a Notice of Appeal, which is somewhat usual in most cases of this lengthy of a sentence. If a sentence is greater than 15 years and one day, the law does not allow a convicted defendant to post an Appeal Bond. Therefore, Jerry Easley was remanded to the Rusk County Sheriff and was transferred the following day to the Diagnostic Unit of the Texas Department of Corrections in Huntsville, Texas, the city where Jerry Easley went to college at Sam Houston State Teachers College. This was certainly not a triumphant return for Easley to his old college town.

Now behind bars at "the big house" in Huntsville, Easley immediately began planning his appeal to this conviction.

Easley Indicted for Arson of the Motorhome (40)

Wɪᴛʜ Jᴇʀʀʏ Eᴀsʟᴇʏ locked down in TDC, many folks breathed somewhat easier. Was this nightmare finally over? While Detective Dan McAnulty certainly felt a bit more at ease, there was a major problem yet facing him. And that was, WHERE WAS SHARON EASLEY AND WHO, IF ANYONE, KILLED HER? The thought of this going unsolved just as the death of Sherry Easley greatly disturbed Detective McAnulty. Always thinking ahead and concerned that somehow Jerry Easley might appeal and win was a thought he did not relish one bit.

Realizing that proving an Arson case on Jerry Easley was possible, he ventured off further into that investigation. While making a case was a distinct possibility, he also hoped that by pursuing this angle, he just might uncover some information leading to the whereabouts of Sharon or her remains. Knowing the unscrupulous individuals that Jerry Easley surrounded himself with, he was secretly hopeful that such information would be out there.

While speaking further with the shady individuals from around the Reeveston garage, he spoke to a man who was known only as Bubba. This man informed him that Easley had on occasion spoken about having vehicles burned for their insurance value to him. This line of conversation led Detective Dan to an individual named Joe Luna, who had worked for another company on Reeveston. While Luna was no longer employed there, it was learned that he and his wife had moved to Alabama.

Charlie Self was an investigator for the Montgomery County Sheriff's Department, who had jurisdiction over the Arson case. Self and McAnulty flew to Alabama and went to interview Luna. Luna was afforded pre-arranged prosecutorial immunity on the Arson case and then spoke freely to the Detectives about the motor home. The following was learned:

Bubba had given his phone number to Easley, who called him "about a job". Easley related that he wanted this motor home burned and in return, Luna could keep the appliances, including the two air conditioning units, generator, refrigerator, and any other items of value remaining. Easley also mentioned that there were women's clothes (Sharon's) still hanging in the closet and that he could also have them for his wife or for whomever. Apparently, Easley did not feel that Sharon would ever need them again. Here again, just as in the many "hits" that Easley had proposed to his employees, he was not one bit bashful in opening himself up to being reported to the authorities.

Luna agreed to this deal and met Easley at an airport storage lot where the motor home had been parked. He drove the motor home to his home, where he parked it in his driveway for a week or more while he stripped everything of value from the RV. In turn, he sold those items to some of his co-workers up and down Reeveston Road. Basically, Luna was "fencing" these items gotten under illegal circumstances. While not opening himself up to other cases, it was apparent to the investigators that Luna was experienced in this art and also had the necessary contacts to rid himself of these items and netting a profit for his efforts. He provided a rough list of the items sold and they totaled nine items which netted him $970.00 cash. His wife admitted to taking some of Sharon's clothing items and was proudly wearing those clothes. Luna still had the microwave oven and two couch cushions from the Cruise Air. Those pillows were brought back to Houston for examination as evidence.

A written statement was obtained from Luna, who also provided the name of the person who went out on Riley Fussell Road to pick up Luna. Luna indicated that they doused the inside of the motor home and then threw a flare inside, which caused an explosion of sorts. Then, they left after watching their handiwork for a short time. A statement of that person was obtained that verified Luna's story. Also, several previous neighbors of Luna's were contacted and they verified the presence of an older motor home in Luna's driveway during that time period in February, 1985.

Based on this information, McAnulty and Self presented this case to the Montgomery County District Attorney. Jerry Easley was indicted for the charge of Felony Arson in July, 1986. While McAnulty had not been successful in learning more about Sharon, there was much satisfaction in knowing that this additional charge would keep Easley in jail while his appeal was working through the system. Should his appeal be successful, which was not likely, at least an additional felony might present Easley from preying on anyone else.

Jerry and Wilma's Jailhouse Marriage (41)

T HERE ARE CERTAIN individuals in our society who just do not desire to be alone. It may possibly be that they just do not function well on their own, or possibly that they wish to have someone else involved in their misery, or happiness as the case may be. There are many and varied reasons for this which is true in all walks of life.

Jerry Easley was obviously one such person. In early February, 1985, his wife of nearly 16 years, Sharon Hammond Easley, went missing under what many believed to be very suspicious circumstances. Jerry claimed he had no knowledge of where she went and even though he related a number of scenarios of what could have possibly happened to her, none really struck as being plausible or true to her family and friends. There were a number of people, from Arizona to Houston, friends and co-workers and family, who were all very concerned about Sharon's health and well-being. They believed foul play was involved and that Jerry was behind it.

In actuality, Jerry really did not make any concerted efforts to report her missing and responded to authorities' inquiries only after being contacted by them. Even then, he seemed rushed and mostly pre-occupied with filing an insurance claim to recover money after the Cruise Air motor home was discovered burned to a crisp in southern Montgomery County.

But as they say, we all have to move on with our lives, no matter what lemons may fall your way. And Jerry likely felt the same way about his life after Sharon.

In addition to the many inquiries being made of Jerry by law enforcement authorities, Sharon's family members and Jerry's son Jon were also asking many, many questions. The motor home destruction, quickly ruled to have been Arson, only added fuel to the fire surrounding Jerry's life, no pun intended.

Bottom line, Jerry Easley needed someone in his life to commiserate with him over the large number of problems he was facing daily in his life in 1985, especially with this trial looming before him. Someone, you know, who would understand him or at the very least, tell him that they understood his pain. You know, someone who would tell Jerry, "I feel your pain".

Over the past several years prior to 1985, Jerry would visit his brother in Elkhart at his business there. This brother was a professional business-man, a person who seemed to care greatly about the small community he had called home from birth. It seemed that a lady worked in this business as a clerk, and her name was Wilma Webber. Jerry at this time was 43 years old, his wife Sharon was gone, and he needed someone. It turned out that Wilma, around the age of 40, was divorced and had been for some time. She too needed some companionship in her rather boring life. Jerry had met Wilma over the years and while being married to Sharon, seem-ingly happy, had never made any romantic overtures to Wilma.

However, this time it was different. Jerry asked Wilma to go out with him, and she agreed to do so. Was it love at first sight? Probably not, but you know as the old saying goes, sometime there is a "lid for every pot".

To say that Jerry was vulnerable would not have been fair to Wilma. Wilma was likely the vulnerable party. No matter how it came about, it happened, and this relationship, strange as it later seemed to be, thrived for a short time. For the rest of the year 1985, Jerry was facing numerous problems in his personal life and Wilma was someone he could turn to. It seemed that there was this HPD Detective Dan that was asking numer-ous questions of numerous individuals acquainted in some manner, either personally or business-wise, with Jerry.

Throughout this courtship of Jerry and Wilma, Jerry's legal problems continued to raise their ugly head. Jerry, through his highly-questionable business dealings, had accumulated a significant amount of money, and even though he was not working, seemed to live rather well on these savings. With his legal problems facing him, he involved Wilma in his personal situation more and more. To her, this was just overwhelming, but at this time, Wilma was "standing by her man". Also, she probably figured WHY NOT? since not much else in her life had gone right for some time now.

After the conviction, Wilma was there for Jerry as moral support if nothing else, as he had been confined to custody during the period of October, 1985, until time of trial. Plus, after Jerry was in TDCJ, he had placed her in charge of his money, more than she ever in her life had access to. Wilma was not required to testify, as she had no actual knowledge of the crime that was laid out there in open court for all to hear what Jerry had been up to. Then, on August 5, 1986, after Jerry had been in TDC custody for three months, a very strange situation occurred. While Jerry was just becoming settled in his new life at TDC, Wilma and Jerry became married in some type of ceremony at which JERRY WAS NOT PRESENT?

No matter how these nuptials took place, no matter where they occurred, or WHY, one thought regarding the legality of this union came to the mind of several people close to the situation. And, that was this: Jerry Easley had been legally married to Patricia Sharon Hammond Bonham Easley since 1969. They had lived together openly as recent as early February, 1985, when Sharon was last seen alive and well by anyone. Even stranger yet, this marriage was called marriage-by-proxy, where someone stands in for Jerry. In this case, it was either Paul Priddy or Jack Terry that stood in for Jerry.

She was gone from the face of the earth under suspicious circumstances, to say the least. Jerry had made no effort to find her or have her declared Dead. In the State of Texas, a missing individual cannot be legally declared Dead until the passing of seven years. Strangely enough, it was later learned that while Jerry was awaiting his trial, he had actually filed for a divorce from Sharon in Anderson County, where as man and wife, they had never resided. This was the home county of Elkhart.

This divorce was granted on July 3, 1986 and had been filed at least 60-90 days prior, which would have placed the date of filing in April or May, 1986. Was Jerry thinking of moving on with his life with Wilma after he was cleared of all charges? Probably so. Yet, Jerry Easley entered into a new marriage approximately 18 months after Sharon was last seen alive. With Jerry Easley facing 60 years, or the rest of his life, whichever comes first, a charge of bigamy was the least of his worries!

In order to better understand the timeline of these marital changes, the following occurred: Sharon missing since February, 1985. Jerry files for divorce in another county in April-May, 1986. Divorce granted uncontested July 3, 1986 and on August 5, 1986, Jerry and Wilma were married with Jerry being in absentia from the proceedings. Maybe Jerry was concerned about a Bigamy charge!

Jerry Easley– Jailhouse Lawyer (42)

RIOR TO BEING imprisoned in May, 1986, Jerry Easley had on several occasions mentioned to family and friends that he would like to go to law school. He had an extensive education on which to draw, as he had already completed several college degrees in the area of education. With those many prerequisites behind him, he felt certain in his mind that with a certain amount of effort, this goal of graduating from law school could be accomplished. However, it was one of those goals that he just never got around to achieving. To him, it was a dream that never came to fruition.

Easley had also studied the law as needed, both criminal and civil. His lawyer and close friend, Mr. Jack Terry, had taken much time with Jerry and taught him how to navigate the law library as needed to deal with his business disagreements. He certainly had used the system on a number of occasions involving business disputes with school districts and more recently and more often, with garage clients. He knew the basics, but as he told several of his cohorts, the system just did not work well for him, for whatever reason.

He reasoned that he would just have to take the situation in hand and deal with it in his own way. Whether it meant forcible eviction without process, so be it. Whether it meant padding a repair bill to the point the vehicle's owner had no earthly chance of paying it and then filing a mechanic's lien on the vehicle, so be it. Whether it meant confiscating a lessee's tools and equipment and forcibly running him off of his premises without due process, so be it. Jerry Easley was used to having his way with or without the legal system. It is possible with the success he had experienced in dealing with these issues, he reasoned that law school was not necessary for a man of his knowledge.

Jerry Easley easily felt wronged in most any situation. Now, at 45 years of age, facing a prison sentence of 60 years with a minimum "to do" of 20 years, the outlook was bleak. With his strange personality, which he had exhibited his entire life, he felt that he had truly been done wrong by not only the criminal justice system, but more specifically by two individuals - Detective Dan McAnulty and Montgomery County District Attorney Charles R. Holcomb. Whether it was Sherry Dean Easley, Sharon Hammond Easley, The Goodrich School Board, or now McAnulty and Holcomb, it was always someone else's fault. It was never Jerry Easley's fault!

In Easley's mind, he had no responsibility for the predicament he was in. It was all the fault of those two individuals. Easley's two wives were either Murdered or missing. Donny Harold had been assaulted in a kidnapping attempt that was intended to end his life far away from witnesses. But, in the end, to Jerry, these facts were not even thought of. In the end, it was McAnulty and Holcomb's fault. And to another extent, it was the fault of his son Jon who testified against him in his trial. That was a hurt that would not go away.

In the very early days of his confinement, he was domiciled with Virgil Otis Griffin, a soon to be four-time ex-con. Virgil was experienced in prison and out, but was not very bright with the books. At Easley's request, Virgil referred him to several inmates known to be very knowledgeable and competent "jailhouse lawyers". These hardened criminals had access to the prison law library and had learned on their own, or from others before them, how to use those resources as well as to navigate the legal system from inside the walls.

One such individual was the infamous Sam Hoover, a former Mayor of the City of Pasadena, a large suburb east of Houston. He had been convicted for his part in the planning and arrangement of the robbery-torture of a wealthy Houston couple in River Oaks. Being a lawyer before being imprisoned, Hoover had an advantage over others inside and was not hesitant to use that to his advantage. There were others that in his job as the aide to a Warden, Easley had the opportunity to seek out and plead his case for assistance. Of course, even inside the walls, those types of favors do not come at a cheap price. Easley, however, was willing and able to pay the price. He had some funds available to him and he was willing to use a portion of those funds to gain access to and learn more about the system.

Now behind bars at "the big house" in Huntsville, Easley immediately appealed his conviction. To counter Easley's actions, McAnulty and Holcomb, through their respective employers, had filed Motions of Summary Judgments. On December 20, 1988, the Court:

(1) Granted Summary Judgments in favor of Dan McAnulty and Charles Holcomb,
(2) No sanctions or attorney's fees were allowed Easley,
(3) Easley's motion for an appointed attorney (for the appeal) was denied, and
(4) Easley's motion to compel production of Documents was declared a MOOT point.

In summary, Jerry Easley struck out completely in his efforts to bring action upon these two dedicated public servants. Round One went totally against Easley. This caused Easley to go into a deep depression, as he was not as astute with the law as he reasoned himself to have been. Then, also he was very lonely for his moral support, Wilma. However, Easley was determined to fight on with his pursuit of justice for himself, although the State of Texas had emphatically ruled on justice in favor of the citizens of Texas.

Easley was actually filing several motions simultaneously, hoping that one would land in his favor. In October, 1986, some five months after his conviction in Cherokee County, Easley's legal efforts were not progressing well for him. However, there existed in the Federal Court System in

Texas one Honorable William Wayne Justice of Tyler, Texas, in the deep East Texas Piney Woods. Judge Justice had become famous for his rulings against the Texas Prison System. He was especially noted for one case, Ruiz vs. Texas, in which one career criminal filed suit for a number of allegations against the State of Texas.

This landmark case brought about many changes in the Prison System, none of which were thought to be of benefit to the law-abiding citizenry in Texas. All of these changes ordered by Judge Justice brought havoc to the system, but were like manna from heaven for the inmates who rode the coattails of Judge Justice's rulings. Many such inmates saw this as an opportunity for themselves and signed on to the Ruiz case in a class action suit. This endeavor later became very, very successful. These rulings meant a total overhaul of the Texas Prison System, costing the State of Texas millions of dollars. Judge Justice became a hero to the law-breakers and was affectionately referred to by them as Uncle Wayne.

As Jerry Easley's frustrations mounted, he chose to pen a correspondence to Judge Justice, who was seated on the bench in Tyler, Texas. He referred in this letter to his previous case, Cause #TY-85-447-CA, further stating that he was being held as a political prisoner. He accused the staff and administration at the Walls Unit of refusing to cooperate with his efforts, having also made preparations for his civil action difficult if not impossible by refusing to allow the necessary references and materials to be delivered to him inside the prison walls.

Further, he stated, the intimidations and harassment as well as the discriminatory definition of contraband made it impossible to work and conduct the necessary preparations and get proper assistance. He implored upon the Judge to intervene on his behalf in order for him to have the opportunity to proceed without hindrance or restriction of his legal preparations for this civil action.

Shortly after corresponding with Judge Justice, Easley apparently became emboldened to proceed forward in his legal maneuvers. In early 1989, he once again filed an Appeal in the United States Court of Appeals for the Fifth Circuit. In this action, termed 89-2147, Jerry E. Easley was the Plaintiff-Appellant and Dan A. McAnulty and Charles R. Holcomb were the Defendants-Appellees. Throughout all of these filings, McAnulty and Holcomb were ably represented by attorneys retained by the City of Houston (McAnulty) and the State of Texas (Holcomb). The representation provided for these two men was only right, as all of their actions in this matter were obviously in the course of their sworn duties. This action taken by Easley was basically an Appeal of the summary judgments granted to McAnulty and Holcomb. This summary judgment was a crown of thorns around Easley's head and he felt strongly that it was just one more example of the injustices previously dealt to him by the system.

Having served in law enforcement, it can be attested to by this author that being sued for your actions while actively pursuing your sworn duties is a very unsettling and disturbing feeling. It was just that for Dan McAnulty and Charles Holcomb, a new ground neither had trod previously in their lengthy and successful careers. They had gone up against previous adversaries, but never against such a man as Jerry Easley. There exists a mutual respect among such professionals as these. When a person, whether on one side of the law or the other, goes up against someone in court, it is usually a matter of who presented the better case to the Judge or the Jury. Harsh words are sometime displayed in court against each side, but when the verdict is reached, those words are usually forgotten and both sides move on with their respective careers. The respect for each other exists as each side remains fully aware of each others' duty to represent their client, be it the State of Texas or the individual charged with a crime.

In 1989, it had now been three years since the verdict in Cherokee County that sent Jerry Easley to prison for a minimum of 20 years. However, he was constantly working to alleviate his situation. Attorneys William A. Worthington and Ramon G. Viada III were eventually listed as counsel in this matter for Jerry Easley. Barbara Callistien from the City of Houston Legal Department represented Dan McAnulty while Leland D. Sutton became the Attorney of record for Mr. Charles Holcomb. Due to the manner in which the City of Houston Legal Department operates, several other attorneys from that office represented McAnulty at one time or the other.

The main issues presented by the Plaintiff here were:

(1) Whether the District Court's disposition should be upheld or overturned,

(2) Whether the District Court did not abuse its discretion by denying Plaintiff the assistance of an appointed trial counsel, and

(3) Whether the District Court erred in granting summary judgments in favor of Holcomb and McAnulty.

With Easley sitting in prison, his mind must have been working overtime dwelling on all of the individuals who were working against him. With him, now it was not just this obsessive Detective Dan McAnulty or this over-zealous prosecutor, Charles Holcomb. Easley's mind kept going back to all of the individuals he had experienced business, personal, or financial problems with over the many years. The trial in Cherokee County haunted him day and night, reliving over and over the testimony of those enemies of his. Reliving the past is the direct cause of resentments which build up in an individual who constantly thinks he was been wronged. And, Jerry Easley definitely had his resentments. One especially haunted him, and that was the testimony against him by his own son, Jon. Easley's family - Mom, sister, and brothers - were there in court and heard all of the damaging testimony dealt against him by his own flesh and blood. Damaging yes, but also very, very embarrassing for this eldest sibling in the Easley family.

Easley's mind was overwhelmed by the memory of all of those who testified against him in the Cherokee County trial. Of course, in his mind, these individuals needed to be dealt with by him. These people needed to pay a price for their actions. Consequently, shortly after his original appeal was filed, he filed his Second Amended Complaint on June 24, 1989. This complaint, of course, named once again McAnulty and Holcomb but was expanded to name the following additional defendants:

(1) Elmer Price and James Hollingsworth - Lessees and customers with whom he had serious business disagreements at the Reeveston garage.

(2) Joe Bailey and John Cossum - Assistant District Attorneys assigned to the Harris County D.A.'s Special Crimes Division, both of whom, while in the lawful performance of their duties, had assisted McAnulty in the preparation of legal papers filed during the lengthy investigation.

(3) Morris W. Hassell - Judge of the 2nd District Court, Cherokee County, Texas.

(4) LeRue Dixon - Easley's own defense attorney at his trial.

(5) Peter Speers III - District Attorney, Montgomery County, Texas.

(6) F.M. (Rick) Stover - Assistant District Attorney, Montgomery County, Texas.

(7) And, of course, the Honorable Lynn Coker and John C. Martin, both State Criminal District Judges from the Montgomery County-Conroe area. They had been deemed by Easley to be extremely prejudicial against him in any and all matters brought before them.

All of these individuals were cited by Easley for their failure to prevent or in some manner aiding in a conspiracy that they knew was occurring or knew was about to occur against him. All of their actions were further described by Easley as violating his rights under the First, Fourth, Fifth, Sixth, Eighth, and Fourteenth Amendments of the United States Constitution. He was on a self-imposed fast track to becoming a competent jailhouse lawyer.

It is a known fact of life that anyone can be accused of or sued over just about anything. However, the problem with this reasoning is that sooner or later, proof has to be brought forth showing that the accusations are, in fact, true. Some of the accusations laid out in court documents by Jerry Easley were as follows:

Elmer Price and James Hollingsworth entered into a conspiracy to maliciously defame him by spreading false rumors that he was engaged in the illegal criminal activity of attempting to hire certain persons to commit Murder. Further, that they went to Assistant District Attorneys Bailey and Cossum, who were introduced by McAnulty. All were in a poisoned conspiracy to locate the "millions" of dollars Easley had secreted and a suggestion of a "Great Monetary Gain" was discussed if he (McAnulty) could locate this hidden fortune of Easley's. The well, Bailey's and Cossum's minds, had already been poisoned by McAnulty and Jon Easley, who interestingly enough, was not on the additional list of defendant's as proposed by Jerry Easley. Easley also accused McAnulty and Holcomb of using the state's witnesses to combine their stories about him and his alleged criminal activities to state such stories before the trial jury, including that of the star witnesses against him, Franky Routt and Norman Donny Harold.

McAnulty was described by Easley as not being able to resist the above proposition, as he was "hung-up" on the solving of unusual Murder cases, most specifically that of Sherry Easley and the unusual disappearance of Sharon Hammond Easley. It was rather obvious that the actions of Detective Dan McAnulty had really taken hold in the mind of Jerry Easley. Easley must have experienced more than one nightmare inside his barren cell with McAnulty the main focus of his terrifying thoughts. And, of course, his beloved Wilma was also constantly on his mind. Knowing full well, he said, of her sexual proclivities, what else was she doing out there while he was so wrongfully locked down?

In addition to the above accusations and in direct reference to the fact that in September of 1986, Plaintiff Jerry Easley was indicted for the offense of Arson in Montgomery County in regards to the motor home being torched there in February, 1985. Easley alleged in court documents that McAnulty had committed the act of perjury before the Montgomery County Grand Jury and had conspired with District Attorney Speers and his Assistant Stover in order to obtain this indictment.

As a result of this on-going conspiracy against him orchestrated by McAnulty, Easley demanded judgment from McAnulty in the amount of $250,000 on each of three counts laid out for the court in his documents, or a total of $750,000. Lesser amounts were demanded by Easley from each of the other named defendants, but it was obvious that to him, McAnulty was the main culprit in all of his problems.

All of these accusations were drawn up by Easley while he was incarcerated, thus comprising a four-year harassment of Dan McAnulty with vexatious litigation. He was hopeful that this bombardment of legal moves would bring the young Detective to submission. Such, however, was not to be. When someone pursues a righteous cause as McAnulty had done, life works in mysterious ways. Sometimes, but not always. But, for now justice had once again been obtained.

The Reality of Sharon's Death (43)

DURING ALL OF the time since the conviction and also throughout the arson investigation, Detective Dan McAnulty had been actively working with Lieutenant Eugene Kellogg of the Cochise County Sheriff's Department, which is headquartered in Bisbee, Arizona.

Lieutenant Kellogg had been assigned by his Sheriff as their lead investigator into the remains that had been discovered in the desert.

With Jerry Easley seemingly locked safely away in prison and his appeals going nowhere, Detective Dan McAnulty and the Arizona authorities continued their effort to identify those remains. The science of DNA had been gradually advancing over the previous 15 years and at this point in time, it was rapidly accelerating. Blood samples were obtained from the Mother of Sharon, Mrs. Freddis Hammond, as well as that of her only two siblings, James and Charles Hammond. These samples were sent to the Arizona Department of Public Safety, whose laboratory was working closely with the Cochise County Sheriff's Department.

DNA profiles were worked up on the bloodstained mattress cover and the foam mattress which had been also recovered from the desert area near where the body parts were found. The official results of that testing were listed as:

THE DNA PROFILES OBTAINED FROM THE MATTRESS COVER AND THE FOAM MATTRESS CANNOT BE EXCLUDED AS HAVING ORIGINATED FROM AN OFFSPRING OF FREDDIS HAMMOND OR A SIBLING OF JAMES HAMMOND AND CHARLES HAMMOND.

While this finding was not considered totally positive, Detective McAnulty began working with Nicole Inacio, Regional Systems Administrator for the western states, which included U.S. territories Guam and Puerto Rico, in an effort to further obtain verification on the evidence. He had previously submitted all known information to NAMUS, which is an acronym for the National Missing and Unidentified Persons System.

It is a customary practice in the identification of these cases to use dental records to positively prove the remains as connected to a missing individual. Such was not the case here in that the skull of Sharon Easley was never found.

Given that the science of DNA was constantly evolving, eventually the results were sent to the University of North Texas (UNT), whose North Texas Center for Human Identification lab was becoming a science leader in this area of investigation. Eventually, those results were positive in determining the remains found in the Arizona desert were that of Sharon Patricia Hammond Easley.

Meanwhile, in September, 1988, with Sharon having been missing for over three years, Sharon was officially declared DECEASED by her family and friends. They had lost all hope. However, McAnulty had not given up on providing Sharon some semblance of justice as well as a measure of both closure and justice for her loved ones. Based on the known evidence at the time, Jerry Easley was indicted in Cochise County, Arizona for the Capital Murder of Sharon. That case was pending when a new District Attorney was elected for that jurisdiction. With Easley locked away for sixty years, that D.A. decided that this case was too expensive to pursue prosecution. The case was dismissed with the understanding that since there is no Statute of Limitations on Murder, the case could be re-indicted if Easley's circumstances changed.

Sharon Hammond Easley 'S Obituary and Memorial Service (44)

HOUSTON CHRONICLE, FRIDAY, September 16, 1988:
"EASLEY - Patricia Sharon Hammond Easley was born December 19, 1942, missing since February 4, 1985, is presumed to be dead. She was a resident of Houston since 1951, received a Master's Degree from Southwest Texas State Teacher's College in San Marcos, Texas in 1966. She taught Chemistry in Houston schools. She also worked as Production Manager for several printing companies in the Houston area. She attended Kingwood Community Church. Mrs. Easley is survived by her step-son, Jonathan E. Easley, Mother, Mrs. Freddis Hammond, two brothers, Charles Hammond and wife Myra of Austin, and James Hammond and wife Cindy of Houston; and aunt, Mrs. Marguerite Hammond of San Antonio; and numerous nieces and nephews."

"A memorial service was held Saturday, September 17, 1986, at 10:00am at Spring Branch Community Church, 9569 Long Point Road, Houston. Pastor Dave Slottje of Kingwood Community Church officiating. For those desiring, memorials may be sent to Camp Peniel, Inc., 4545 Bellaire Blvd., Bellaire, Texas 77401."

"Hymns sung at the service were "Like a River Glorious" and "Because He Lives". Solos by Tim Hammond were a "Hymn Medley" and "Finally Home.""

"Those that knew Sharon well spoke at the service about the Sharon they knew. Those were Ed Stewart, Alice Whitelock, Marguerite Hammond, Nita Frank, Donnie Ellis, and Jonathan Easley."

"Precious in the sight of the Lord is the death of his saints".

Sharon's likely knowledge of Jerry's involvement in Sherry's brutal Murder and her unwillingness to come forward with the truth over those many years certainly would not in any manner qualify her for sainthood. However, she certainly did not deserve the brutal death she suffered, or the manner in which her remains were disposed; that manner being like that of an animal thrown on the side of a road in the Arizona desert. As near as can be determined, whatever human remains that were left after the testing were interred in a pauper's grave in Arizona.

The funeral visitation registries for Sharon's parents were unavailable for review. However, what is known is as follows: Mr. A.E. Hammond, Sharon's Dad, passed away in 1977 at the age of 62. This was during a period in Sharon's life where she was somewhat estranged from her parents due to the actions of her husband and his attitude toward anyone that she was close to. In the early 1980s, Mrs. Freddis Hammond, Sharon's Mom, made the comment that this was the first time she had seen her son-in-law in 12 years. This would lead one to believe that while Sharon had been allowed to be with her Mom and family at the time of her Dad's death, that Jerry Easley was not present. Mrs. Freddis Hammond passed away in 2010 at the age of 96 years. Both parents are interred at Memorial Oaks Cemetery in West Houston.

Jerry and Wilma's
Jailhouse Divorce (45)

To SAY THAT the marriage of Jerry Easley and Norma Burdick Webb was strange would be the understatement of the century. Sure, there had been such arrangements under which one party of a marriage was confined in prison for a lengthy period with no immediate outlook for release. Usually, however, these were situations where the marriage had taken place much prior to the conviction or the beginning of the prison sentence. In that type of situation, the spouse of the incarcerated person usually still loved the spouse or there were financial considerations or concern for the children. This marriage between Jerry and Norma was completely different and proved itself each and every day to have been entered into under very, very strange circumstances.

Following his conviction, Jerry had arranged for his good friends on Reeveston Road, Louise and Dwight Moore, to be responsible for some of his financial matters. Jerry had several siblings to whom he appeared to be very close to, yet he relied on these friends to handle some of his finances. Stranger yet was the fact that Dwight Moore had not spoken very well of Jerry, having even once stated that Jerry was a vindictive, revengeful man that he just as soon not have anything to do with anymore.

Anyway, he had trusted Louise to take control of some of his savings and instructed her to provide some income for Wilma while he was locked up and actively working on his appeal. Jerry was not without hope that his conviction would eventually be overturned. No one was sure what exactly that hope was based on, but nevertheless, Jerry had this hope and probably needed it each and every day as something to hang on to.

This worked well for Wilma for a time, as she had not previously ever been accustomed to such a windfall. She was receiving $1,000.00 a month from Jerry, by way of Louise and Dwight, which along with some odd jobs she was able to complete, she was living well, or as well as she likely ever did. In the dollar value of 1986, Wilma could well be living "high on the hog", as East Texans are prone to say.

At some point in time after Jerry's incarceration in May, 1986, Wilma was able to purchase a relatively late-model used car for cash. These funds apparently came from Jerry's stash. However, throughout the next several years, communications between Jerry and Wilma became stagnant. After all, he was locked up and his appeal was not proceeding well at all, at least not from his point of view. Here, Wilma was free, and spending some or a large portion of Jerry's money. He had known Wilma for some time, and he very likely had other thoughts about the lifestyle she was enjoying while he was in the situation that he was in. Was she being "true blue" to Jerry, as she had promised to be? These were not good times for Jerry. But, he needed someone and that was Wilma.

Of course, Jerry had made this bed and now he "was forced to sleep in it". Whatever his motivation to maintain this unusual marital relationship, that reason was unknown to anyone who was remotely aware of the situation. His family members were especially puzzled by this arrangement.

Then, on March 1, 1990, three and one-half years after this strange marriage, Wilma filed for a divorce from Jerry Easley. It is unknown how often Wilma had visited Jerry, her on-paper-only husband in prison, but this was deemed to be a serious blow to Jerry. Without a doubt to anyone, the marriage had obviously been consummated prior to his arrest and conviction. Jerry, who had experienced aspirations in his free life to study the law, had now immersed himself in the further study of law while being incarcerated. After all, what better to do with his time?

While he had centered on the most important point of all, his appeal, he had gained a considerable knowledge of the inner-workings of the law library that was made available to him while in prison. That was criminal law, and now, he felt the necessity to gain further knowledge of the civil laws, specifically domestic relations, or more specifically, divorce. And, that he did.

Being served in prison for divorce must have been devastating for Jerry Easley, and with no option of gaining outside legal assistance in the matter, Jerry worked feverishly to file responses to the divorce request from the petitioner, Wilma. Jerry would become the Respondent in this civil action filed by Wilma, and while there were filing fees in order for him to properly and legally respond, he had adequate funds available for that purpose. In his mind, this divorce was worth fighting and at least there were not the usual outside legal bills to cover the associated expense.

With unlimited time on his hands, which also obviously somewhat relieved his mind regarding his terrible situation in confinement, he totally immersed himself in this effort to save his marriage. Jerry, who had become married on two previous occasions, had never been in a situation of dealing long-term with a recent ex-wife. Unfortunately for all but him, his ex-wife and a present wife either were murdered or turned up missing. This was new ground for Jerry, and he was determined to plow this new ground.

This marriage, which could not have ever been further consummated after the actual nuptials at which he was not even present, was apparently worth saving in Jerry's mind. Could it have been that no one, in Jerry Easley's mind, not a woman or anyone else, was ever allowed to walk away from Jerry Easley? This could possibly have been a motivation on the part of Jerry. This was not the way things were supposed to be with someone like him, someone that constantly needed to be in charge of his own destiny, someone who had controlled people all of his life. Up until now, that is.

In the month following Jerry's being served with divorce papers in prison, he used his limited (not in his mind) knowledge of the domestic relations statutes to respond to Wilma's claim for dissolution of the marriage.

Jerry got his "jailhouse lawyer" practice in full swing, and much, I am sure, to Wilma's discontent, he began flooding the court with petitions. These petitions, ad nauseam, are listed below. Jerry had nothing else to occupy the long days in TDC, and he likely figured, WHY NOT? He knew she had access to his money, yet he likely thought that there is no way she would expend the amounts of money to answer all of the many petitions he flooded her and the Court with.

The Divorce Petition was filed in the 2nd 9th District Court of Montgomery County, Texas. Wilma, 44, who at time of filing, officially declared Montgomery County as her place of residence and of course, Jerry, 49, resided against his own free will in the TDC Ellis Unit One, Huntsville, Texas, Walker County. The petition rightfully stated that the marriage took place on or about August 5, 1986 and the couple ceased to live together on February 27, 1990. The wording "ceased to live together" was another strange phrase as Jerry had been in Custody the ENTIRE time from the date of marriage until February 27, 1990, two days prior to Wilma filing for the divorce. It is unknown what occurred on or about these dates that could have precipitated the divorce filing by Wilma.

The dates listed were nearly as confusing as anything else in this marriage and the petition for divorce on the date listed was only several days prior to the filing. In the Petition, Wilma stated that "the marriage had become insupportable because of discord or conflict of personalities that destroys the legitimate ends of marriage relationship and prevents any reasonable expectation of reconciliation". Wilma Gail Webber (Easley) chose as her legal counsel one Ronald L. Meeks of Willis, Montgomery County, Texas. At the time of this filing, Wilma was agreeable to pay any and all of her own legal fees in this matter and was requesting to take back her previous name of Webber. She was ready and completely willing to move on with her life and do whatever was necessary to end this fiasco of a marriage.

Jerry began filing a flood of legal documents in response to the request for divorce. This flood of official court documents prepared by Jerry

Easley were all filed on March 22, 1990, and consisted of nine different and varied filings. In his original answer, it was his request for Wilma to meet the burden of proof that he is TEMPORARILY confined to TDC. To Jerry's way of thinking, being under a 60 year sentence while in your mid- forties was temporary.

Jerry further responded that true enough, "they were joined together in the bonds of holy matrimony on or about the 5th of August, 1986 although he was not present at the ceremony. He specifically denied any separation between the parties as husband and wife since the inception of the marriage. This was totally laughable as they had never lived together after that ceremony. The conditions attendant upon this marriage have remained constant (this was basically true and laughably so) and that Wilma Easley has condoned such factors as being part of the accepted conditions of this marriage and no change in said conditions constitute any grounds for divorce and/or separation from this marriage commitment and agreement or arrangement". Jerry denies specifically that this marriage has become insupportable because of discord or conflict of personalities between them that destroys the legitimate ends of this marriage relationship and prevents any reasonable expectation of reconciliation.

In a following section of the Response, Easley further states that the parties are domiciled in Anderson County at all times during the pendency of this marriage. This was most certainly a false statement in that his only connection to Anderson County was that was his childhood home of origin. He was convicted in Cherokee County and incarcerated thereafter in Walker County. He also stated that he shall establish that the allegations of Wilma are the result of undue influence and irrational behavior occurring from stress and anxiety, constituting psychological and sociological aspects of a nervous breakdown. Easley also attempted to advise the court of the character, reputation, and instability of Wilma to deal with reality while undergoing the current state of stress. Further, Jerry Easley requested that prior to any actions taken to dissolve this marriage, that testing and counseling be conducted in an attempt to reconcile any and all "imagined marital conflict".

As had been the pattern of Jerry Easley throughout his adult life, finances played an important role in his behavioral issues with people in general. Here again, he portrayed Wilma as destitute at the inception of this marriage with no assets and a considerable amount of liabilities. This may have very well been true as Wilma had been married and divorced several times and had not attained any advanced education. She had always been married or worked menial or other clerical jobs.

Easley, who had previously placed money at the very top of his priorities, played the "money card", openly declaring that since his conviction, he had undergone a community liability of approximately $25,000 in legal fees. The majority of these fees, if not all, were expenses incurred in connection with the appeal on his conviction. Was he actually expecting to regain some of those fees from a destitute woman? Knowing Jerry Easley, he was very probably expecting this remuneration from a woman he knew had limited income potential.

Other allegations in Easley's original response were that Wilma had committed adultery and fraudulently converted personal and real property to her own use and benefit. Then, he got really down and dirty by stating that Wilma's carnal lust for obsessive sexual gratification was the primary reason for this cause of action. He was portraying his personal knowledge of what he perceived to be her unusual sexual appetites and using them by making them a matter of court record. All of this was being done in an effort to win her back. Strange, indeed.

Jurisdictional issues were a focus of attention on this filing for divorce. Being filed in Montgomery County was felt to be a real problem for Easley as it was his sincere feeling that there were three District Court Judges in that County who had previously sat in on proceedings involving him and that it would be impossible for them to be impartial in their rulings. They were the Honorable Judges Lynn J. Coker, John C. Martin, and James H. Keeshan.

All three of these respected Jurists were perceived by Jerry Easley as prejudiced against him, probably his feelings surfacing from a guilty conscience as well as the frivolous lawsuits, civil and criminal, that he had brought forth over the years. While Jurists such as these three are bound by oath to not carry their feelings over from one case to another, it would be naïve to believe that the chatter around the Courthouse did not exclude previous suspicions about this man Jerry Easley and his ongoing legal difficulties.

While he did not have the proverbial "leg to stand on" in his attempt to recuse or disqualify these three Jurists, he had extremely strong feelings on these jurisdictional issues. Also, the prosecuting District Attorney on Easley's Conspiracy to Commit Capital Murder trial, was none other than the current District Attorney for this Judicial District, Charles R. Holcomb. It was common knowledge around the Courthouse that Easley had filed a Federal Lawsuit against not only the primary investigative Detective, HPD's Dan McAnulty, but also against Charles Holcomb. There were no positive results for Easley as a result of this lawsuit which was filed and later dismissed in the United States Court of Appeals for the Fifth District out of New Orleans, Louisiana.

The Motion for Recusal and Disqualification of these Jurists was filed on, March 22, 1990. In not any particular order, Easley filed also on this date the following motions:

MOTION FOR RECUSAL OR DISQUALIFICATION OF JUDGES - This motion outlined the perceived bias that Easley felt that the Judges in Montgomery County had not only shown against him in the past, but more importantly that they would continue to show such bias. He strongly felt that his civil rights would be violated should any of these Magistrates be allowed to rule in these proceedings.

DEMAND FOR A JURY TRIAL - Easley cited the Texas Family Code covering this request and all others that followed. He was aware that in order to obtain a jury trial, he was required to make a monetary deposit. However, he further begged the Court to waive this requirement as he was unable to do so with property or otherwise.

MOTION FOR CHANGE OF VENUE - Easley requested venue to be moved to Anderson County and cited reasons for such being that he had the right to be sued in his County of Residence as well as where the cause of action occurred. Further, that Norma had "forum shopped" by filing in Montgomery County, where she full well knew that Easley was well-known, not well thought of, and where he obviously could not receive a fair and impartial hearing. He went on to say that they had resided in Anderson County during the marriage. Since he had been incarcerated the entire period of the marriage, this could hardly have been factual.

APPLICATION FOR TEMPORARY RESTRAINING ORDER AND TEMPORARY INJUNCTION - This petition was basically requesting a full and complete accounting of all assets pertaining to the marriage. Easley stated that he was in possession of information that Wilma had removed and concealed his assets in an effort to deprive him of such. This petition was one that would likely have been in order in any divorce case and he was attempting to recover as much as possible the assets he had willingly granted to Wilma during the marriage. He was now requesting of the Court that Wilma be required to pay reasonable attorney's fees and expenses associated with this legal action initiated by her.

MOTION TO REQUIRE SURETY BOND - Easley requested that since Wilma was the sole custodian of all of his assets, she should be required to post a Security Bond in the amount of $100,000. He reiterated that it has come to his attention that Wilma has removed and/or secreted from the Court assets that belonged to him. Easley did in fact have a legitimate concern in this area as it had come to his attention that a bank account in his and Wilma's name had been closed on the day the divorce action was filed. In another very strange allegation, he indicated that Wilma has failed to provide him with funds for his support and personal needs. Of course, his personal needs for food and clothing were provided to Jerry by the State of Texas. A bond in this amount was totally out of the question for Wilma to have met should she be required to do so.

MOTION FOR LEAVE TO PROCESS IN FORMA PAUPERIS - Pauper is the key word in this motion as Easley was proclaiming that he was in effect, a pauper. He requested of the Court that he be permitted to proceed without payment of the normal fees, costs, witness fees, subpoena expenses, bench warrant fees, and expenses of witnesses to travel to court to testify. He continued to say that he was a pauper in State of Texas custody and since the date of the marriage, he had trusted the Petitioner with his assets and that she had either squandered such and/or secreted his assets.

MOTION OF APPOINTMENT OF COUNSEL - Once again, Easley brings out the fact that he is "temporarily" incarcerated in the Texas Department of Corrections. He states that he is without funds and has been "called upon" to defend himself from this action taken by Wilma. Further, Wilma has access to the funds and is requesting the Court to appoint counsel for him to adequately defend himself from the actions taken by the Petitioner (Wilma). In the alternative, he requests that Wilma provide him the necessary funds needed to properly defend himself against her requests for the dissolution of the marriage.

MOTION FOR BENCH WARRANT - Easley states the necessity of him being physically present at any and all court proceedings. Unless a change of venue is granted him, he would need to be in Montgomery County and since he is incarcerated in Walker County, it would become necessary for the Court to order him to be Bench Warranted from custody to the court proceeding. He further requests that after any proceeding that he would be allowed to attend, he be returned immediately to his unit in Huntsville where he would have immediate access to the law library there in order to conduct research into what had occurred in the court.

One could only wonder, if each and every prison inmate anywhere, not just in the State of Texas, were granted all of the conveniences Jerry Easley was requesting, countless logistic and transportation problems, including guard hours, would need to be dealt with in order to accommodate these requests. One could also wonder how ridiculous and laughable these requests were viewed when considered by the Court. According to Easley and his wishes, his conviction and imprisonment should not cause him any other inconvenience in his personal matters.

If it was Easley's intent to wear Wilma and her attorney down with motion after motion, he apparently succeeded. With mounting legal bills facing her, on April 2, 1990, Wilma, through her attorney, filed a MOTION FOR NONSUIT, which was approved by Judge John Martin. Wilma and her attorney were overwhelmed with Easley's jailhouse filings and as a result, Wilma just basically gave up. She was just unable to legally continue her efforts to remove herself legally from this man and from this ordeal she had gotten herself involved in.

On April 5, 1990, Wilma dropped the divorce action. If she remained married to him, she would then become the widow of Jerry Easley should he pass away.

Wilma was contacted by this author, but refused to respond to phone calls. Correspondence was sent to her and her response was to please leave her alone, as "this was a long time ago, and she desired it to be forgotten". That request was honored. While her version of the events is not known, she has been displayed as honorably as possible. Detective McAnulty indicated that he attempted to contact Wilma after Jerry was convicted but she did not wish to talk with him at that time as she was obviously afraid of Jerry and wanted some time to pass before she wanted to be interviewed.

Suspicion arises as to why Jerry Easley went to the lengths he did to maintain this marriage on paper, at least. He was facing a lengthy incarceration, one of which he may not ever be released from. Yet, he pursued every possible avenue legally to avoid the divorce. Was he just merely practicing his jailhouse lawyer activity to remain busy? Or did he wish to remain married to Wilma to prevent her from ever testifying against him?

Easley Still A Danger
Behind Bars (46)

AFTER JERRY EASLEY was convicted in May, 1986 and sentenced to 60 years in the Texas Department of Corrections, most people that had prior dealings with Easley rested somewhat easier. They were obviously thinking that the havoc that Jerry had wreaked on so many lives, both physically and emotionally for so many years, not to mention legally, was over. After all, Easley was then 45 years old and under his sentence, he was required to serve at least 20 of those 60 years. That would make him 65 years of age should he survive prison life for that long of a period. Most thought that he would not be able to survive inside those surroundings where he would not be able to exercise his usual control of the lives of anyone who disagreed or crossed him. Behind the walls, it was he who would be controlled by the system.

People who knew him were already calculating the number of years until he could get out of prison. Of all the people who were concerned, one of those was his own son, Jon. Jon was painfully aware that since he had testified against his Dad in the Cherokee County trial, that he had become an enemy of his Dad. And Jon was well aware of what being an enemy, whether or not you had done anything to deserve to be such, meant to his Dad. Jon had not only felt his Dad's wrath on a personal basis, but had also observed his Dad's infliction of wrath on other people who he felt had done him wrong, including Sharon.

In reality, Jon had testified against a man who he felt was not only responsible for his Mom's death, but also involved in the disappearance of his Stepmother, Sharon. Jon really did not have much of a choice but to do what he did when he testified about that terrible night in Jacksonville in 1983. To make matters worse, Jon was aware that his Dad's family held very harsh feelings towards him because of his testimony. As they say, "Blood is thicker than water". But, again, what was a 20-year-old to do when he knew what he knew, when he had experienced all of these tragedies in those few years?

Jon stated in a 1989 newspaper article that he felt like he was on his Dad's list. While Jon's math may have been somewhat off, his feelings of fright were not off much when he stated that he had only 13 years before he would feel the wrath of his Dad in the worst way imaginable - to be on his hit list.

When Easley was sent to prison in May, 1986, he was sent to the Diagnostics Unit, where he underwent numerous evaluations in an attempt to determine what skills he possessed. The thinking here by the prison system is to find a suitable position or job in which the inmate can become a productive person for the entire system. Also, the goal was to assign the inmate to a job that he can become comfortable with according to his skills. Keeping a man somewhat occupied in a task was considered to be much better than to have him spend his waking hours working out in the weight room or watching television, and all the while building up resentments against those who live the free life on the outside.

After diagnosis, Easley was assigned to be a bookkeeper for the Prison Major in charge of this particular section. During this period, a Virgil Otis Griffin was assigned to be Easley's cellmate. Now, one would have to wonder regarding the wisdom of this move, placing a four-time convicted felon to live and co-habit in such close quarters with an educated former school superintendent, although one who was also a convicted felon of a violent crime. No matter what the reasoning was on the part of the prison system, this was the situation as it existed shortly after May, 1986.

There was another person who was concerned about Jerry Easley behind bars. That was Houston Detective Dan McAnulty, who had basically been a thorn in Jerry's side and was THE law enforcement Officer solely responsible for Jerry finally paying the price to society for some of his wrongdoings. Dan, a college graduate, had studied Psychology and through his extensive investigation of Easley's many sordid activities, felt he had come to know Easley inside and out. More importantly, Dan knew that Easley was always bent on revenge towards anyone he felt had wronged him, whether they had or not. It made no difference to Jerry Easley. Paul Nix, the veteran Homicide Detective who had not only studied Jerry Easley and investigated him thoroughly, felt the same way about Easley. He and Ed Horelica had, on many occasions, advised their young protégé to take Easley very seriously, that he was a dangerous man to be reckoned with.

McAnulty, being the consummate detective he was, took a certain amount of pleasure in investigating Easley to the extent he had - obtaining a conviction. However, Dan had several other reasons to continue his investigation. Very simply put, those reasons were Sherry and Sharon. In his mind, even though Easley was locked down for at least 20 years, there was the matter of the UNCLEARED 1969 Murder of Sherry Easley as well as the unresolved disappearance and probable death of Sharon Easley.

Having been a Homicide Detective for a total of eight years, McAnulty was well aware of the responsibilities that accompany those duties. He was painfully aware of the fact that Sherry's killer had not been brought to justice. Also, the details of Sharon's disappearance remained a complete mystery, leaving Jon and Sharon's loved ones without any closure. Justice delayed is justice denied.

He, like many dedicated and conscientious Homicide Investigators, had envisioned both Sherry and Sharon crying out from their graves (Sharon's remains withstanding) for someone to speak out loudly and clearly for them. Of course, while Sherry's earthly remains were in her grave at Woodlawn Cemetery in Houston, Sharon was, well, who knows where her earthly remains were? She was still missing at the time. Her cry, whatever it may have been and wherever it might emerge from, was lingering in the back of the mind of Detective Dan McAnulty. He frequently was reminded of this as Nix and Horelica had schooled him well on the responsibilities of being a Homicide Detective.

Being assigned to the Special Crimes Division of the Harris County District Attorney's Office, McAnulty was assigned a very heavy case load. He served at the discretion of several Assistant District Attorneys and while responsible to them, he was also allowed a reasonable amount of investigative discretion in regards to other cases that had come to his attention. Easley, being locked down for now, did not satisfy Dan. He knew that there was more to learn about Sherry and Sharon and in general, about Easley's sordid activities. McAnulty was not one to give up without pursuing more about this protagonist Jerry Easley.

After Easley was in custody in Huntsville for several months, McAnulty continued his investigation by determining who had been in close contact with Easley inside, centering on who might have been a cellmate. This inquiry led McAnulty to learn of the existence of one Virgil Otis Griffin, a four-time ex-con who had been in and out of custody his entire adult life. He was an alcoholic as well as a drug abuser, when he had the opportunity to practice his addictions. It was the experience of many Investigators that while being confined in jail as was Jerry Easley, some prisoners would open up to those in similar situations as they. This was McAnulty's thinking when he initiated this latest inquiry.

McAnulty learned that Griffin had been released from Huntsville in July, 1986, having received one more chance to go "straight". However, once again Virgil had not chosen to do anything different. It was learned that "Old Virgil" was already listed as a parole violator as of January, 1987. Having been paroled less than six months previously, it appeared that the State of Texas Parole Board had erred again by opting to trust "Old Virgil" on the outside.

McAnulty and his working partner at the time, HPD Homicide Detective Kenny Williamson, learned of an address in north Houston where one of Virgil's ex-wives was residing. Going to that address,

McAnulty was completely surprised to observe a familiar vehicle parked in the driveway. It was none other than a Z28 Camaro that had been driven by Jerry Easley prior to his conviction. Registration was run on the vehicle and it was verified that the vehicle was registered in Jerry Easley's name. What a surprising development!

This Z28 Camaro was just another of the many vehicles that Easley had filed a mechanic's lien on and had obtained ownership because the original owner could not afford to pay the inflated repair bill of Easley. If Easley wanted it, he had figured out a way to get it.

At this point, rather elated with this new development, Dan and Kenny were able to determine Virgil was in the house. It took a short time, but they were able to coax Virgil into surrendering to them on the parole violation warrant. He was placed under arrest and taken to their offices and questioned.

In a completely unrelated incident to Virgil Griffin, an ex-con who had been a later cellmate of Easley was spotted in the area where son Jon was living. Upon being questioned by police, he admitted that he had been given $1,000 and a car to "do something about Jon". However, after further investigation by law enforcement, it was decided that this man's testimony by itself would not be sufficient to make another case against Easley. He was considered not to be a credible person that a jury might believe.

As one could well imagine, Virgil Griffin was not an easy subject to interview. With his record, he knew full well that he was once again facing some time in the big house in Huntsville. When he realized that McAnulty was the Detective he had heard so much about from Easley, he knew very well that he did not want to return to the prison system with any type of reference to him being a snitch. Virgil was a big man, six foot four inches tall, weighing nearly 200 pounds. He could usually handle himself if pushed by another inmate, but now at the age of 45, he no longer wanted any physical battles to accompany the misery of being once again locked up inside those walls.

As reluctant as he was to speak to McAnulty originally, the Detective had a calm interviewing demeanor which eventually led Virgil to open up about what he knew regarding Jerry Easley. Of course, he was vigilant about not incriminating himself in any new offenses he may have committed during his six months of freedom. With his extensive criminal background, he walked a tight line, which McAnulty not only recognized but also appreciated and understood. The detective made it clear to Virgil early on in the interview that his main focus, actually the only focus, was to learn more about Jerry Easley. The lengthy interview of Virgil by McAnulty and Williamson revealed the following:

Easley began early on in his incarceration of having difficulties with prison life, not totally surprising for a 45-year-old highly educated narcissist with a long history of demanding his way in life, whether it be with spouses, children, or business associates. He was very "whiny" and constantly complaining to other inmates about his new life in "the pen". Easley was very distraught about being separated from his latest love, Wilma. He was obsessed regarding her being able to date other men while he was confined and actually cried tears over this sad situation he found himself in.

Being this way was perceived by the other inmates as insufferable and weak as well as someone to avoid as each and every inmate had their own crosses to bear and situations to deal with on a daily basis while being locked up. Listening to someone else constantly complain and profess their innocence was not something most inmates cared to deal with. The best way to handle someone like Easley was just to avoid them and be seemingly cold to them.

After being the Major's bookkeeper for a short time, Jerry was transferred to a different job, this time as a medical clerk in the prison hospital. Easley became very upset about this change in jobs, telling Griffin that "he was not going to put up with this". This job change affected Easley's routine of spending many hours in the prison law library. Of course, Griffin just laughed at this and told Easley that in the pen, you do what you are told to do, not what you want to do. This was the manner in which Griffin originally dealt with Easley.

However, after being forced to listen to Easley speak about his education, how he had been a school superintendent, had come from a good family, was raised in the church and how his ex-wife had cheated him out of all of his money, this must have gotten to Griffin. Even Griffin, the hard-nosed convict who had experienced a number of incarcerations, began to sympathize with him. Griffin probably just tired of hearing Easley's complaints and decided to deal with him in another manner. After all, Griffin was looking at a parole in the very near future.

Easley never mentioned to Griffin which one of his murdered wives had done this to him. Of course, Griffin had no knowledge of anything other than what information Easley chose to provide him with. While Griffin was beginning to relate to Easley and his many problems, he was also thinking of ways in which he could use Easley to his own advantage. This was a classic case of one con attempting to con another, something that happens each and every day, inside and outside the walls of custody.

While Easley's obsession over Wilma occupied much of his time, he was also adamant regarding the appeal process on his conviction. Jerry, for whatever reason, possibly over his numerous illegal activities over the years, had spent considerable time in law libraries in Houston. His attorney and long-time friend, Jack Terry, had on occasions accompanied Jerry and assisted him in learning the system.

Faced with quite a bit of free time in prison, Jerry inquired of Griffin regarding who were the most experienced "writ writers" or "jailhouse lawyers", as they were referred to. Griffin referred him to several, the most prominent one being the former mayor of Pasadena, Texas, Mr. Sam Hoover. Not exactly broke financially in prison, Easley hired Hoover or others to assist him in researching the appeal process on his conviction. Griffin related that Easley had several angles he intended to pursue on an appeal, the most common one, that he had been inadequately represented by ineffective counsel. When Easley, who wanted out of jail tomorrow, learned that most appeal processes took at least two years, he became depressed and continued to whine to Griffin about this distressing news.

On Easley's side of the equation, he very soon recognized Griffin's prison savvy as well as his obvious "street smarts" and began to confide in "Old Virgil", obviously sensing that he was someone who could be trusted.

Griffin was due to be released shortly and the cell friendship of Easley and Griffin only lasted several months until July, 1986, when Griffin's actual release date was announced.

Griffin, who had been released from prison on at least three occasions prior to this release, departed The Texas Department of Corrections this time with several advantages previously unknown to him. This time, he left with the promise of two items: (1) The use of a vehicle and (2) The promise of $1,000 to be given to him after his release.

It was obvious that Griffin had either played a scam of monstrous proportion on Easley or that Easley was basically unprepared to deal with individuals who were as devious as he was. Either way, when Griffin left TDC in Huntsville, he left having taking advantage of Easley. Griffin left with the small amount of money provided to all released inmates and purchased a bus ticket to the small East Texas town of Elkhart, which just happened to be Jerry Easley's hometown. It was also the home of Easley's Mother.

Prior to Griffin leaving prison, with a reluctant and suspicious TDC Chaplin assisting but also monitoring the call, Jerry Easley made a collect call to his Mom, Mrs. Cora Easley, in Elkhart. He advised her to let Virgil Griffin take for his own use the Z28 Camaro that he had left there in Elkhart. This must have been a budding five-week friendship that had bloomed and blossomed between Easley and Griffin.

The history of this vehicle was unknown to Mrs. Easley but it was felt that it might have been obtained through the Easley Enterprises automotive garage that Jerry either owned or operated for a number of years in North Houston. Easley was aware that the Z28 needed a state inspection as well as a vehicle registration renewal and told his Mom to make sure that Griffin had the funds to complete these requirements.

Easley's prison wife Wilma met Griffin at the bus station and took him to Mrs. Easley's home. Here, Griffin played the part and spoke at length about Jerry and his adjustment to life inside the "Walls". Wilma and Mrs. Easley were weeping continuously over Jerry's plight in prison and the more Griffin described how difficult it had been for Jerry to adjust to his new life, the more sympathy there was generated for Jerry.

Griffin recognized the weakness of both these ladies as they wept and sympathized over their loved one's problems. He played it out to the fullest, feeling as if it was his duty to inform the family of Jerry's situation. The Easley family rightly suspected that Jerry would have a difficult time adjusting to prison life, but what Griffin was relating to them even made them more concerned. Griffin did his duty in meeting his new friend's family and then set out the next day to make the Z28 legal on the streets of Texas. He did not stay one minute longer than he needed to in this hick town of Elkhart.

The second part of Griffin's windfall from Easley was a letter of introduction to a long-time friend and confidante, Mr. Paul Priddy, who had also been somewhat of a spiritual mentor to Jerry Easley. This letter further instructed Mr. Priddy to give Virgil $1,000 from a fund that Easley had entrusted with him. Mr. Priddy, although very reluctant to do so, went along with Easley's request and took Griffin to a bank in Pasadena, Texas and assisted him in completing the transaction.

There is an old adage used earlier in this book which is something along the lines of, "if it is too good to be true, then it probably isn't". Truer words were never spoken as even the most naïve person would wonder what "strings" were attached to these gifts.

Of course, Virgil Otis Griffin had his own agenda after receiving his windfall assets from his cellmate of only five weeks. Well, now what else is a four-time ex-convict heroin addict/alcoholic expected to do with the "free" use of a sporty vehicle such as the Z28 and $1,000 in cash money? He could have taken advantage of this situation and used the money and vehicle to obtain gainful employment and begin a different lifestyle than those previous lived out, all of which always seemed to find him back in the same situation as before - prison. Well, what else was "Old Virgil" supposed to do under these circumstances? So, Griffin's obvious choice was to get a girlfriend and a bunch of heroin and booze and spend a week in a motel partying down. And he did just that. Old habits are hard to break.

In the midst of all of the fun Virgil was having, he neglected to fulfill one of his most important but reasonably simple obligations to the State of

Texas upon his release from full custody. And that was to report to his designated State Parole Officers, who had been assigned by the Parole Board to be his contact in times of difficulty there in the "outside world". All of this fun, together with this blatant neglect to even follow the simplest and basic rules of freedom, would only catch up with a parolee after a period of time. And, so it did with Virgil.

In the State of Texas, when a parolee does not comply with the rules set out for him, just as not even reporting to his Parole Officer, a warrant is issued for his or her arrest. This is commonly known in the criminal justice system as a Blue Warrant. There are many, many reasons for which such a warrant was to be issued, many of them much more serious violations than Virgil was guilty of in this case. However, he had shown no respect whatsoever for the source of his freedom and having been provided yet another chance out there in the free world. Virgil was typical of many ex-convicts and even though they would be very reluctant to admit this problem, they are sometimes just totally incapable of functioning in a normal man's society. Some actually thrived during their custodial periods of life but did not function very well at all on the outside. Virgil was such an individual.

After hearing this long and interesting story from Virgil, McAnulty began to lean on him to tell what it was that Easley wanted him to do for him. McAnulty had come to know Easley very well, having investigated him over a long period of time. This could not be, in McAnulty's reasoning, just good-hearted Jerry Easley doing something for someone else out of the goodness of his heart. Virgil brought up the snitch problem to McAnulty, who explained that there were ways to protect him from such a reputation when he returned, ways such as having him assigned to a different prison facility as that of before. Virgil, even as savvy as he was, somewhat bought this idea from the persuasive Detective and further related the following:

Easley told Virgil he needed two people taken care of on the outside. McAnulty knew full well what was meant by "taking care of someone". However, he pushed Virgil a bit further and eventually Virgil admitted to

McAnulty that it was Easley's desire to have several people on the outside killed.

Number one was his son Jon, as Easley was deeply affected by his son's testimony in the Cherokee County trial and indicated to Virgil he did not want to see his own son testify in another trial against him. McAnulty questioned him further as to what, if any, trial Easley was speaking of? Then, Virgil dropped the bomb on McAnulty, stating that Easley was very concerned that McAnulty would continue his "vengeance" on him by attempting to pin the Murder of his wives on him. In Easley's world, McAnulty was out for "revenge".

Number two on his list was none other than Detective Dan McAnulty, the Detective who has been causing Easley a lot of problems for some time now. This had to have been a shocker to the veteran Detective – a prison inmate putting out a contract on him for rightfully and lawfully doing his job. McAnulty was a family man, having been married for 18 years with a son and a daughter. This was a very stressful time for Dan.

Having digested what Virgil had just dropped on him, Dan came to understand what Paul Nix had previously told him about Easley, that he would have to kill him if he found him around his house and family. He came to feel the same way and even though Easley was locked down, Dan began constantly looking over his shoulder. The stress of investigating and imprisoning Easley resulted in Dan now awakening on many mornings with a smile and saying to himself, "It's a good day - Jerry Easley is in the penitentiary". Dan had never before felt that way about the many other crooks he had investigated.

There was a Number three, him being the District Attorney who had successfully prosecuted Easley in the Cherokee County trial - Mr. Charles Holcomb. While Virgil was relating all of this to the two Detectives, he was on occasions laughing and making a joke out of the entire matter. When asked why, Virgil stated that he had no intention of doing anything that Easley was asking him. He just wanted the car for a short time and to enjoy it as well as the money from Easley. He continued to make light of Easley's requests, saying that there was no way he would do a hit on anyone, especially for that small amount of money. Just kidding, he added. Actually, as bad as his record was, he had never been investigated for Capital Offenses before.

The Detectives, prior to arresting Virgil on the Parole Blue Warrant, had thoroughly researched him and all of his known criminal activities and arrests. While Virgil was a low-life scum bag career screw up, he had no record of being violent towards anyone except, like he said, on occasions slapping a girl friend or ex-wife, but only then because they really needed it. Even with his intimidating physical stature, he had never used it inside prison other than for his own protection and defense.

Virgil reluctantly told McAnulty this tale of deception between he and Easley, but adamantly refused to ever testify against Easley should any charges be brought against him regarding the "hits" on Jon Easley, Dan McAnulty, and Charles Holcomb. Without his testimony, there was no evidence to prosecute Easley on any charges. Of course, what McAnulty was really searching for was any conversations Virgil and Easley may have had regarding Sherry or Sharon. Virgil consistently denied that Easley had ever mentioned anything about his ex-wives other than that one of them had taken all of his money. That wife, Wilma, had to have been the one he was referring to. After all, it was common knowledge that his first two wives, Sherry and Sharon, were dead.

The results of this investigation were documented and presented to the proper prosecutorial authorities within several jurisdictions. All authorities agreed that without Griffin's cooperation, no prosecution could proceed at this time. Based on this situation, the best law enforcement authorities can do in such cases is openly advise the "targets" of the situation and to be aware of such in all of their daily activities. In this case, Jon, Detective McAnulty, and District Attorney Holcomb were already well aware of the situation.

Jerry Easley Dies in Prison, 2003 (47)

AFTER HIS APPEALS were exhausted, Jerry Easley languished in prison, a broken man. He became ill and was admitted to the Michael Unit Hospice Unit of TDC. He was pronounced dead on 2/23/2003. The apparent cause of death was lung cancer. His body was released to the Herrington Funeral Home in Palestine, Texas. He is buried in an Easley family plot in the Strong's Memorial Park near Slocum, Texas, only four miles east of Elkhart. He is interred near his parents and other ancestors. His Dad, Mr. F.C. Easley, passed away in 1964. His Mom, Mrs. Cora Easley, passed away in 1989 after seeing her oldest son convicted of a heinous crime and sent to prison basically for the rest of his life. There is also a marker there for several other immediate family members.

The Dean and Hammond Family, 2018 (48)

SHERRY DEAN'S PARENTS are interred in Woodlawn Cemetery near the intersection of I-10 and Antoine Drive. Her sisters, Naomi and Betty, have passed away. Brothers Troy and David are still alive, as is her very close sister, Glenna, and the younger sister, Doris, as of the writing of this book in early 2018. There are also a number of nieces and nephews that never had an opportunity to know Sherry.

Sharon Hammond's brothers James and Charles are still living. They also had children that were deprived of a relationship with their Aunt Sharon. The Hammond parents, Mr. E.A. and Mrs. Freddis, are interred at Memorial Oaks Cemetery, I-10 near Eldridge.

Jonathan Easley and His Family, 2018 (49)

J ON RESIDES IN West Houston near Katy with his wife of 28 years, Jill. They are the parents of three children, who are Jon-18, Josh-16, and Bethany-11. Jon is the Chief Engineer of Facilities at a large downtown Houston hotel and has been successful in that area of responsibility for a number of years.

Detective Dan McAnulty, 2018 (50)

IN 2018, DETECTIVE Dan McAnulty, now 69 years of age, is retired and lives in Kingwood, Texas, with his wife Maria. Dan is a native of Beaumont, Texas. He came to Houston, Texas, and embarked on a law enforcement career in 1969 at the tender young age of 19. Dan was the eldest child of a family of four children when his Dad passed away rather suddenly when Dan was only 17. He assisted his Mom greatly from that time on and then struck out on his own with his young wife, Ethel, who later become the Mother of Kristen and Dan, Jr. He continued his education after completing HPD Academy Class #40 in May, 1969 and earned his Bachelor's degree.

Dan completed his 20 years with the Houston Police Department in 1989. His devotion to duty eventually took its toll on his marriage and he and Ethel divorced. He took his HPD retirement and was immediately hired at the Harris County District Attorney's Office as a Captain of Investigations. Dan continued his excellent and rewarding career, basically continuing where he left off in the Special Crimes Division. For a number of years, Dan was assigned to the Public Integrity Section of Special Crimes. In that capacity, Dan's tenaciousness led to a number of convictions of elected officials in Harris County who had violated their oath of office in order to financially benefit themselves. Dan retired from Harris County after completing over 40 years of service to the citizens of Houston and Harris County.

Dan met his second wife, Maria, while he was assigned at the D.A.'s Office. Maria just recently retired from the Harris County District

Attorney's Office after serving as a Chief Prosecutor. She had served over 40 years prosecuting criminals in Harris County. Dan and Maria's marriage was blessed with a daughter, Emily.

In 2018, Dan's oldest Daughter Kristen is a schoolteacher and also the mother of two children. She and her husband reside in Kingwood. Dan Jr. is a Senior Property Tax Representative and also resides in Kingwood. Dan and Maria's daughter, Emily, is currently attending Texas Christian University in Fort Worth, Texas, with an eye toward attending law school.

While this book is dedicated to the memory of Sherry Ann Dean Easley, Patricia Sharon Hammond Easley, and in honor of Jonathan Edward Easley, I feel inclined to include the excellent and dedicated career of one Dan Alton McAnulty Jr. Were it not for his tenacious investigative nature, this entire criminal episode of over 17 years would have never come to a prosecution. To Dan McAnulty Jr., law enforcement hats everywhere are off to you.

THE END!

ABOUT THE AUTHOR

A veteran of three decades in the Homicide Division of the Houston Police Department, Nelson J. Zoch is well qualified to write about police procedure and murder. Working closely with the detectives who investigated the murders of Sherry and Sharon Easley, as well as the officer who worked the aborted kidnapping of Jon Easley's college roommate, he has traced the elements of a true story that is far more fascinating than many crime novels. In the tradition of Truman Capote's *In Cold Blood*, Zoch has brought a nonfiction tale to fascinating life.

Made in the USA
Columbia, SC
05 January 2019